~

Lost Delta Found

Rediscovering the Fisk University–Library of Congress
Coahoma County Study, 1941–1942

John W. Work
Lewis Wade Jones
Samuel C. Adams, Jr.
Lost Delta

Found

Rediscovering the Fisk University-Library of Congress Coahoma County Study, 1941–1942

Edited by Robert Gordon
and Bruce Nemerov

Vanderbilt University Press
NASHVILLE

Published 2005 Vanderbilt University Press
First Edition 2005

Printed on acid-free paper
Manufactured in the United States of America

10 09 08 07 06 05   1 2 3 4 5
Frontispiece: "Son" Sims and Muddy Water, courtesy of the Center for Popular Music, Middle Tennessee State University, John W. Work III Collection.

Library of Congress Cataloging-in-Publication Data

Work, John W. (John Wesley), 1901–1967.
Lost Delta found : rediscovering the Fisk University-Library of Congress Coahoma County study, 1941–1942 / John W. Work, Lewis Wade Jones, and Samuel C. Adams; edited by Robert Gordon and Bruce Nemerov.
　　p. cm.
　　ISBN 0-8265-1485-5 (cloth : alk. paper)
　　1. African Americans—Mississippi—Coahoma County—Social life and customs—20th century. 2. African Americans—Mississippi—Delta (Region)—Social life and customs—20th century. 3. African Americans—Mississippi—Coahoma County—Music. 4. Blues (Music)—Mississippi—Coahoma County. 5. Gospel music—Mississippi—Coahoma County. 6. African Americans—Mississippi—Coahoma County—Folklore. 7. African Americans—Mississippi—Coahoma County—Religion. 8. Delta (Miss. : Region)—Social life and customs—20th century. 9. Coahoma County (Miss.)—Social life and customs—20th century. 10. Coahoma County (Miss.)—Religious life and customs.
　　　I. Jones, Lewis Wade, 1910–　　II. Adams, Samuel C.　　III. Gordon, Robert, 1961–
IV. Nemerov, Bruce.　　V. Title.
F347.C7W67 2005
305.896'07307624—DC22
2004029428

To John Wesley Work IV

CONTENTS

❧

The Manuscripts

INTRODUCTION TO DELTA MANUSCRIPTS

27

❧

"The Mississippi Delta" by Lewis W. Jones

❧

John Work's Untitled Manuscript

John Work's Music Transcriptions

127–222

"Changing Negro Life in the Delta"
by Samuel C. Adams

CONTENTS

LIST OF

ILLUSTRATIONS

ACKNOWLEDGMENTS

This book would not have been possible without assistance, guidance, and inspiration from the following people: Tara McAdams; Doug Seroff; Jessie Carney Smith, University Librarian, Franklin Library at Fisk University; Beth Howse, Special Collections Librarian, Franklin Library at Fisk University; John Work IV; Frederick Work; Alice Marie Jones Johnson; Evelyn Adams; Mayo Taylor; Matt Barton; Jeff Todd Titon; Charles Wolfe; Betsy Phillips; Sue Havlish; Dariel Mayer.

Bruce Nemerov wishes to acknowledge the support of the Center for Popular Music at Middle Tennessee State University and its director, Paul F. Wells.

PREFACE

Early in the research for my biography of Muddy Waters, my friend Bruce Nemerov at the Center for Popular Music in Murfreesboro, Tennessee, sent me his article on John Wesley Work III.[1] The Center holds some of Work's personal papers and many of his personal field recordings. John Work, he explained, was the *other guy* on the trip when Muddy was first recorded, and Work had written a manuscript that included dozens of transcriptions of the recorded music. The manuscript and transcriptions had been lost in the 1940s and Bruce asked me to keep a lookout for them.

I only sort of knew what he meant. That is, I knew about Alan Lomax making the trip to the Mississippi Delta in 1941 and coming away with the first recordings of Muddy. I'd heard *The Plantation Recordings,* the collection of Muddy's diverse material from the 1941 and 1942 trips, and I was just getting familiar with the interviews included on it. The "other guy" conducted two of the four interviews with Muddy. Hmm, I thought, should be interesting.

As my research continued, I was further attracted to Work's work because it implied real documentation of Muddy. Researching an illiterate person from a chiefly oral culture was rife with difficulties. Information in Muddy's world was exchanged through stories told from mother to son, from friend to friend. I knew that no matter how hard I looked, what doors I knocked on, cousins I turned up, rocks I turned over, I'd never find a box containing Muddy's childhood diary, no bundles of correspondence expressing his innermost thoughts. Work's meeting with Muddy might mean I'd find field notes.

I found more than that. The name given to the whole of the research was The Fisk University–Library of Congress Coahoma County Study. The study produced great recordings and detailed documentation of the people, lives, and lifestyles of the Clarksdale, Mississippi area. (A four-page questionnaire was completed by scores of residents, among them Muddy and his family.) As I began to explore the files, I found that the evolution of the study, and the story behind it, were as revealing as the results.

I was searching for written documentation specifically on Muddy, but the correspondence, reports, and paperwork I found would have gripped any researcher. This was no pretty picture of institutional cooperation; instead, there was name-calling, hostility, deception—and major accomplishments to boot. I took a left turn from Muddy and explored the study—in the archives of the Center for Popular Music, in the Special Collections Department of the Fisk University Library, in the Library of Congress, and in the Alan Lomax Archives at Hunter College in New York. Aside from Nemerov's article, there was little else published except for Alan Lomax's *The Land Where the Blues Began,* his 1993 account of what had happened fifty years earlier.

Yet the goal of the study was to have been a book based on the project's findings, written by the Fisk participants and jointly edited and published by Fisk and the Library of Congress. Correspondence indicated that the manuscript had been completed in the mid-1940s by John Work, was then submitted to the Library of Congress, and there it was misplaced, recovered, and misplaced again. Lomax's book decades later proved a poor substitute. Despite winning the National Book Critics Circle Award, it was full of historical inaccuracies, the most obvious being the conflation of the two trips into one.

The relative importance of these inaccuracies can be argued, but what my research was revealing was more important: another perspective on these trips existed, another perspective on history. "What does it really mean when the plantation Negro says that he does not remember old folk tales, but enjoys telling a worldly story? What does it mean when he says that he has no time to sing? What does it mean when a woman says that the burial association is better than the church?" These are questions asked by Fisk graduate student Samuel C. Adams, who lived in Coahoma County while participating in the study. In searching for Work's manuscript, I first found Sam Adams's (which was unidentified and which I originally mistook for Work's), then Lewis Jones's, then finally Dr. Work's. The research and analysis by these three had never been released. Until now, all we knew was this white man's perspective; even research done by the African-Americans that Lomax incorporated had been filtered through his viewpoint. Lomax was responsible for a lot of great work, but he did not work alone.

More than sixty years later, here are the facts—the writings of the principal participants of the Fisk–Library of Congress Coahoma County Study. Reading them is like finding old pictures of someone you've always known. The pictures reveal new aspects of an old friend, a deeper sense of dimension. The pictures are worn, and you study the wrinkles—where's this photograph been and why have you not seen it before? The picture's history has become part of the story, and you're hungry for clues, for information, for more and more character. Suddenly, you're struck by things you'd never noticed, by how this lifelong friend you thought you knew well now looks so very different.

—Robert Gordon
Memphis, 2005

INTRODUCTION

Lord, the people was all dancing, enjoying their life so high
Lord, the people was all dancing, enjoying their life so high
Just in a short while, the dance hall was full of fire.
　　　—"The Death of Walter Barnes" by Baby Doo Caston

JOHN WESLEY WORK III

When a fire ripped through an April 23, 1940 social gathering in Natchez, Mississippi, two hundred citizens were burned alive, and many others were scarred for life. Among the dead were Walter Barnes and most of his orchestra, the Royal Creolians, who had been hired to play for the dance. The carnage was so great that the story garnered front page coverage from many mainstream newspapers across the country—despite the fact that segregation reigned and all the victims were African-Americans.

In Natchez, nearly 60 percent of the 16,000 residents were black, and few families went unscathed by the tragedy. Musicologist John Wesley Work III, a professor at Fisk University in Nashville, read the United Press wire story on the front page of the *Nashville Banner* (see Appendix 1). He considered the cultural ramifications of the event and wrote to the president of Fisk: "I would like very much to have the opportunity of collecting songs in that area next spring. At that time, the anniversary of that fire, there undoubted will be many folk expressions and memorials and I believe that research then would be fruitful."[1]

African-American vernacular music had not been collected until the nineteenth century, and then not scientifically. Professional minstrels—whites in blackface—were driven by commerce to learn songs and vocal and instrumental technique from slaves. Abolitionists and post-Civil War Freedmen's Bureau workers, affected by the sentiments in the "Negro spiritual," collected such songs and made early transcriptions. By the third decade of the twentieth century, collections by Henry Krehbiel, Natalie Curtis Burlin, Guy Johnson, and other whites enlarged the base of published African-American vernacular music. Academics and religious leaders had also taken an interest in vernacular song. Three such men were associated with Fisk University: the Work brothers—John II and Frederick—and Thomas Talley. Collections by John Work III's father and uncle emphasized African-American religious expression, finding it a worthy representation of the race to white society. Professor Talley, in addition, collected game, dance, and children's songs. John Work III followed his father, uncle, and Talley but with a different emphasis. Work would not focus solely on song collection, as his predecessors, white and black, had done. Work was also interested in social context, performance practices (including instrumental accompaniment to songs, something usually ignored by previous collectors of African-American music), and song creation. The Natchez tragedy would be an opportunity to study all three.

Indeed Work's prediction was correct: the Natchez fire was quickly memorialized in song. Black musical groups cut several memorials to fallen comrade Barnes, including songs by Gene Gilmore, Baby Doo Caston, and the Lewis Bronzeville Five. More than a decade later, major blues artists recorded tales of the event—including Howling Wolf's "Natchez Burnin' " and John Lee Hooker's misdated "Disaster of '36." These, however, are the tributes by people far from the event, and Work was interested in how the community itself would commemorate such a tragedy.

John Work III came from a musical family. His grandfather, John Wesley Work, was born a slave in Kentucky in 1848.[2] First known as Little Johnny Grey, he was bought or leased by Colonel Work of Nashville, Tennessee. With his master, John Wesley spent some of his youth in New Orleans, where he attended rehearsals of the opera company, learned to read and write English and speak French, and developed his beautiful tenor singing voice. Sometime before the Civil War, upon his return to Nashville, John Wesley was asked to organize and train an African-American choir at Rev. Nelson Merry's First Baptist Church. The choir included three future members of the original Fisk Jubilee Singers.[3]

Fisk University was founded in January, 1866, in the immediate aftermath of slavery's abolition. The school's initial financial woes began to diminish when, in 1871, the Fisk Jubilee Singers began a fundraising tour. Response to their presentation of spirituals was so strong that Fisk could soon build Jubilee Hall, the South's first permanent structure built for the education of black students. Fisk always measured itself by the highest standards of American education, and its alumni include W.E.B. DuBois, the social critic and co-founder of the NAACP; writers James Weldon Johnson and Arna Bontemps; and Booker T. Washington was on its Board of Trustees. (Contemporary alumni include Thurgood Marshall, John Hope Franklin, and Nikki Giovanni.)

John Work's two sons, John Wesley II (b. 1872) and Frederick Jerome (b. 1879) were born in Nashville and attended Fisk. Upon being hired by the university in 1898, John Wesley II reorganized the Fisk Jubilee Singers, and thereafter taught history and Latin in addition to music. He led Fisk's male quartet, which recorded for Victor Records in 1909 and 1911, for Edison in 1912, and for Columbia Records in 1915 and 1916. His book *Folk Song of the American Negro* was published in 1915. Despite its title, the book uses only Negro spirituals as examples of black American music. It does, however, include in its text discussions of African song, American folk song, transmigration, character and peculiarity—all in all, fairly dense stuff. The book identified the Work family name with African-American vernacular music. It was an identity his son would not forsake.

John Work II suffered a heart condition, and collapsed at Nashville's Union Station as he

John Work was a gifted composer and educator. One of the first African American academics to argue the value of African American folk music, he preserved this heritage both in his book, *American Negro Songs and Spirituals,* and through his work with the Fisk Jubilee Singers. c. 1950. Courtesy of Fisk University, Franklin Library, Special Collections.

was about to board the New York train on September 7, 1925. His wife Agnes held him in her arms as he died. John Wesley Work III, a student at the Institute of Musical Art (now Juilliard School of Music), brought his mother, sisters, and brother to New York to live after his father's death.[4] Fisk soon reclaimed its own. The new university president, Thomas E. Jones, asked Agnes—herself an alto of some renown—to return to Nashville to train student singers. She had sung at Fisk as a student under Adam Spence and professionally as a member of F. J. Loudin's troupe which toured Britain in 1897–1898. By January 1927, she was again a valued member of the Fisk community. But tragedy struck the Work family the next month when Agnes suffered a fatal stroke while singing with a mixed octet in St. Louis.[5]

Shortly thereafter, John Work III was called to Fisk to assume his mother's duties and given a faculty appointment in the music department, teaching undergraduate composition. In 1932 he was awarded a Rosenwald Fellowship that he used to study music at Yale.[6] He returned to Fisk in 1933. His work at Yale stimulated his interest in the roots of African-American music. Yale professor and friend George Herzog wrote in a letter dated November 19, 1935:

> . . . glad to know more about your researches . . . especially interested in your saying that you plan, in your present work, to take up the statement of collectors who have questioned the purity of Negro folk-song. That is a question which has interested me all along. Whatever the ultimate origin, African or not, of American Negro folk-song I personally believe little has survived from Africa, and that most of it grew on American soil. It is a distinct contribution of its own, and not a copy of European-American folk songs. It is here, I believe, that men of great scholarship like Guy B. Johnson and George Pullen Jackson may not see the problem in full perspective . . . happy to know that *you who have so much more*

access to the material and a more intimate acquaintance with the background are interested in a similar approach.[7] [emphasis added]

Herzog encouraged Work to study Negro folklore using principles of comparative musicology. Jeff Todd Titon, professor of music at Brown University, points out that Herzog

> was the leading comparative musicologist in the USA then. Herzog, who was undertaking similar projects among American Indians in the 1930s, and publishing them in folklore journals, provided at least a model for Work. Field recording, musical transcription, and then comparison and interpretation based on musical analysis was the core of their enterprise, but comparative musicologists like Herzog in the United States and Constantin Brailiou in Eastern Europe were also paying attention to cultural contexts, noting down sociological as well as musical data. Developments in the academic fields of folklore, comparative musicology, and sociology were not the only influences upon Work's collection of Black folksong. Ideas of race, class, gender, and heritage, as well as the power of institutions, money, technology, and authority, all shaped the conceptions, collection, and presentation of American folk music between the Wars.[8]

Work's desire to study vernacular music in its social context—what would come to be called ethnomusicology decades later—meant that working solely in the ivory tower of Fisk's music building was too confining. He was preparing for field work.

Herzog was also interested in Work's growing collection of opportunistically gathered folk songs. By all accounts, Work had a fine ear and could scribble a lead sheet for most folk tunes on first hearing. Four- and eight-measure music manuscript fragments in the margins of later notebooks give evidence of this practice. No record of Work's early collection survives, though Herzog wrote, "Since you state that the size of the collection is such that publication of the whole is at the present difficult, it is evidently a collection that ought to be made known, even though only through a reference by number of melodies."[9]

Work also took advantage of the fact that Fisk, in the 1930s, functioned as a training ground for teachers from rural African-American school districts throughout Tennessee, Alabama, and Georgia. During the summer Educator's Sessions at Fisk, Work taught not only music education technique but also the value of vernacular music in schools. As a result, teachers from rural schools in the South became good sources and local contacts. Work's colleague at Fisk, chemistry professor Thomas W. Talley, had used such sources in compiling material for his 1922 book, *Negro Folk Rhymes (Wise and Otherwise)*.

In 1938, one of Work's rural contacts directed him to "Sacred Harp singing," an unusual form of music and social custom. As Work described it in *The Musical Quarterly* (January 1941):

> My interest in this music was aroused in the summer of 1938 by Miss Ruby Ballard, supervisor of Negro Schools in Dale County, Alabama, who was in attendance at Fisk University. She described a musical activity, entirely new to me, which was deeply embedded in

John Work's first field recordings were of shape-note singers. Though he learned about the musical form from his students at Fisk University and though the research was in furtherance of his scholarly goals, he, himself, financed the trip to the Sacred Harp Singing Convention in Ozark, Alabama on September 24–25, 1938. Work is third from the left. Courtesy of Center for Popular Music, Middle Tennessee State University; John W. Work III Field Collection.

the culture of the section. She told how neighbors gathered in the evenings to sing; how birthdays, anniversaries, and holidays were celebrated principally in singing. Frequently music makers from the entire county gathered for a singing festival which might last from one to two days. Once a year singers from all the counties in the section would meet for two days. Early in September she wrote that the Alabama State Sacred Harp Singing Convention would meet in Ozark on the 24th and 25th of the month. Immediately I made plans to attend.

Work scrupulously describes the performance practices of the shape-note singers. However, one significant detail is missing from his article. He had returned to record the singing at a meeting at Dothan, Alabama, on November 28, 1938. It was his first effort at field recording.

Fisk owned a disc recorder, though based on aural evidence the institution did not have the funds to maintain the machine.[10] Nor was it able to supply Work with sufficient recording blanks. In a letter to W. D. Wetherford of Fisk's Humanities Department, Work asked for use of a car, movie equipment, and sound equipment for a Sacred Harp project, stating "I have already made three trips at my own expense."[11] Work had been financing his own research; now he was beginning to search for institutional support.

In 1938, Work also presented the results of his private research. He delivered a talk titled "Negro Folk Music" as a part of Fisk's annual Robinson Music Lecture Series.[12] Work addressed topics including spirituals, blues, and instrumental music, approaching them from a musical, historical, and sociological perspective. In discussing the influence of tradition on audience "attitude" (a sociological term, he noted), Work revealed the wide range of his musical experience as well as a well-honed sense of irony:

> If I were to select the one singing occasion I have witnessed which received the most applause I would mention a program I attended in a large metropolitan center some nine years ago. Because of the deductions I am leading you to make, the occasion and place must remain nameless as must the performers. The occasion was highly cultural. An outstanding Negro soprano and pianist were on the program as well as our own Dr. James Weldon Johnson and an eminent professor from one of the country's largest universities. Also on this program was a Negro quartet. Nine years of constant search for an adjective to describe the singing of that quartet have provided no more fitting one than "terrible." The voices of the group were unusually poor. The harmony was of a particularly inferior grade. As an instance of this, the bass ignored a fundamental musical law observed rigidly by every musical unit—whether the bass instruments of a symphony orchestra, the bull-bass in a hill-billy band, or the bass in a barber shop quartet—that the bass must end on the tonic note. No matter how much wandering he might do in the body of the piece he obeys the fundamental urge to end on the tonic. The bass of this quartet did not end on "do." He only wandered. He was typical of the other members. The quartet was supposed to sing two spirituals—"Good News the Chariot's Coming" and "Steal Away to Jesus." But this quartet with all its bad harmony and voices were forced by the most tumultuous applause to sing six songs before they were allowed to leave the stage. From the standpoint of applause they easily overshadowed all other personalities on the program. The reason for all this? The tradition that America likes to see four Negroes together—singing. The audience, if you would like to know, comprised over a thousand university people!

Not only did Work illustrate how the reception of a performance is shaped by audience expectation, but his view of the distinction between "authenticity," or that which is genuine and grounded in practice (though perhaps unfamiliar) and "tradition," or that with which we are familiar and accustomed, was even more pointed:

> The Hall-Johnson Choir has established a tradition of performing the spirituals to which many influential important New Yorkers subscribe. When the Fisk Choir with its own established tradition of performing the spirituals went to New York in 1933, one of the prominent newspaper critics roundly scored it for not singing the spirituals as well and

in the manner (what he meant was "tradition") of the Hall-Johnson Choir. I am perfectly sure that if the Hall-Johnson Choir were to perform in Nashville, many Nashvillians would condemn it for not singing in the Fisk tradition. And yet, if it were possible to transport a chorus from some rural church in the deep South which could sing the spirituals in an authentic manner with the slow tempi, the ejaculatory style, and the absence of any graduations in dynamics to New York or Nashville, both places would find it uninteresting and disappointing. Authentic as it might be, it would not be traditional.

At the same lecture, Work discussed the blues, anticipating by more than a decade the "blues as poetry" literary model. Work also is the first academic trained in the European tradition to express appreciation for the purely musical values displayed in the accompaniments to blues song—an appreciation both evident and useful when transcribing the Coahoma field recordings four years later. From the 1938 lecture:

> We have in the form of the blues an unexpected phrase balance. As distinguished from orthodox forms which balance phrase by phrase, designated by the terms "antecedent

One of John Work's ongoing jobs at Fisk University was to teach music composition and theory to undergraduates. c. 1950. Credit: Fisk University, Franklin Library, Special Collections.

phrase" and "consequent phrase," the blues has two antecedent phrases balanced by one consequent phrase. The verse can illustrate this phrase balance easily. Let's quote from a well-known blues:

> When I was home the door was never closed
> When I was home the door was never closed
> Where my home is now the good Lord only knows.

You noticed that the second line was merely repetition. This is a feature. This repeated phrase has an important esthetic function in the form. It is definitely a tension factor making the third line, the release line, more welcome.

This word structure is simple enough but the music is infinitely more complex. There are still three lines but they are each different and have a preconceived harmonic basis. Practically every blues conforms to a rigid harmonic mold. This is supplied by an accompaniment which is usually very highly embellished and highly rhythmical. In no manner must this accompaniment be considered subordinant to the singer. It is just as important. Together they form an integral whole. Actually to many the accompaniment is the more interesting. In authentic performances no written music is ever used and the accompaniment resolves itself into improvisation which, in the hands of the better instrumentalists, becomes a demonstration of genuine skill and imagination.

For most of 1939 and 1940, bound to Fisk and Nashville, Work located and collected primarily from local musicians. Of the forty-one folk musicians listed in his notebooks, there exist audio samples of twenty-four.[13]

John Work, using Fisk's recorder and dime-store recording blanks, was on his way to building a notable private collection of recorded Negro folk music. Call-and-response singing at a folk church in Pulaski, Tennessee; a South Carolina ex-convict singing a work song; the Alabama Sacred Harp; banjoist Ned Frazier and fiddler Frank Patterson singing and playing nineteenth-century dance tunes and minstrel songs; Jesse James "Preacher" Jefferson playing blues on the harmonica—these were the start of the collection Work envisioned. Classically trained, comfortable with theory, an accomplished composer, John Wesley Work III was asserting the importance of the self-taught musician, championing the authentic, the indigenous, the vernacular.

THE FISK–LIBRARY OF CONGRESS COAHOMA COUNTY STUDY

John Work's interest in folk music sparked one of the earliest, most important, and comprehensive studies of a folk music culture in the United States. His intention to study the Natchez community became, ultimately, the Fisk–Library of Congress Coahoma County Study, a series of field trips during 1941 and 1942 that resulted in, among other things, the first recordings of blues musicians Muddy Waters, David "Honeyboy" Edwards, and Son House; recordings by several other musical greats including Sid Hemphill; and detailed documentation of a society.

A large-scale folk music study could not be financed with an assistant professor's salary, so John Work again sought to enlist the university administration in his cause. On May 25, 1940, he formally introduced the idea of a complete folk music study in the first of three letters to Fisk University president Thomas Elsa Jones. Following Herzog's methods, the study, Work explained, would include social context, performance practice, and repertoire provenance, and was to be carried out at Natchez, Mississippi, scene of the devastating fire the previous month.

Thomas Elsa Jones, a white Quaker, was president of Fisk from 1926 to 1946. Born in Indiana in 1888, he was educated at the Hartford Theological Seminary and Columbia University. At Fisk, he appointed African-Americans to positions of power and relaxed rules that had prohibited male and female students walking together on campus or from going downtown on their own time. Jones attracted many leading academics to the school faculty, which became two-thirds black by 1945.[14] Despite Jones's liberal policies, Work never developed a close personal relationship with the president.[15] According to Work's wife Edith, Work was "not comfortable" with President Jones, who, despite his record of recruiting and appointing blacks, passed over Work for advancement to positions he was well qualified to hold. Jones denied Work the opportunity to direct the Mozart Society (the university chorus) and three times passed him over for the chairmanship of the music department in favor of whites.[16] This lack of rapport would profoundly affect the Coahoma study.

Within days of the Natchez proposal, Jones and Work met to discuss the project, and others from Fisk's faculty were brought in. Harold Schmidt, chairman of the music department, often had spoken of a research branch for his department. Dr. Charles S. Johnson, famed head of Fisk's social sciences department, was also in favor of an intensive study within a limited territory (Johnson had already led several such studies); he encouraged Work to include folk tales, religious practices, foodways, and occupational lore with his music study.

All the ideas were incorporated into a proposal Work sent to Jones on June 21, 1940. He explained that Natchez was selected because of April's tragic fire: "To the abundance of folklore natural to the community, a new body of lore is due to be added. It is the ballads and music arising out of the holocaust of last April . . . the impact of this terrible fire with its religious implications on the minds and imagination of the unlettered Negroes of that region must of necessity be of such weight as to stimulate the creation of a tremendous amount of folk expression."[17]

The excitement about capturing that "tremendous amount of folk expression" was growing. Five days later, after a meeting, Work wrote to Jones: "As you will recall, we mentioned the possibility of our tying up with the Library of Congress and its tremendous project in Americana folklore research. Both you and Dr. Weatherford [professor of religion and humanities] had a definite feeling that the Lomax people would be interested in seeing their materials put into use at such a place as Fisk University. It certainly would be to our advantage to have the opportunity to work with these American folklore collectors because of their wide experience in this field."[18]

This note reveals how the Library of Congress—where Alan Lomax was employed—was brought into the project: Fisk was developing the study and needed a partner with greater resources. The Library was an obvious choice, and all the Fiskites were enthusiastic. The Library's participation was itself significant. Perhaps the study's greatest contribution was institutional validation of the African-American vernacular as a legitimate and important culture. To many African-Americans, secular music had long been considered not only a low art but also a sin. With few exceptions, Fisk and most of "Negro" academia had emphasized Eurocentric musical practices. As Lomax wrote a year later, "This marks the first occasion on which a great Negro university has officially dedicated itself to the study and publication of Negro folk-songs . . . [the study] will lay the basis, it is believed, for contemporary music history, for a new approach to the field of folk music, for a practical working knowledge of the musical life of people, which will be equally useful to scholars, professionals and administrators in the field."[19]

So it was that on June 29, 1940, President Jones wrote to Jackson Davis of the General Education Board, New York:

> I am submitting herewith an appeal for a special grant to enable Mr. John W. Work, of Fisk University, to pursue studies on the Negro folk ballads in Natchez, Mississippi, and selected areas in the South.
>
> Mr. Work is the son of the famous John W. Work who published one of the first volumes of Negro spirituals and directed the Fisk Jubilee Singers for many years. John Work, Jr. [John Wesley III was known as "Junior" at Fisk], was composing such as "The Tennessee Lullaby" and arranging Negro spirituals while he was yet in his teens.
>
> He has published many choral numbers and arrangements of spirituals. He has just had accepted for publication by Simon, Howell & Co., a volume entitled "Negro Folk Music" which will be off the press in October.[20]

Work's trip was already broadening; Natchez was one of the "selected areas" to which he would travel to document the role of music in the culture. The appeal also indicated that initial contact with the Library of Congress had been made:

> It has already become evident that such a study would be of much interest to the Library of Congress, to John and Allen [sic] Lomax, and to others who have been working in this field. Exchanges of material, comparison of recordings and general collaboration between Fisk University and the Library of Congress have already been agreed upon in case the project can be carried out. In celebrating the 75th Anniversary of the founding of Fisk University, from May 1st through 8th, 1941, it is hoped to present, together with other American music, Negro ballads as they are being created today.[21]

The General Education Board declined the grant proposal, but the researchers were not deterred. Fisk enjoyed the validation brought by its association with the Library of Congress, as well as their superior equipment and resources. Meanwhile, Lomax hoped to work with Fisk's Charles S. Johnson, whose book *Shadow of the Plantation* (1934) was an impressive sociological portrait of a specific region.

Johnson, in addition to directing Fisk's department of social sciences, was also author of *The Collapse of Cotton Tenancy* and *Statistical Atlas of Southern Counties*. A Virginia native (b. July 24, 1893), Johnson earned his Ph.B. at the University of Chicago in 1917 and was a World War I veteran. After the Chicago race riot of 1919, Johnson was appointed executive secretary of the Commission on Race Relations by the governor of Illinois. When the Laura Spelman Rockefeller Memorial Trust endowed Fisk with funds to create a social research program in 1927, Johnson was lured to Nashville. By the mid-1930s, he was the African-American superstar in the social sciences, becoming the first black trustee of the Julius Rosenwald Fund in 1934 and the first black elected vice-president of the American Sociological Society in 1937. In 1946, he would succeed T. E. Jones and become the first black president of Fisk. Johnson was the scholarly power through whom Lomax might gain credibility in academic circles.[22]

Aiding Johnson at Fisk was Lewis Wade Jones, who would become an important player in the Fisk–Library of Congress Coahoma County Study and a contributing author to one of the project's manuscripts. Lewis Jones worked closely with Johnson as a research assistant, supervisor of field studies, and as a departmental instructor. Born in Cuero, Texas, on March 13, 1910, Jones, who was African-American, received his undergraduate degree from Fisk in 1931. He spent the next two years at the University of Chicago as a Social Science Research Council Fellow, returning to Fisk at the end of 1932. He joined the military in 1943, then took a faculty position at the Tuskegee Institute School of Education; he stayed there until his death in 1979, at which time he was a professor of sociology and director of the Tuskegee Institute Rural Development Center. As the Coahoma project took shape, it became clear that Johnson would not be taking an active role; Lomax would be working in the field with Lewis Jones.

This development should have surprised no one. Johnson's survey method, beginning with *Shadow of the Plantation* in 1934, had been to create a questionnaire and then put assistants in the field. For the Coahoma study, he seems to have adapted social and statistical models used in 1938 and 1939 to gather the data that would be published in 1941 as *Growing Up in the Black Belt: Negro Youth in the Rural South,* arguably his most important book.

So, Johnson assumed an advisory role in the Coahoma study. His lack of direct participation and leadership was unfortunate for Work, to whom Johnson had been an ally and friend.[23] He'd been instrumental in securing the Rosenwald Foundation money that allowed the publication of Work's book *American Negro Songs and Spirituals* (1940). He would later appoint Work director of the Fisk Jubilee Singers (1947), and then chair of the music department (1951), making Work the first African-American in that position. The two were even neighbors in the faculty-occupied houses that lined the Fisk campus. Had Johnson assumed more control of the study, it seems likely that Work would have enjoyed a more active role in the fieldwork.

The next record of events is dated nearly a year after the General Education Board grant application. On April 29, 1941, Fisk opened a weeklong celebration of its seventy-fifth anniversary. That first night featured "A Program of Negro Folk Music: Blues, Ballads, Spirituals, and Work Songs by the Golden Gate Quartet and Josh White." The commentators were Sterling Brown from Howard University and Alan Lomax from the Library of Congress. Lomax probably attended Work's anniversary week program; Work began with praise for Lomax and Brown, and for their "program of Negro folk lore that surely must be regarded as one of the great cultural events in Fiskiana . . . So comprehensive was that concert and lecture that this program can hardly be more than an echo of it."[24] Aided by fiddler Frank Patterson, guitarist Ford Britton, and banjoist Nathan Frazier, all local amateurs, Work set out "to establish the thesis that in each of your communities there is an abundance of significant folk lore of which you have been generally unaware but which can easily be discovered and usually made available for the community's appreciation and education."[25] Despite his humble appraisal, Work's program must have had an inherent strength comparable to the professionalism of Josh White and the Golden Gate Quartet. The field recordings Work made of the Frazier/Patterson duo (now in the Library of Congress Archive of Folk Culture and selectively issued on compact disc by Rounder Records in the U.S., and entirely by Document Records in the UK) are considered by scholars and musicians among the finest examples of black string band music.

Lomax's presence allowed face-to-face discussion of the field research project. Evidence of the meeting at Fisk is found in a letter from Lomax to President Jones dated July 1, 1941, and in a mid-September 1941 summary statement by Lomax. This meeting marks the beginning of a major change in the trip, a shift in the control of the project from John Work to Alan Lomax. In attendance were Charles S. Johnson, John Work, John Ross of the drama department,[26] President Jones, and Lomax. In the July letter, Lomax wrote from Washington D.C., "My report of the project discussed by us at our last conference in Dr. Johnson's office has been warmly received in the Library. I think that it would be best to carry out a survey of the type discussed in the Mississippi Delta Counties, and to help Dr. Work in his recording in Nashville and vicinity."[27]

Work's response has not been located, but his attempt to regain control of his study can be gleaned from Lomax's July 30 letter:

> Dear Mr. Work, I think you have gotten things rather mixed. When I was in Nashville, I discussed two separate projects; one, a survey project to be worked out with Dr. Johnson, and, two, a small recording project to be initiated in Nashville by yourself with your fiddlers and local singers at once. I am still very anxious that you begin work on this. (I thought that it might be possible eventually to extend this to include field work.) . . . I am in correspondence with Dr. Johnson about the survey recording project which we plan to initiate sometime in October. I hope to work with you in this connection also."[28]

Had John Work been more highly valued by President Jones, had Charles S. Johnson been more personally present in the project, had Work himself been of a more aggressive nature[29]— then the project's initiator might not have been told, in effect, "Don't call us, we'll call you." Even the palliative for Work's demotion—the Library of Congress would repair Fisk's recorder, allowing him to make better recordings on his field trips—came with a hitch. He would be required, in exchange, to donate twenty discs from his private collection for deposit with the Library. Not only was Work's vision being commandeered, so were his recordings.

Lomax's later account of the study's origin makes no mention of a project being conceived before his involvement. In *The Land Where the Blues Began,* he wrote: "It was clear that Southern blacks would not readily confide in a white folklorist. Therefore, *I approached Fisk University* [emphasis added], the Princeton of black colleges, with the idea of doing a joint field study with my department at the Library of Congress. The aim was to establish a center for black folklore studies at Fisk . . . Charles S. Johnson, head of sociology at Fisk, liked my notion of doing a study of an urbanizing cotton county as a way of accessing the continuing importance of traditions. For this reason we picked Coahoma County, the cotton capital of the Delta, as the site."[30]

Oddly, Lomax omits mention of Charles S. Johnson's recently published *Growing Up in the Black Belt,* a study of Coahoma and seven other Southern counties. A chief point Johnson addressed was the modernizing influence of urbanization on plantation culture and the survival of traditions. Johnson may have welcomed, and even steered to the Delta, a folkloric addendum of his sociological survey, but Lomax's claim of co-authorship seems overextended.

Lomax's own correspondence reveals a less unilateral process than he would claim fifty years later. Three weeks before the initial outing to Coahoma County, Lomax wrote Johnson: "A number of people have suggested that southwestern Tennessee, which is slightly more stable than the Delta area, would be a better region for work than the one we have thought of already."[31] Even two days before the expedition was to begin, the team was making preparations to work in Ripley, Tennessee, and Carthage, Mississippi (which is in the hill country and not the Delta). On August 21, Lomax wrote Johnson: "I hope that by [August 25] Doctors Jones and Work will have consulted about revivals in Tennessee and Mississippi and will have a recording schedule laid out."[32] Also perplexing is that on the same day, Lomax revealed an altogether different plan to his superiors at the Library of Congress. "The purpose of this trip is . . . to record Negro revivals in the region of northwestern Mississippi."—referring to the Delta, not Carthage.

Work, probably finding Lomax's planning too haphazard, resumed his own pursuit. His foremost interest was songs and musical styles, and Lomax's trip—now conforming to his desire for scholarly validation—was becoming increasingly sociological.[33] Work may have feared that songs were being forsaken. He already knew that good material and social context would be found at an annual gospel revival in Ripley, and at a traditional fiddlers' meet in Carthage. Having lost control of the original project, Work seems to have begun planning and fundraising for a new, separate expedition. On August 22, Work wrote to the Fisk comptroller requesting $78.20 for a twelve-day trip to Ripley and Carthage. His budget does not include money for blank discs; that form of institutional support was to come through Lomax. By controlling the flow of blank discs, Lomax could prevent Work's independent expedition.

Aware of Work's plans, and possibly concerned with keeping Charles S. Johnson's good will, Lomax mollified Work in a letter of August 23, making Work's new trip seem the team's primary interest. Writing from D. C., Lomax praised him for the 1938 Negro Sacred Harp songs that Lomax had just coaxed from Work for donation to the Library. He closed: "I shall see you the morning of the 25th, ready, I hope, for our trip to Ripley." By inviting himself along, Lomax was subsuming Work's new trip as he had the Natchez one.

On August 24, 1941, Alan Lomax arrived in Nashville. With him was his wife Elizabeth, who would assist him with the field recorder, which filled the back of their car. Lewis Jones and

John Ross from Fisk's drama department would have to travel separately. Arrangements were made for John Work to meet them in Clarksdale on the twenty-eighth, a Thursday. Before departing on that day, Work—holding steadfast to the potential of his vision—wrote a letter to President Jones outlining his plans for a separate recording project, also twofold. First, he wanted "to record and study unique or interesting folk activities; i.e. camp meetings, Revivals, barn dances, fiddler's meets, etc." in nearby communities; as well, he was interested in "interviewing creative individuals in the various communities and recording their songs." He also wrote, "Following his discussion with you, Mr. Alan Lomax has agreed to aid in these projects by supplying me with phonograph discs. I have just received a letter informing me of his sending me 50 of them this week." In return, Lomax demanded, however, that the recordings Work would make on these discs be donated to the Library of Congress; he promised to make copies for Fisk (a promise unfulfilled).[34] In closing, Work revived his original idea for recording in Natchez, stating his desire for approval of the requested $250 for the year's work, and "that this amount of money will permit a trip to Natchez, MS next Feb. I understand that these projects described are subordinate to the larger folk song project in which the Social Science Dept. and Mr. Lomax are collaborating, and in which I will also serve." The good soldier, Work then marched out to the field.

For better or worse, the project was underway, with Lomax in charge. The plan was to begin with a preparatory week-long trip in August 1941, which was to be followed by a more in-depth trip several months later. Recordings were to be made both times. After the first visit by Lomax, Lewis Jones, Ross, and Work, Fisk dispatched two graduate students—Samuel C. Adams Jr. and Ulysses S. Young—to Coahoma County for the fall 1941 semester, allowing time for in-depth field research. During the short preliminary trip to the Delta, Jones and Ross seem to have been left to their own devices in surveying the plantation culture for future study. Lomax, as far as can be determined, did not supervise Lewis Jones as he did Work. Jones most likely reported directly to Charles S. Johnson at Fisk.

Lomax's summary of what had been Work's idea is compelling: "the agreed upon study was to explore objectively and exhaustively the musical habits of a single Negro community in the Delta, to find out and describe the function of music in the community, to ascertain the history of music in the community, and to document adequately the cultural and social backgrounds for music in the community."[35] Coahoma County had a population of nearly 50,000 in 1940, but it boasted only one city, Clarksdale, with a population of 12,168.

As the Library of Congress guide to *The Library of Congress–Fisk University Mississippi Delta Collection* states:

> This project was the first racially mixed field study in the Deep South. Racial tension was high in the Delta at the time of the study, and cooperation was necessary. Fisk University needed the backing of the federal government in the form of the Library of Congress, while Alan Lomax needed the help of black scholars to overcome racial suspicion and to facilitate rapport with informants.

Lewis Jones was an instructor in the Department of Social Sciences at Fisk University from 1932 to 1942, where he worked closely with Charles S. Johnson. In 1949 the two co-wrote *A Statistical Analysis of Southern Counties; Shifts in the Negro Population of Alabama*. After leaving Fisk, Jones moved to the Tuskegee Institute School of Education, where he was a professor of sociology. This photo comes from the 1958 Tuskegee University yearbook. Courtesy Tuskegee University Archives.

Rapport *did* exist between the informants—who were not all of the same socioeconomic class—and the academic blacks. Work, Jones, and Adams were all southern-born and living in the south under the same Jim Crow laws as the Mississippians, a fact not lost on the locals.[36]

Work and Lomax worked from Friday August 29 through Wednesday, September 3, in Clarksdale, Hollandale, Stovall, Money, Mound Bayou, and Lake Cormorant. They recorded church services, spiritual singing, oral histories, and secular songs, including blues by Muddy Waters, Son House, and Willie Brown. But the only aural evidence of Work during that week is the instantaneous disc recordings of the project's most famous byproduct, McKinley Morganfield, aka Muddy Waters. Work conducts two of the four interviews with "Stovall's famous guitar picker." In the second, Lomax interrupts after several minutes, commandeering the questioning. In subsequent recordings, Lomax's is the only interviewer's voice heard.[37]

John Work—a trained musician and a member of the ethnic group being studied—was kept from the heart of the project and, after the trip, retired to a room in the social sciences building at Fisk to transcribe the discs. From the enthusiasm in Work's voice and the relaxed responses of Muddy Waters in the few moments when Work has control of an interview, one can only wonder what may have been gathered had he been allowed to truly "facilitate rapport with informants."

As noble as an interracial team was, it was not without its own problems. Underlying conflicts become evident in these two perspectives on some of the participant's roles. Lomax wrote about Lewis Jones, who had picked cotton in rural Texas as a child: "No plantation boss could resist the sincere but respectful Prof. Jones (call me "Looey" and I'd feel more at home) when he knocked at the back door and, hat in hand, asked them to help him in his study of the 'colored' problem. The toughest cracker overseers have confided their troubles and their secrets to Jones."[38] And Jones (as recounted by Lomax) perfectly understood the impossibility of the Fiskites doing this work without a white person's presence, and how that presence affected them: "Every Negro got to have his white man, his boss, to look after him when he get in trouble with the white world. Now I don't know about the rest of you, but this [Lomax] is *my* white man on this trip . . . We are registered in the minds of the authorities who control the destinies of everyone in Coahoma as Lomax's colored folks."[39]

The 1941 Coahoma outing resulted in twenty-five sixteen-inch disc recordings, totaling approximately twelve hours. The material ranged from church services to blues to interviews. The experience familiarized the researchers with the issues of field recording, and allowed them to better prepare for their next recording trip. Lewis Jones returned almost immediately (September 9) to Clarksdale, and on his first evening he went to five juke joints and listed the songs he found on each club's jukebox. (See Appendix 5.) Jones was, at that point, laying groundwork for Fisk graduate students to work from September 25 to the end of October on the "socio-musical survey," and for Lomax and the Fiskites to return to Coahoma in late October or early November for two or three weeks to finish the study. Lomax wrote, "The records will then be brought to the Library, and copies sent to Fisk University for transcription and study by various members of the faculty. By the middle of December Dr. Johnson and I look forward to having the material well in hand for final editing . . . The projected field work will result in a study, jointly edited by Dr. Johnson and his assistants, and by Alan Lomax, which will be published under the sponsorship of Fisk University."[40] Five hundred and eighty dollars had been spent to date, with an anticipated total budget of $1,947.90 (revised on October 2 to $1,573.65).

Despite the expectation to return in six weeks, nearly a year would pass before the study was resumed. The first delay came on September 16, when Johnson wrote Lomax: "I have just had a long distance telephone call from Lewis Jones in Clarksdale, Mississippi . . . This is the most feverish year that the section has experienced so far as cotton picking is concerned . . . [Plantation owners] are urging that the actual recording that may require some time be done after November 1st. They said around November 15th."[41] Jones wrote, "When we left here seventy-five cents a hundred was being paid for cotton picking, and today they are paying $1.50. [Ultimately prices went to $2.00, the highest since 1926.[42]] People have quit their town jobs and gone to share in the first cotton prosperity in a long time." He had plans to do some picking of his own for the first time in sixteen years: "I hope I'll pick enough to pay for the overalls I'll have to buy. Talking with the pickers all day should yield some materials and some leads."[43]

Meanwhile, Fisk held a training seminar over the weekend of September 20–22 "to acquaint the graduate students, who are to carry on the field work, with the field of Negro folk-song and its problems."[44] Two graduate students—Samuel Adams, from the Sociology Department, and Ulysses Young, a Fellow in Anthropology—then joined Lewis Jones in Coahoma County. Adams was researching his masters thesis, *Technology, Secularization, and the Rural Negro,* for which he was awarded a degree in 1947; Young, a fellow, would not have been required to submit one. The two coauthored the very informative "Report on Preliminary Work in Clarksdale, Mississippi." (See Appendix 3.) Adams later went on to become the U.S. ambassador to Niger.

By October, John Work and his student assistant Harry Wheeler were transcribing the recordings from the first trip. They created a laboratory of their own, allowing for the careful atten-

After receiving his Master's Degree from Fisk University, Samuel C. Adams, Jr. attended the University of Chicago, where he received his PhD in 1953. He had a long and distinguished career in public service, highlighted by his appointment to the post of Ambassador to the Republic of Niger in 1968–1969. This photograph is from that time period. Courtesy of National Archives.

tion the transcriptions needed. The laboratory was given space in the sociology building, Charles S. Johnson's domain, rather than the music building. The lack of participation by the music department after the initial meetings attended by department chair Schmidt, a white man, is puzzling. Did Schmidt, like many trained in the Eurocentric canon, feel the subject unworthy? This viewpoint is still common in many university music departments.

Plans for the November 15 return were in place as late as October 29, when Johnson wrote Lomax about the continuing field work of Adams and Young: "[They have been] spending continuous time in Coahoma County, getting acquainted, working in the cotton fields, talking with persons, visiting churches, juke houses and pool rooms, etc. . . . I am having copies made of their field notes and interviews, and a copy will go to the Library of Congress [[45]] . . . Dr. [E. H.] Watkins [Ethnology and Cultural Anthropology] and Mr. Lewis Jones have spent two periods in Coahoma County since you left, and they are giving rather close supervision to the two field workers."[46]

The November return was finally put off, due to a combination of events—mainly the weather and, for Lomax, other pressing work in Washington. Then, in December, Pearl Harbor was attacked. In a January 1942 letter to Lewis Jones, Lomax recounted his recent suggestion to Johnson that they terminate the Coahoma study: "possibly the study we had outlined was a bit utopian in the situation of the present crisis, and asking [Dr. Johnson] whether he thought so, and wondering whether we had better tackle some other job at this moment . . . I'd like very much to spend the money which has been set aside for this project for some sort of meaningful study which would be carried on in collaboration with Fisk University."[47]

Meanwhile, John Work continued transcribing, and the Fisk field workers continued collecting data. Samuel Adams wrote Dr. Johnson on January 8, 1942:

Family schedules and musician questionnaires have been filled out for all of the rural families for an area of about seven miles. (All of the Negro plantation families between the school and the city, a distance of about 4 1/2 miles; and all of the families for about 3 miles going in the other direction from the school.) Not including work done previously, up to date forty families have been contacted. In addition to the filling out of the family schedules and musical questionnaires, an inquiry has been made and information secured from individuals on folk stories, tales, songs, folk practices, religious practices and on general plantation poverty and folk practices in regard to midwivery. It is felt that within another week the King and Anderson Plantation area can be completed.[48]

Four days later, Adams wrote again, revealing a sense of the students' living conditions. They'd completed another fourteen reports. "At present we are living with a Mr. Downs here at the school. We have lived here with him for a period of three weeks due to the fact that since Mr. Wright and his son have married they require the use of their home. At present Mr. Downs does not fully appreciate the arrangement. He has been nice, congenial, and cooperative, but he complains of not being able to sleep due to the fact that he has two other people bunking together in his bed with him, and at first the matter of the electric light burning late at night."[49]

Six months after the first Coahoma trip, Lomax filed a report on the Library's work with Fisk. It reads, in its entirety:

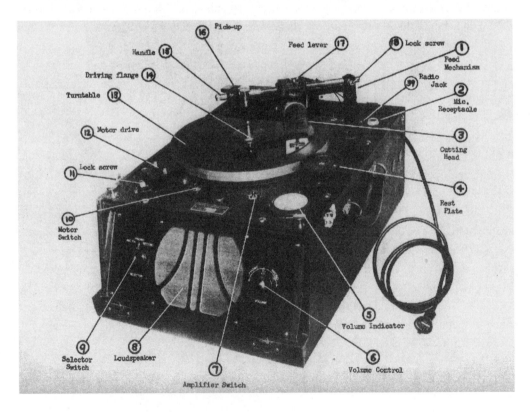

March 2, 1942. Archive of American Folk-song, Music
Secretary's Office
Dear Miss Caton:

In cooperation with the Fisk University Departments of Sociology and Music, the Archive made a trip to Coahoma County, Mississippi, last summer and recorded there about twenty 16-inch slow speed records of Negro music including many items which will eventually be published by the Archive in record form. This trip was preparatory to an exhaustive investigation of the folklore of this county by Fisk research workers.

On the way back to Washington, according to plan, I stopped to record some of the best ballad singers of the Virginia mountain area, obtaining from them also much material which is being used in our publication of folk songs.
Respectfully yours,
AL
Assistant in Charge
Archive of American Folk Song

Lomax also had some accounting to take care of. To receive reimbursement for payments to artists in 1941, Lomax needed witnessed chits, and he'd neglected to procure them during the

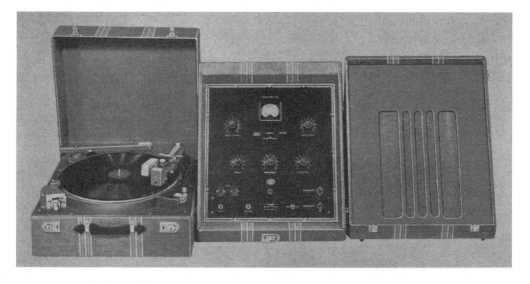

(Opposite): Presto Model D disc recorder. This was a portable 12" turntable model complete with built-in amplifier and speaker. John Work used the Fisk machine for the Sacred Harp and subsequent field recordings as well as student recitals and Jubilee Singers rehearsals at the University. (Above): Presto Model Y disc recorder. Model Y was a bulky component system with a 16" turntable, amplifier, and monitor speaker. The Library of Congress' unit had a modified power supply that could operate from either alternating current or batteries, allowing it to run off a wall circuit or a car battery. Courtesy of Alan Graves, personal collection, www.televar.com/grshome

trip.[50] Around March 10 he sent copies of these chits to John Work for witnessing, and Work passed them along to Lewis Jones and John Ross for signatures.[51] Lomax had waited seven and a half months to tend to this errand, but ten days later, on March 20, he sent a note to Dr. Johnson asking him to hurry the matter and blaming the Fisk professors for the delay: "The whole darned United States Accounting Office and the war effort are being held up by this procrastination."[52]

Lomax received his signatures and his money but he did not expedite matters when others needed help. On March 17, Lomax sent Muddy Waters a form notifying him of the inclusion of "Can't Be Satisfied" and "Country Blues" in a Library of Congress album, for which Muddy would receive a twenty-dollar check. Muddy wrote Lomax three letters over the next ten weeks inquiring about his money. ("I. thought I. wood write you all about my check I. am. still , wating on it but I haven got any answer from. you all."[53]) Nine months after being told of his recompense, Muddy received the promised two copies of the record; while there is no record of the payment, Muddy remembered receiving a twenty-dollar check.[54]

By the second week in July 1942, the return trip to Coahoma County was imminent. Lomax arrived in Nashville on the thirteenth and spent the evening with Work, reviewing his Nashville area recordings. These included sides by the fiddle and banjo team Frank Patterson and Nathan Frazier who had appeared at Fisk's seventy-fifth anniversary program. Another of the thirteen discs contained a sermon, "Dry Bones in the Valley," which was prefaced with the song "Don't Let Nobody Turn You 'Round," sung by Nashville's Fairfield Four, a quartet that would go on to fame on network radio and records. Lomax's notes indicate no recognition of the significance of any of the music Work collected. "Rest of evening with John Work getting his records ready for deposit and trying to work out his problems—mostly of incompetence, laziness and lack of initiative on his part. Violently hot all day in this filthy and ugly old town."[55]

By midday Thursday, August 16, Lomax was headed to Memphis—without John Work or Lewis Jones. Work was not expected, but Jones's absence is more peculiar. The tension between Lomax and Jones is evident in Lomax's field notebook, in which Lomax writes, "Lewis Jones at 12 o'clock refused to begin the trip with me to Coahoma, deciding to wait now until Sat morning. More and more convinced he really resents me."[56] By the seventeenth Lomax was in the Delta, and by the nineteenth Jones, with Fisk music student William Allen (who owned the car) and a student observer Margaret Just Wormley in tow, had joined him.

For the rest of July and the first half of August, the crew worked the Delta. Lomax etched seventy-six discs with blues, hollers, sermons, spirituals, gospel songs, quill (panpipes) tunes, ballads, and stories. John Work did join Lomax for a week (July 26–30) in the middle of the trip, and was present when Muddy Waters and his family filled out the general musical questionnaire.

Lewis Jones and his students continued the statistical and ethnographic study of the towns and plantations in the area. On August 15, after recording a fife and drum picnic, the frazzled group—"the dust and heat and fatigue finally got me," Lomax wrote in his notes—headed back to Nashville.[57] John Work had spent most of his summer there, teaching educator's sessions to support his extended family for which he had assumed responsibility after his parents' deaths. He also spent time composing and arranging music, which would garner him both Composer's Guild awards and the honor of directing the world-famous Fisk Jubilee Singers.

If he had spent some time that summer pondering his role in a project that he'd conceived and been virtually evicted from, he may have received some solace in thinking of his mentor Dr. Herzog. Herzog's methodology in comparative musicology, according to Jeff Titon, "recognized a distinction between the collector or traveler who gathered the music, and the scholar or scientist (and this is how Work must increasingly have seen his role) who transcribed and analyzed it and prepared it for publication. He may have regarded Lomax's role as principally that of collector, not as scholar—and in so thinking he would have been exactly right. Work probably regarded his scholarship, and the published work that was to come out of it, as pre-eminent and far more important than Lomax's collection of the material. Indeed, Lomax was incapable of Work's kind of scholarship, and Work knew it."[58]

With the fieldwork completed, preparation for the monograph began immediately. On July 24, 1942, President Jones wrote Work: "In accord with our recent conversation, I understand that you will put into shape for publication the results of the Coahoma County folk music study." Work responded on August 18 with a detailed plan for transcribing the records, correlating the interviews with the music, interpreting the gathered materials, conferencing with other authorities in the field of folk song, and editing and assembling the book. He received authorization from Fisk on September 22 to begin the task.

On October 7, however, a proprietary dispute began: "I am still not clear as to what role the Library of Congress is to have in the completion of the study," Lomax wrote Fisk's president. "Our investment in the project was a considerable one and I should be embarrassed to make a report on the basis of the plan attached to your letter of September 22. It is not clear where the editorial supervision of the project should lie or how the monograph should be laid out."[59]

President Jones responded to Lomax, October 19, 1942: "I have discussed with Messrs. Johnson and Work the cooperative relations that can and should exist between the three agencies in developing this volume. I think we have a general understanding and there is no disposition, I am sure, on the part of any one to take advantage of the other." Note Jones's reference to "three agencies"—Lomax earlier had nominated himself and Charles S. Johnson as authors. It must have become apparent to Johnson and President Jones that a musicologist—a third agency—was needed.

Further, Johnson was not likely interested in putting his name on the Coahoma study. Though musically compelling, the trip's sociology was not up to his standards. Only one hundred plantation families were surveyed for the project; for *Shadow of the Plantation* (1934), Johnson questioned 600 families. From 1938 to 1940, Johnson directed a survey of over 2,200 black youth of eight counties across five states; the data became the basis for *Growing Up in the Black Belt* (1941).[60]

Labor continued. The Library began duplicating 196 twelve-inch acetates from 1942. Fisk developed a folk culture seminar, calling in their most prestigious faculty members as guest instructors, including Professor Thomas Talley from the chemistry department, author of *Negro Folk Rhymes (Wise and Otherwise)* (1922), and George Pullen Jackson, professor of German at Peabody University, author of *White Spirituals in the Southern Uplands.*(1933) Ten students signed on for the course of nineteen seminars, ranging from "Characteristics of a Folk Culture" to "Dance Music and the Blues," which covered "Sex and love in the culture. The family pattern and love-making conventions. The red light district."[61]

Late in October, Fisk's president learned by happenstance of Lomax's departure from the Library of Congress, and thus from the project. Jones was writing to arrange a meeting during a forthcoming trip to Washington D.C. The meeting was held with Dr. Harold Spivacke, the Library's Chief of the Division of Music, and recapitulated in a letter from Spivacke to Jones in November. The body of the letter is six numbered points. The first is: "All relations between Fisk University and the Library of Congress in connection with the Coahoma County Study are to be between us personally for the time being at least." Point two: "For the present it does not seem necessary to set up an advisory committee, but consultants will be called in from time to time as needed." Dr. Charles S. Johnson had long been removed and Lomax was gone from the project. Lewis Jones was preparing for his military induction. Only Work kept his eye on the ball and kept it moving forward. He continued transcribing the discs, taking notes on their contents and meaning. He is the subject of point five: "Dr. Work is to submit samples of his transcriptions." The heads of the institutions were not sure what to make of the project, but they clutched it close.

Work was relishing his task. Four days before Spivacke's letter was written, Work sent President Jones a five page memo reporting on his transcription progress, including the completion of all the records from 1941. Most interesting is his commentary on technique, which shows a devotion to the actual and not the romanticized: "With my assistant Mr. Harry Wheeler, we have transcribed 20 spirituals, 2 blues, a sermon by Rev. Ch. H. Savage, and a prayer. In transcribing the spirituals I made an earnest effort to transcribe the songs just as they were sung—not as I thought they ought to be sung . . . It is more important however to recognize that these sermon-poems are intoned. And the audience's response to these is due more to the preacher's tone and the pitch than to the words. Therefore, I point with a great deal of pride to our transcription in musical notes of the folk sermon recorded at the Mt. Ararat church. To do this accurately and comprehensibly required practically all of three weeks."[62]

Work was also moving toward his interpretation of the data: "I have studied or am in the process of reading these new books: *Father of the Blues* (Handy), *Our Singing Country* (Lomax), *Lanterns on the Levee* (Percy), *Folk Songs of the South* (Cox), *Slave Songs from the Georgia Coast* (Parrish), *Folk Songs of Mississippi* (Hudson), and magazine articles."[63]

Professor Work continued on his tasks, submitting to President Jones on February 10, 1943 samples of his transcriptions and two essays. Jones sent a copy to Mr. Spivacke. In June 1943, Jones met twice with the Library in D. C. In July, John Work was nearly done with his manuscript. In a report to Jones, he wrote that this would

> consist of 158 transcriptions of folk songs; a folk sermon found among the Negroes of Coahoma County; a catalogue of the disposition of the records (whether transcribed or not); and a treatise consisting of 10 chapters, bibliography, two indexes (general and classified); a biographical appendix; and a preface describing the transcribing process.

I received from the Library of Congress 196 duplicate recordings of folk material gathered by Mr. Lewis Jones and Mr. Alan Lomax in the summer of 1942 . . . I am reasonably sure that for the first time a Negro folk sermon was transcribed in its musical symbols . . .

Last month [June 1943], I went back to Clarksdale for the purpose of interviews to fill in certain gaps in the materials and to obtain some pictures of Delta scenery . . . I believe that the Mississippi Folklore Project will prove to be more and more important. Unquestionably we have the most important and comprehensive Negro folk music collection in America (or in the world probably) except that in the Library of Congress . . . Also we have preserved, by a stroke of good fortune much valuable Negro music and speech that due to the disruption of the Negro rural life in the South by the war might have been lost forever.[64]

By the end of July 1943, Work had turned in his manuscript and transcriptions, and was already considering changes. Work wrote President Jones on July 30:

In studying the treatise on the Mississippi folklore project which I have submitted to you, you will observe that there is no introductory chapter describing the organization of the project with reference to the valuable contributions to it made by the Library of Congress and Fisk University. Also none of the essays I have written attempts to present the sociological background of the area studied. I felt that the first should be written by you or some person whom you might designate to write it.

Mr. Lewis Jones has written the sociological part and while his organization principle is at variance with mine, I do not believe it is in conflict with mine. Such differences, or duplications which might occur could be easily harmonized I feel, if the project is to evolve as a one-book affair. If it is to become a two-book project, my volume would need a preface.[65]

The Lewis Jones manuscript is, indeed, simply his thirty-two page introduction tacked onto John Work's manuscript, minus Work's indexes and transcriptions. (The longhand versions of much of Work's paper are in his microfilm files at Fisk.)

The project seemed on course for a grand finish. But within two months, the bungling had begun. The Library's Botkin wrote to John Work on September 21, 1943: "No one here seems to know anything about the manuscript which you say President Jones was to have brought to Washington in July." It was soon recovered, though only briefly: "Your completed manuscript reached me only a few weeks ago and I have not had a chance to go over it thoroughly," Botkin wrote Work on November 10. "The Library has by no means lost interest in the project but the project has lost two of its collaborators, Alan Lomax, who is too busy, and Lewis Jones who, I understand, is in the Army . . . I still think the main job, which is one of correlating a large body of diversified data into a unified whole, still lies ahead." Dr. Spivacke wrote Work that same day, assuring Work that his interest in the manuscript was not diminished, and that he awaited Dr. Botkin's report on the paper and his own opportunity to read it.[66]

The paper trail then drops off dramatically. Lewis Jones, who had been inducted into the army on October 13, 1943, served until October 8, 1945. On November 23, 1945, the Fisk graduate student Samuel Adams submitted his thesis *Technology, Secularization, and the Rural Negro.* Three weeks later, President Jones received a letter from Duncan Emrich, the new chief at the Library's Archive of American Folk Song: "I have recently assumed the position left vacant by Dr. Botkin . . . The manuscript being prepared by Dr. John Work . . . seems to have been left at somewhat loose ends . . . We do not have a copy of the manuscript."[67]

President Jones wrote Emrich on December 26, 1945: "It was expected that Mr. [Lewis] Jones's study would be integrated with that made by Mr. Work and a volume brought out under either the auspices of Fisk University or the Library of Congress; or jointly. As both Mr. Jones and Mr. Lomax were inducted into the armed forces, Mr. Work completed the first draft of the manuscript which was submitted to Messrs. Botkin and Spivacke for review and suggestions as to what could be done with the study. Neither of these gentlemen were able to do anything about it at the time so the matter rested there. I plan to come East in January and hope I may have a full talk with you regarding the completion of the study, if this seems advisable."[68]

Record of the project stopped for two more years, resuming December 18, 1947, when Lomax first attempted to exploit the research himself. He wrote Work requesting permission to "bring a portable machine and copy off some of the material I need from the Coahoma recordings." Work, whose manuscript had been mishandled, apparently inquired as to the purposes of the copies, for Lomax replied on January 2, 1948:[69] "Dear Mr. Work: I believe you know why I want to get copies of the Coahoma records. I need the material for a book on which I am presently engaged. The records are not suitable for commercial exploitation and that is not my interest in them."

Lomax's book was completed five decades later, during which time many of the recordings made in Coahoma County found their way onto commercial releases, legal and otherwise. The first usage was a year after the first trip, when Lomax included Muddy Waters in a Library of Congress album of 78 RPM discs. In the 21st century, musicians have experimented with some of the recordings, adding rhythms, beats, and other instruments.[70] Among the more prominent artists recorded are bluesmen Son House, Willie Brown, David "Honeyboy" Edwards, and Muddy Waters; fife and drum leader Sid Hemphill, and gospel singer Bozie Sturdivant of the Silent Grove Baptist Church.

Alan Lomax contributed greatly to our knowledge of American culture. He made great field recordings. His immense legacy of recordings is testament to his negotiation of circumstances—in domestic and international cultures. The intensity of the performances confirms the intimacy he created for the recording situation.

When Lomax published his book in 1993, John Work was mentioned three times: in the preface, he was mentioned in association with the musical transcriptions; in the sole text mention, he was present at the recording of Muddy Waters; in the acknowledgments, his name is listed with Jones and Adams. Adams is not otherwise mentioned; Jones, who is cited several times, is the only one portrayed as an actual participant in the research.

When Lewis Jones and John Work were cobbling together the "final report," Adams's manuscript was not yet written. However, Adams did have access to the Jones and Work writings, and he employs—without attribution—the River, Railroad, and Highway metaphors that Jones had been using since at least 1942. To a modern, proprietary eye, it is surprising that Adams would use another's work without citing the source. However, Jones was Adams's teacher; they both worked in the specialized field of social science at Fisk, where a spirit of cooperative scholarship would have been imperative. It's all but inconceivable that Adams was trying to get away with anything.

But fifty years later, when Lomax published *Land Where the Blues Began*, his audience would have had no idea about his sources. Adams's text was available to Lomax who, in *Land*, used photographs of the Dipsie Doodle and a hand drawn map of a Clarksdale neighborhood, both of which first appeared in Adams's master's thesis. Lomax does not attribute his source. (Lomax also used Work's photograph of a sharecropper's cabin, unattributed; Work's handwriting can be seen bleeding through.) In much the same way that Lomax reconfigured the population and cultural expression of Coahoma County by focusing on the uneducated artists over more educated spokespeople, by favoring "tradition"—spirituals—over an authentic presentation of current church practice, he disavowed the community of scholars that worked with him. (See Editors' Introduction to the John Work manuscript). As Adams, Jones, and Work repeatedly make clear, Coahoma County was a diverse community that included educated black Southerners able to articulate their ideas about their home. By devaluing their contributions, by emphasizing the culture of powerful but less articulate artists that he—Lomax—is required to "explain" or "interpret" for mainstream America, by not citing the major contributions of black Southern scholars who helped him with his work, Lomax creates an appealing but static and nostalgic portrait of black Southern America.

Coahoma County was a vital, active, and evolving world. Several of the Fiskites wrote optimistically of the expected results of their work, and though nothing of the study was published during their lifetimes, their expectations—a basis for contemporary music history, a new approach to folk music, a working knowledge of the musical life of people—were not incorrect. There are many details, facts, and descriptions that may have been lost without the study, including Work's discussion of Charles Haffer's broadsides. The early musicological analyses seem almost prescient—especially Work's focus on the songs "John Henry," "Frankie and Albert," and "Stagolee." The graduate seminar based on the study's findings brought together many of the area's most prominent African-American academics, creating a think tank that must have sent ripples throughout the world of African-American cultural study, arming a new generation for the task of research and analysis.

Every bit as important as what went on back in Nashville and Washington D. C., was the effect of the researchers' presence on the Delta people. These rural citizens, with little money and little means for travel or communication beyond the distance of a field holler, lived in isolation. Seeing their lives as the focus of study by outsiders must have heartened many individuals, validating their culture and affirming their way of life. The outsiders' presence surely had that impact on Muddy Waters, who felt that if he were important enough to be recorded in Mississippi, he might be talented enough to make a career in Chicago. As its creators hoped, this study did mark a turning point in the appreciation of African-American culture.

History has been indifferent to John Wesley Work III. His ideas and initiative, his research and analysis have been appropriated by others, his contribution not acknolwedged. In the texts of Alan Lomax, John Work is barely mentioned. Work's personal field recordings—those other than from the Coahoma Study—have seen only pitiable release: the occasional Library of Congress issue, a small folk collection here and there. Several were released as part of Rounder Records' "Alan Lomax Collection." Those not deposited in the Library of Congress are in the archives of the Center for Popular Music, Middle Tennessee State University.

After Dr. John Work died from a heart attack in 1967, his widow Edith maintained his personal papers and recordings in their Nashville home. Mrs. Work engaged Fisk archivist Beth Howse to organize and microfilm most of the paper items. When Mrs. Work became ill in the late 1980s, the collection was stored in a commercial storage facility. There, it was inadvertently lost. Fortunately, Work's manuscript and all of his 158 transcriptions had been preserved on microfilm in the Fisk Library's Special Collections.

Sixty years may have passed since these manuscripts were intended for publication, but the information is right on time. Today, as casinos dot the land and satellite antennae take Delta inhabitants far from their shotgun houses without having to leave their sofas, their culture is changed. This record of the historical past helps us see how the past lives in the present, and also how that past came to be.

THE MANUSCRIPTS

~

INTRODUCTION
TO DELTA MANUSCRIPTS

While these manuscripts were always *intended* for publication, they were never *prepared* for publication. Before a publisher could be found, before even a publication agreement could be reached between Fisk and the Library of Congress, the manuscripts were misplaced, set aside, or filed away, and the authors moved to other pursuits. The details of final drafts were never addressed. The manuscripts reprinted here are the last drafts produced, and except for the most basic copyediting, we have left them intact rather than guessing how the authors might have done their final tweaking.

A book was always the end goal of the study, and this compendium is as near to that goal as can be achieved; with the addition of the Adams manuscript, it actually comprises more than was originally intended. That the manuscripts were found in the Lomax archives six decades after they went missing may reveal much about how research is, and is not, shared, attributed, and published. Like an old photograph rediscovered, this work opens a window into the past, one that had been boarded up, revealing a vision rich with cultural detail. Six decades lost, the recovery of this research helps us not only to see a vanished way of life but also to understand how fragile our sense of the past is, how each version we construe is only the latest draft, how important it is to recover as many of our storytellers as we can.

~

"The Mississippi Delta"
by Lewis W. Jones

EDITORS' INTRODUCTION

This manuscript, a noncirculating original, was found stashed in the back of a file cabinet drawer in the Alan Lomax Archives at Hunter College in New York. The manuscript of 119 typescript pages had a soft powder-blue cover identifying it as a product of, and the property of, the Social Sciences Institute at Fisk University. It has since been returned.

The manuscript is titled "The Mississippi Delta" and the author is given as Lewis W. Jones, though the authorship claim is misleading. The manuscript is actually the culmination of the Coahoma study, the draft unifying the sociological and the musicological perspectives. It is John Work's long text with an introduction by Lewis Jones. Only the first thirty-two pages are by Jones; the remaining eighty-seven are a verbatim copy of Work's manuscript. (There are drafts in Work's hand on microfilm at Fisk confirming his authorship.) It is not clear who assigned sole authorship to Jones. "The Mississippi Delta" did not include Work's transcriptions or indexes. This document may be what was sent to the Library of Congress in July 1943—and lost, and found, and lost again. Confusion would have resulted from searching for John Work's manuscript when it had Lewis Jones's name on it. It may have been picked up by Lomax on his 1948 return to Fisk. In 2001, Robert Gordon rediscovered it in the Alan Lomax Archives while researching his biography of Muddy Waters.

As was discussed in the previously cited July 30, 1943 letter from John Work to Fisk president Thomas Jones, Work focused on musicology, Jones on sociology. Lewis Jones intended to draft a much longer introduction. His outline of his projected work is included as Appendix 4, "Memorandum to Charles S. Johnson from Lewis W. Jones; Folk Culture Study in Coahoma County. Mississippi; August 20, 1942." His intention was to document three periods of social life in the Delta. Working from the premise that, "the river and the levees are responsible for the economic life of the delta," Jones designated each generation by its mode of transportation: The River (roughly 1860–1890), The Railroad (1890–1920), and The Highway (1920–1940). Jones was unable to complete his proposed treatment due to service in the armed forces, and the manuscript sent to the Library of Congress contained a survey of the three generations and fuller analysis of only the River generation. His writing is vivid with detail about river and levee camp life, clearing the jungle, and other aspects—secular and religious—of a vanished time, gleaned from the memories of those remaining few whom he terms "The Pioneers." "I been all over here in boats," says one subject early in Jones's text. "I can go now and show you places that have cotton and corn on them now where I used to fish."

The South is often mythologized, and many visitors go there to confirm their assumptions. But Jones was bred in the South —as were Work and Adams—and he is quick to disabuse a reader who may have more exotic expectations. Early in the work, Jones writes about the landscape "which usually disappoints the traveler who had had some vague romantic vision." Jones is positioning himself against the kinds of romanticized notions associated with visitors like Lomax, and he begins his essay with hard, fast, and concrete details—a geographical tour. Proceeding through ever-smaller divisions of territory, he takes us from the vast region to "an average working community"—Coahoma County. His specific descriptions of work and play enhance the cultural portrait he creates, especially for readers coming decades after the passing of this way of life. Jones's presentation of the River generation indicates how strong his portraits of the succeeding generations would have been.

The Mississippi Delta

by Lewis W. Jones

Social Science Institute

Fisk University

Nashville, Tennessee

I

The Delta

Though its Chamber of Commerce advertises Clarksdale, Mississippi, as "the Heart of the Delta," the Negro citizens of Clarksdale regard the town as one half of a world categorically divided into "The Delta" and "The Hills." This distinction, for the Negroes, requires no elaboration: "In the Hills" is a matter of fact response to the frequently posed question "Where do you come from?" Clarksdale Negroes, when referring to "The Delta," have in mind the area between Memphis and Vicksburg along the Mississippi. Outsiders—those who recognize other deltas—distinguish this one as the Yazoo–Mississippi Delta, a region whose boundary wall is one of hills rising from one hundred to three hundred feet above the flood plain of the Yazoo River. The area covered by the Delta is approximately 8,000 square miles of level, low-lying land, taking in eleven entire counties* and a portion of eight others.† The whole is encompassed by the Mississippi River on the west and a run of hills on the east. The effect is that of a vast oval about one hundred and eighty miles long and roughly seventy-five miles wide. This oval is almost exclusively agricultural, yielding one of the richest cotton crops in the United States.

In its natural state the oval was subject to the overflows of the Mississippi. The alluvial deposits of the river gave the soil a reputation for fabulous richness. In 1840 the

---

*Tunica, Coahoma, Quitman, Bolivar, Sunflower, Washington, Humphreys, Leflore, Sharkey, Issaquena, and Tallahatchie.

†DeSoto, Tate, Panola, Grenada, Carroll, Holmes, Yazoo, and Warren.

Delta produced 39,000 bales of cotton, and by 1850 it was producing a total of 42,000 bales annually. After small levees had been built, production increased to 136,000 bales in 1860. The population in the region made proportionate growth: in 1860 there were only 6,606 people in Coahoma County; in 1940 the single urban center of the county, Clarksdale, had a population of 12,168. In 1940 there were four other incorporated centers in the county: Friars Point, with a population of 940, Jonestown with 706 inhabitants, Lula with 503, and Lyon with 339. Coahoma County's population in 1940 was nearly 50,000.

The smaller incorporated places are in many instances no more than plantation headquarters. There are, for example, Farrell, Sherard, Rena Lara, Hillhouse, Bobo, Coahoma, Cloverhill, Hopson, and Matteson plantations. Small as they are, these centers are of great importance to the Negroes who live on and near them; they are the sources of food, clothing, and recreation. As social centers these plantations are also the scenes of numerous dramatic incidents, the incidents of the normal working community of the average working man.

An average working community is Coahoma County; the working man in Coahoma County is the farmer; the average farmer, like thousands of his peers, lives in a house close to the cotton fields. These simple folk do most of the work and most of the living; the patterns of their lives are remarkably alike. Indeed, their names and their jobs are their most distinctive possessions—"Jim Smith be my name, what might be your'n? I'm making a crop with Mr. Higgins." Work for all is the code; the women and children chop cotton in the spring, pick it in the fall. Young men drive tractors covering acres that formerly took many men and mules. During the week all are busy traveling between cotton rows with a sack, a hoe, a plow, or a tractor.

On Saturday the people who live and work in the cotton fields fill the streets of the "New World" in Clarksdale, or they mill in and out of the stores in Jonestown, Friars Point, and Lula, or they crowd the commissaries at Hopson, Stovall, Sherard, or one of the other plantations. At night, on Saturday, there may be dancing at Mrs. Baugh's, or Stovall's, or at New Africa. Every Sunday there is a church meeting within walking distance of the houses. There is the Green Grove Church, Mt. Ararat, New Hope, and a score of others in the area. On week days the commissaries, the stores, and the churches are empty and the sidewalks are bare, but there is heavy traffic on Saturday and Sunday—people are walking, or riding in wagons, or driving automobiles of various makes and models. These, then, are the ordinary people, the folk, working and living in the Delta.

The oldest generation of the Delta folk is composed of those who have lived past their seventieth and eightieth birthdays. There are not many and they don't do much work, but they do a lot of living in their memories. They are the people who cleared and settled the Delta. Phineas MacClain, who lives on Sherard's plantation, is a typical example. He doesn't work much now but he does not appreciate the changes that have come—changes requiring so little work from a man "making a crop." "They" are doing things to him that he can't understand when they "break your land, plant your crop, and plow it and don't turn it over to you 'til it's ready to chop, while you set around doing nothing." When settlement time comes, after his wife and grandchildren have picked the cotton, he finds the costs of cultivation charged against him in the accounting. This seems to him unusual and unnecessary. He feels that if anybody knows about the cultivation of cotton planted in this land, he is the person. He knows all about cotton and all about the land in which it grows.

> I been right here since '79. Life then and now like no life at all. There's been changes in the system of living, changes in everything. One thing different now from then—I been all over here in boats. I can go now and show you places that have cotton and corn on them now where I used to fish.

Phineas MacClain thinks the old days were happier than the present ones. He doesn't think much of the levees or of the drainage system; the overflows that came regularly when he was young were, to him, beneficent. He remembers everything that has happened to the land and to the people for a period of sixty years. He remembers the early planters who set out to develop the swampy forests into cotton plantations: the Lombardys, Mr. Sherard, Mr. O'Neil and others of their generation. MacClain worked on the levee under Old Man Dabney, the engineer, and the contractors who built different sections of the levees. His associates were Negroes who built the country and made reputations for themselves by buying land or perhaps by cutting somebody's throat! Some of his contemporaries can join him in recounting stories of Coahoma County when it was on the frontier. Others, as one of the oldest generation expressed it, "don't have their real mind no more." They recall, now and then, that they played "ring games" in the moonlight, singing and cutting capers, but they have forgotten the words or the tunes they sang. They went to the dances but can't remember, as Phineas does, the figures and popular dance tunes. Some of them gambled, but they have forgotten the game-talk and the gamblers' songs. Theirs at that time was a creative world. They cleared the forest, built levees, traveled on the waters of the Mississippi in skiffs, made bumper crops of cotton, danced, gambled, loved and killed with what seems to have been tremendous zest.

The next generation came when the country had been opened up. They are people, now between the ages of fifty and seventy, who found the frontier pushed back, the river dwindling in importance, and the era of the railroad beginning. A levee system, protecting the lands of the country from overflows, had by that time been completed. The railroad lines were crossing the county and cotton growing was in boom. When Mrs. Frank Reed came to this section of the Delta, Phineas MacClain's generation had put the Sherard plantation into cultivation. Mrs. Reed and her husband were tenants on that plantation until they were able to buy a place for themselves. She and her son are perhaps the most successful among the few Negro farm owners in the vicinity of Sherard. Their lands were purchased from the railroad company when they were selling land which had been given to them by the Government as a subsidy to encourage construction. Mrs. Reed describes the first time she came to the spot where she now lives. It was a cane brake covered with what she claims was "the biggest cane you ever saw," protected from the flood waters by a levee "no bigger than the railroad dump." She and her husband built a one-room house with a "stick and dirt" chimney and set up housekeeping with "two children and a box of meat."

People belonging to this second generation are now old, but they are still strong and vigorous. Having come with the first orderly regimes established after the frontier, they still represent order. They frown alike on the violence of the pioneer life they found and the disorderly life of the present. Mrs. Reed, referring to one of the pioneer heroes, remarked, "I just couldn't stand him. He was the kinda man didn't have no respect for nobody—for himself and nobody else. He was a devil." The present, in contrast to the orderly past which she helped to develop, seems confused and disorderly to her as well as to her contemporaries. Their world reached its flowering around the first World War and suffered a collapse later which has never been quite understood.

In the active lives of the second generation the church became the dominant institution of the community. In the church buildings, most of which were built by this generation, the congregations uniformly sang the long "Dr. Watts" hymns, enjoyed (prior to their exclusion, as Negroes, from politics) political rallies, and supported vigorously the numerous lodges which grew out of the church organization. These people helped bring order into the life of the area and witnessed this same order disappear into the chaos of the present. All, therefore, that is still established and considered normal in the Delta is indebted to this generation.

The third generation is composed of young adults between the ages of thirty and fifty who came to maturity in confusion. Their memories of an orderly world are those of their childhood and youth. Cotton growing for them has not departed from the "old way," nor has the church become weakened in its expression of the true faith by the introduction of "a form and a fashion." Theirs has been a rapidly changing world. They have no pleasant memories of the isolation and stabilization before motor transportation arrived; they have enjoyed the freedom of movement the "good road" brought as they rattled about in the second-hand cars their cotton money bought. Sixty cent cotton, six cent cotton, "parity checks," and tractors have been among the many surprises in their economic life. Electric lights in the church and electricity to make their nickels bring music out of "Seeburgs" and radios are their pride. For them there is no stable past against which to measure the present day; there is only a succession of changes in their way of working and living from war to war.

Youths and children try to get a grip on life in the midst of a disintegrating past and a fascinating present. For them the new has as much place as the old. As they acquire the culture, they receive the traditions from the past and the technology and the organization of the present and even absorb the conflicts between the two. They pick cotton, play their games, follow their parents through a routine of living, and go to school. They sing the songs currently popular on the radio and the juke boxes and learn others as they hear them sung by older people at home and in the fields. Theirs is the task of discovering a pattern of living which conforms with their opportunities as well as with the varied inheritance from their elders.

These are the people of the Delta. Their lives are intimately related to cotton and cotton growing. Cotton guides the use of the seasons and the day for them, as it has done for others through sixty years. The winter and the early spring are respectively the wet season and the idle period. Then comes the period for the plowman, with his mules or tractors, to prepare the land and plant seed. As soon as the cotton plants stand a few inches above the soil, the struggle to "keep ahead of the grass" begins. Women and children swing their hoes from dawn until dusk, destroying weeds and grass which thrive among the young plants. Midsummer has come before hoe and plow can be laid aside. The plant is then mature and no further cultivation is required. There is a period of waiting while the bolls develop and burst open, presenting the fruit to the harvesters. This season of waiting is called the "lay-by" and is given over to festive occasions and group activities in the area. The revivals, lodge meetings, conventions, and associations are held during the lay-by. When the harvest is ready, from dusk to dawn all available black hands hurry among the cotton leaves and fill the long white sacks. Haste is essential to gather the harvest before damaging rains fall or the chill winds bring winter and another idle season. The order which cotton imposes has known modification with changing skills and practices over a period of sixty years. With all the shifts and changes "The Delta" remains basically "The Delta"—different from all others, despite technological and community changes.

II

The River and the Levee

Travelers going south from Memphis observe what seems to be a hill west of the highway or railroad. Passing from view only to reappear closely for several hundred yards, the "hill" then curves away until it is dimly outlined in the distance for a few miles before it disappears. This hill is the levee, a grass-covered, gentle slope which usually disappoints the traveler who had had some vague romantic vision of the Mississippi levees. Each time the levee curves near the roadway, the traveler scrutinizes it more closely, deciding that it is going to appear as a low hill for the extent of the trip. The more curious, anxious to see beyond the levee, and thinking perhaps that the river washes its further side, can find a road leading to the levee summit. They may drive along the roadway found there and the chances are that even though they reach the top of the levee they will not see the river. Between the levee and the river are small fields, waste land, and trees; it is only through the trees along the river's edge that the waters of the Mississippi may be seen.

The river and the levee are responsible for the economic life of the Delta—the river made the Delta a rich agricultural area and the levee made it possible for man to exploit it. The people know that the river is responsible for soil that can produce bountifully. But the river has enriched the soil according to a scheme of its own and not in accord with man's plans or needs. Following its ageless pattern, it continues to heap up riches which bring fear and suffering instead of profit and pleasure to the people whose welfare depends on it. This is the same wayward but useful river which preceded man and man's plans—plans that included the creation of the levees. For since first discovering the rich deposit of top soil that the river brought from thousands of miles away, men have sought to use it.

In their attempts to keep the annual overflow off the occupied land, the natives employed a simple device. They set up earthen barriers to hold the waters in bounds. But the waters of the river, chafing always against restraint, gathered in volume time and time again to destroy the man-made hills placed along the river's course. The optimism and ambition of man have been great enough to prompt him to rebuild after each disaster; finally a barrier forty feet high, and four hundred feet broad at the base was achieved. Still, the river gathers force behind it and the men who created this mountain-like barrier still fear the potential and incalculable power of the river.

Beyond the levee the waters of the Mississippi are placid. Now there is no traffic on the river reminiscent of its past glory as one of the busiest thoroughfares in America. But many years passed while the process of imprisoning the river and substituting other means of transportation went on. Through these years countless individuals continued to travel on the river and to pile up its levees. The folk, white and colored, have great admiration and respect for both the river and its levee—both are a part of their lives. Successful struggles with the one and the building of the other are remembered with pride. To those who lived through its building, the levee is something more than a grassy hillock. Many of them worked to raise the mound of earth behind which they could live and farm with a minimum of fear.

Some of the men of the oldest generation worked on the first levee construction undertaken after the war of the rebellion. They had none of the powerful machines used today but raised these early levees by wheelbarrow loads of earth. Over a span of sixty years one old levee worker surveyed the improvements in machinery that made possible higher and stronger levees.

When they first started building levees all the work was done with wheel-barrows. I rolled many a wheel-barrow up there. Went from wheel-barrow to slips—a big shovel with two mules hitched to it. There'd be one man to load, one man to drive it, and one man to stay on the dump and dump it. It would never stop, just come right around. Then they went to wheelers. A wheeler was like a slip, only it was bigger with wheels. It would carry three or four times as much as a slip. It had levers on it. You hitched two mules to it. From wheelers they went to wagons and carts hitched to four mules. Then they used a turning plow and a belt. Then they come to the present time with these trucks, dippers and tractors.

There is a long step from the early days, when sweating Negroes and Irishman built their small mounds of earth pushing wheel-barrows, to the days when giant shovels lift a ton of earth with one scoop.

The machines were constantly being improved but the organization for levee construction did not experience such rapid changes. Contractors undertook the construction of sections of the levee and assembled equipment and workmen in that unique institution—the levee camp. It was wild and lawless. To build the levee ruthless bosses drove hardworking, gambling fighting workers. It is difficult to get at facts behind the legend and lore of the levee camp, but for the folk of the Delta the legend and lore are the facts. The boss of the levee construction gang on the sections of the levee was called "captain" and was notoriously careless of the cost in carrying out the contract. The maxim of the levee boss, according to many legends, was, "kill a nigger, hire another; kill a mule, buy another." The Negro workers reflected the attitude of the boss when following the huge, wheeled shovels called "wheelers" they sang:

"Captain, Captain, My hands is cold."
"God damn your hands, let the wheelers roll."
       or
"Captain, Captain, Is the money come?"
"None of your business, don't owe you none."
       or
"The collar's creaking the hame-string's crying,
Captain say, 'hurry, hurry'
But I'm going to take my time."

The violence of the levee camp is hardly equaled in any descriptions of work life in the south. The bosses were belligerent and tough and the men they worked were hardly less so. Conflicts between the contractors and the workers have a considerable place in the legends of the levee camps. Some of the bosses are reputed to have refused the wages promised when they employed workers. The workers they hired were as tough as their job. One old man reports that "the levee bosses would hire anybody; they didn't care who worked for them." Many of the workers they hired didn't care whom they worked for. One contractor, who was supposed to have promised a pay day "when it snowed in Mississippi," looked across the counter of the commissary one day into the muzzle of a Winchester held by Black Snake who informed him "snow done fell; we gonna have a pay day." There is the story of how Dollar Bob collected wages to buy his woman a dress.

> Red Willie told Dollar Bob
> She wanted a red dress cost a dollar a yard
> Dollar Bob said, go to bed girls, don't say a word
> You gonna get that dress if it's in Vicksburg.

Practically all of the story tellers have at least one story in which a "bad nigger" got the best of the levee boss. Phineas MacClain told this one:

> They used to work you on the levee and wouldn't pay you. A big nigger come along and Idaho asked him if he wanted to work. He said, "How much do you pay?"
> "$2.00 a day."
> "How much is board?"
> "Three and a half."
> "When is pay day?"
> Idaho said, "I paid off yesterday and I pay every two weeks. It'll be Saturday after next."
> He went to work and I believe he worked three days that week and four days the next week. Saturday came and Idaho didn't pay. This feller asked some of the niggers when they paid off.
> A nigger said, "They don't pay off here."
> He said, "He gonna pay me."
> He found Idaho in the commissary. He asked him when he going to pay off. Idaho said, "Next Saturday."
> That nigger said, "No, you gonna pay me off today."
> Idaho said, "All right, I'll go over to the tent and get it."
> That nigger knowed he was up to something and he said "You ain't going nowhere. You gonna pay me right here in the commissary now. I heared about you and I walked all the way from Vicksburg to work for you."
> Idaho paid him and he said to Idaho, "I'm going to Friars Point and don't tell nobody you can't find me cause I'm telling you where I be if you think you want me."

The old levee workers had admiration for the bad bosses but the bad nigger that came along occasionally was a hero.

The violence of the levee camp was not confined to the conflicts between the bosses and the workers. The bosses would advance them money for gambling and for liquor when they didn't pay off, and those who received their wages often promptly lost them gambling on Saturday night. One levee worker, in reference to this habit said, "When that happen, he'd go to the Commissary Monday morning and take up a pair of pants and shirt, throw the old ones away and work for another week, maybe lose his money agin, and do the same thing." The Negroes killed each other following quarrels that developed at the gambling table or over one of the women that followed the levee camp. One levee worker was called Walking Tom because whenever the levee camp moved he'd walk and let this woman Red Mamie ride in the Wheeler. In the late afternoon, usually around four o'clock according to levee workers, they would begin singing. These songs were songs about love and women. One of these quoted was:

> Old Sam Henry, workin on the levee,
> Dis work am heavy
> Goin to make some money and give to my honey
> Working on the levee, sleepin on the ground
> Giving my baby money, and she's foolin around.

The history of the river and the levee is not all told in the story of the enterprise, the ingenuity, or the energy of a few men, but in the work of many men and their lives around the levee camp. The only record of these is in the fireside tales carelessly heard by their grandchildren, tales often unsuitable for children's ears.

Making a breach in the levee ranked in the Delta with horse stealing in the wild west. When the pressure of the waters on the levee threatened to break through, there was always the temptation to make a breach with explosives, turning the waters on the land at some spot to jeopardize someone's property. The levees on the Arkansas side of the river were reputed to be weaker than those of the Mississippi side. When the river was at flood stage, watchmen were placed on the Mississippi levee to prevent anyone's relieving the pressure on the Arkansas levees by loosing the waters into the Delta. Men with reputations for marksmanship were usually given the jobs of watching. There is a George Adams who had such qualifications and who was once engaged by the chief engineer on the levee to do a stint of watching. The watchmen went in pairs and George was accompanied by his pal, Jordan. One night, after they had been watching for some time, they heard the approach of a skiff. According to George Adams' story, "A skiff come up there with two niggers and two white men in it. The white men stayed in the skiff with the guns and the niggers come up on the levee and commenced boring. Them niggers was boring too!"

The watchmen were being rewarded for their vigil. Somebody was actually preparing to dynamite the levee. From where they lay just over the levee on the landward side, George and Jordan were watching preparations being made to plant a charge of dynamite that would make a breach in their levee. The Negroes completed their boring and the white men came up to inspect their work. One of them said, "Drop it in there." Then George rose up from his spot of concealment. "I rose up and I say, 'I'll drop you in there! I'll kill your soul if these bullets will kill it.'"

George and Jordan lighted the lanterns which were the signal to announce trouble, and soon other watchmen came and a messenger was dispatched to Rena Lara to bring old man Dabney, the chief engineer. In less than two hours a crowd had gathered and a decision was reached concerning the punishment of the levee breakers from Arkansas. In George's words:

> They put plows around them men's necks and took them out in the river and drowned them. They heaved them in the river like chunks of wood. Old man Dabney said, "You was gonna cut the levee so people would drown, I'm gonna let you see how it feels."

George had helped build the levee; he had fought and gambled in the levee camps; old man Dabney was the engineer to whom the contractors were responsible. In a period of crisis they had saved their levee in a manner in keeping with the turbulence that marked life among the levee builders.

When the first levee building was undertaken, during the early settlement of Coahoma County, the life of the people was focused toward the river, the principal avenue of communication and trade. The most important town was Friars Point, at old Port Royal. Other trading posts were Burke's Landing, Malone's Landing, and Sunflower Landing. Famous river boats plying between New Orleans and Memphis paused to deliver and take on merchandise as well as passengers at the Coahoma County Landings. Older people have fond memories of the *Kate Adams*, the *Western Bell*, and many other famous steam boats.

It was in the northern end of the county that Grant undertook the task of making his way to Haines Bluff by the Yazoo Pass and on through the Coldwater, Tallahatchie, and Yazoo Rivers. Between Friars Point and Coahoma there is a splendid monument to the vagaries of the river in Moon Lake, a great stretch of an abandoned bed of the Mississippi. Near Sunflower Landing is the legendary spot from which DeSoto first saw the river. Through this section of the Delta the Mississippi River is rich in lore and legend.

To the folk, the river is more than a geographical fact. They have had to live with it and know it more intimately than a passing Grant or DeSoto. Their favorite fishing spots are "blue holes," small lakes whose beds were formed by the rush of waters through a break in the levee. They have trudged the levee at night watching for "sand boils," or signs of the water's penetration of their guardian barrier. Their most complete and intimate knowledge of the river has been gained by navigating its winding waters in small crafts. An old man who cannot now pull an oar recounts a trip by boat which is one of the characteristic incidents of life along the river, in the days when the river was the main thoroughfare for all sorts of travel and traffic:

Old settlers in here were the Parks. Denny Parks' daughter married a man named Ben Lombardy. His father lived at Hillhouse. It must a been '82 or '83. Water was all over the land. You could scarcely find land. It was along in February, his father got a congested chill and died.

Ben Lombardy sent for me and Griffin Sanders to take him down there to Hillhouse. We got a skiff and the way we had to go, it was twelve miles. Just before we got there the old man died. When he found it out he said, "Well boys, we have to go back." That was twelve miles against the current.

Friars Point was our trading point then. He said "Boys, we got to go to Friars Point to get a coffin for the old man." Friars Point is eighteen miles. He give us a drink of whiskey. We got to Friars Point about three o'clock that evening. He give us fifty cents to get supper and went off and stayed and stayed. He come back about dark. We got the coffin and started down the river sixty-six miles to Hillhouse. We had all the advantages of the current going back and we got to Malone's Landing just a little fore day, making a trip of 120 miles in a skiff that day.

The folk, going about their ordinary affairs in the small crafts at their disposal, had to share the river with the big boats carrying the regular river traffic. One ancient traveler tells of tying his dug-out to a tree on the bank to keep from being swamped by the waves made by the passing *Western Bell*. Another was "thrown around like imagination," until pitched into a thorn tree which saved him from being swamped. Sometimes they made trips on the big boats and enjoyed the amusements they occasionally brought to the Delta. When the river went on rampage they battled with it to save the marooned farmer or the farmer's unfortunate livestock. Beyond the levees, the Mississippi does not today seem to be the same whirling, untamed, and almost personal being that the stories of old settlers suggest.

III

The Pioneers

The oldest person found in Coahoma County was Lucy Adams. A hundred and four years old, blind, and unable to control her memory, she would sit in her rocking chair and entertain herself for hours by singing in an uncertain and quavering voice. Usually she sang only snatches of songs and sometimes she confused one with another. Her favorite was one she said her grandfather had sung:

Mary's the bosom bearer and Jesus is her child
    Mary's the bosom bearer and Jesus is her child

Keep your lamp trimmed and burning
    Keep your lamp trimmed and burning
For your work's most done.
- - - - - - -
Sister don't get weary
    Sister don't get weary
Sister heaven's just before you
    Sister heaven's just before you
Keep your lamp trimmed and burning
For your work's most done.

    - - - - - - -

Brother don't get weary, etc.

Another song she liked, but of which she could remember only a fragment, was:

In the morning when I rise
Get up in the morning like a turtle dove
I don't want to stay here no longer.
    - - - - - - -

When I come to study my cause
I'm afraid I'm not borned of God
I don't want to stay here no longer.

These and others she sang were not Delta songs for she had but recently come from the hills and her memories, therefore, were those of other Mississippi sections.

The true Delta old people are younger, ranging in age from seventy-five to ninety years. There are nearly two hundred of them in Coahoma County but they are seldom seen unless they are sought. They sit on their porches in summer, before the fire in winter; their memories are good and they have lived most of their adult lives in Coahoma County to which they came as pioneers. Phineas MacClain, as an example, has been a farmer in Sherard Community for sixty years. George Adams, the retired bad-man, lives at Farrell. "Dr. Tom" at Cloverhill, Jim Neal in Clarksdale, and Rev. James Chambert at Lyons are representatives of the pioneer group. There are no memories of slavery in the Delta among them. This section of the Delta has little history in lore or writing prior to the rebellion of 1861. The 6,606 people enumerated in the census in 1860 seem to have been concentrated largely on the ridges east of the Sunflower River. Along the Mississippi there were a few plantations but these had not been fully developed. Slave labor was used but few Negroes remained after emancipation.

In the decade of the war, the increase in population in Coahoma County was small;

about 500 more people were recorded in the county census of 1876 than for 1860. In the decade of the seventies there was a considerable increase. The census of 1880 showed a white population of 2,412 and it showed too, that nearly six thousand freedmen had been added to the Negro population. The oldest Negroes in the county had migrated there between 1870 and 1890. The memories of slavery preserved in the tales of the oldest generation belong to areas other than the Delta, the earliest accounts of this area are these describing it as a frontier.

When the pioneers came, the Delta was regarded not only as mysterious but tales were circulated advertising its damages. Most of the stories had to do with the river on rampage—"they had stories in the hills about overflows with people drowned and houses floating down the river." These accounts, describing the Delta as a sinister spot where life and property were constantly in jeopardy, gave way in the seventies to equally exciting stories about wealth to be had there. An old woman explaining the circumstances which prompted her family to migrate to the Delta said:

> The cause my father and my relatives coming here was people come down here and come back with so much money. They come back to the hills and make folks think greenbacks grew on trees and they had ponds of molasses here, and folks in the hills believed it.

Others reported that the same myth reached as far away as Georgia and set the credulous on the move. There was considerable unrest and movement on the part of Negroes throughout the south in this period and some sought their fortunes in the flood-washed but rich delta.

Most of the Delta was virgin land in 1870. It was necessary to lay the axe to the forests before the plow could fulfill the destiny of one of the world's richest cotton areas. The people needed to develop the Delta came from the older settled areas where they had been concentrated in slavery. One who came from the vicinity of Meridian said:

> This country was built up out of hill people. It was just territory when the Civil War was fought. Wasn't nobody in here much.

Another old man seemed to have wandered away from Alabama in his youth. After some aimless moving about he finally came to settle in the Delta.

> I was born on the Edwards Plantation near Montgomery, Alabama. After freedom come, I left. When I come from Montgomery, Alabama I struck Mississippi and turned left, went to New Orleans for a few days. Being shrewd and a good laborer I turned right and come up here and settled in '80 on the Sherard Plantation. I come in the fall and help gather the crop, and then right away I occupied farming.

When Stack Mangham's father came from Georgia, the only land in cultivation on the Clark Plantation was a narrow strip on the east bank of the Sunflower River. Upon their arrival to inspect a tract of newly purchased land, pioneers found it necessary to mark their path through the forest.

Some ideal soil and climate characterized the Delta, nearly all of the earliest settlers came with the express purpose of developing cotton. Even gamblers, in the pre-levee days, applied their winnings to the expense of harvesting their crops—always, of course before the "high-water" covered the land. These planters took the risk of reaching the safety of the higher ridges ahead of the flood rivers. But coping with "high-water" was not the most arduous of their tasks—they had to haul their harvested cotton over newly made paths to distant steamboat landings. They had to clear the land, and later build levees and railroads, both essential enterprises auxiliary to the basic cotton economy.

In clearing the land of the forest, owners of plantations hired gangs of wood choppers while small farmers of forty and eighty acre tracts had "log-rollings." The sound of axes rang through the Delta as an accompaniment of simple rhythmic woodcutters' songs. A popular one was:

July and August, Tu Lum
July and August, Tu Lum
July and August, Tu Lum
Two hottest months in the year, Tu Lum.

July and August are traditional wood-cutting months because they are the months of the "lay-by," the period between the planting of cotton and its harvesting. When cotton growers have done all that they can with plow and hoe, there is this interval of waiting while nature ripens the fruit. The time is used for incidental jobs—clearing new fields, for example.

In the frontier days, wood cutting frequently took on the character of a contest between the pioneers. Typical is this story told of two rival plantation owners who were clearing land at the same time. The two gangs of woodcutters were working near enough for one to hear the crashing of trees felled by the other. Chuckling, Phineas MacClain gave this account:

Ooten claimed his niggers could outwork Oneil's niggers. Oneil heard about it and made Ooten do his niggers awful bad. Oneil would come in the night and cut his trees half through and the next morning Oneil would be falling trees before Ooten's niggers got started.

Ooten thought Oneil's niggers was outworking his niggers and it made him awful mean. He would whip his niggers almost to death.

The control exercised by the employer over his wood cutters was similar to that exercised over levee workers and other gang laborers. Stimulated by their rhythmic songs, encouraged by their wages, and driven by physical punishment, the Negro woodcutters made acre after acre of forest land suitable for the cultivation of cotton.

The woodcutters made a sport of clearing land when it was done as a "log-rolling" on one of the small farms. The owner would provide a big dinner and plenty of liquor. Throughout the day the guests at the log-rolling would have a "big time with the men trying to show their manhood." Skill with the axe was a source of pride, but tests of strength came in moving the logs and piling them together. A routine was developed in which four small sticks were forced under a log and eight men, grasping the ends of the sticks, would lift and carry the log to the pile. This procedure required cooperation. "All the men would move together when somebody call—'Hands on your pole! Bow and Come! Bow and Come!'" There would be logs too heavy to be lifted by the usual eight men, claimed "they didn't have no grip in their hands and would wear a cuff." The "cuff," a leather device strapped to the wrist, was so designed that the end of the pole fitted into a leather loop. Others participated in the log-rolling by wearing a "bull band." This fitted over the shoulders with a loop into which the pole fitted. The strong had little sympathy for the weak and thought it a good joke to let the wearer of a "bull-band" fit the pole in his harness and release their holds, thus leaving the victim pinned to the earth by the weight of the log. Many acres were placed in cultivation on days when clearing land was more sport than work.

The Negro pioneers became operators of cotton farms under a variety of tenure arrangements. Some came to the Delta with complete organizations for plantation operation. For example, John H. Sherard came to the Delta from Alabama bringing tenants and skilled craftsmen with him. In his group there were a carpenter, a brick mason, and a blacksmith. Other Negroes drifted in alone but found no difficulty in securing employment because laborers were scarce. Still others came to work on the building of the railroad or the levee and remained to farm. A rather interesting arrangement was reported by one early settler:

> This in here from Greenwood to Memphis was trees and cane. White people came in here and took up land and let you have it for seven years to work and furnished you what you need to clean the boogers, bears, and mosquitoes out of it.

While the area was still frontier, its destiny as a plantation region seemed unquestioned. Plantation owners seeking more fertile soil found it here, and Negro farm workers found better working conditions than those existing in the older plantation areas.

The plantation system in this period was in its most benevolent phase, if the reminiscences of the old men are to be trusted. The region did not attract all the workers who were wanted and the plantation owners made many concessions to retain tenants once engaged. When a tenant was secured he was given an attractive contract.

> When a man got a man in here he tried to keep him. He didn't force him but he tried to do so many things to make him stay. If land was renting for ten dollars an acre, he'd give it to you for nine dollars and the rough land free. We could sell our own cotton.

Sharecropping as a system had not developed and the tenants enjoyed some independence and a voice in the management of their business transactions.

Agriculture then had all the disadvantages expected in the cultivation of new lands. However, the fact that they were new lands had its compensations, one of which was bountiful production. According to one account:

> In the old days we made a bale of cotton to the acre. In '86 I made eighty-four bales. In '90 I had sixteen bales of cotton out-of-doors to be disposed at my say so. I sold three bales under Cleveland's administration and didn't get a hundred dollars for them but I lived better than I do now.

According to the practices obtaining, the landlord received his share of the crop and the tenant was free to dispose of his part at his convenience and according to terms agreeable to him.

The lands were not intensively cultivated and the farmers enjoyed the contribution of forest and stream to their subsistence. In those days "bear tracks in your cornfield was more common than pig tracks now." Deers, turkeys, small animals and fowls were a part of the abundant wild life. The streams and lakes contained an ample supply of fish. One of the tall tales of the time declares that "fish was so plentiful if you go out in the river in a boat and take a light the fish would jump in your boat." There were ample woodlands and pasture so the game and fish, together with the production of food crops, made low priced cotton no serious problem.

Some disadvantages were the short growing season and the limited transportation facilities. No drainage system had been developed and the wet season was long. Sometimes it was late in the spring before crops could be planted. The latest beginning of preparation for planting recorded was that in which the farmer said, "I run my first furrow the fifth day of May and then couldn't go all the way through, but I made eighteen bales of cotton and two hundred bushels of corn that year." Difficulties in getting cotton to market were due to the poor roads and the fact that local market centers were all on one side of the county. The river was the chief avenue of transportation and distances from the farms to the steamboat landings were great as well as taxing because of the poor roads. In the dry season "it would take six horses or three steers to haul three bales of cotton. You'd have to cuss and holler and everything to get to the river." In the wet season there was another problem:

> Mighty near all the crop caught in here after Xmas you have to boat out. It would take a skiff and two men to boat two bales of cotton out. When the weather got bad you'd have to wait for the water. The mud was so bad you couldn't haul it.

Life was strenuous, the country was wild, tools were crude, conveniences were few, but the people had a good time. There was leisure filled with diversion and recreation for everybody. The pioneers took their recreation seriously. Everybody enjoyed the picnics which were almost a weekly occurrence in midsummer. In the lay-by, the favorite season for the annual celebrations of the organizations in the communities, the roll of the drums and shrill note of the fife were frequently heard entertaining the picnickers. Most of the other recreational activities were divided into those for the sinful and those for the religious people. The log-rolling and the quilting were entertainment for all, without distinction. For a quilting, the women gathered and worked all day getting the quilt completed and the men were invited in the evening. There would be food and perhaps "ring plays" but the distinctive feature of this occasion was "christening the quilt." The new quilt would cover a man and he would chase the women until he caught one, whereupon his stumbling and blundering chase was rewarded with a kiss. The "ring play" is no longer practiced but was a favorite form of recreation for the pioneers. On moonlit nights they would gather in a well-swept yard and sing and go through the antics of the "ring play." Of the plays reported there was one in which a man would get in the center of the ring and the group would sing "there's a stove pipe waiting for me" and then call a girl's name. The girl would join the man in the center of the circle and kiss him. Then another man would take the center of the ring, the group would sing again while he was joined by a partner to go through the routine again.

The favorite pastime for the religious was the "Rock Daniel." At church entertainments, after the quilting, or at parties given by religious people, "the rock" was a prominent feature. A man and a woman facing each other would place their hands on each other's shoulders and rock while singing familiar religious songs. Sometimes at the conclusion of a church service, the members would remain and have "a rock."

For men, gambling was a popular activity. There were regular gambling houses at the steamboat landings and on the boats, but a table might be set up any place. According to one story:

> We went over to Malone's Landing to meet the boat to get a new engine for the gin. Between the levee and the river was a crap table. The road curved but a path come right by the table. I saw a man or thought I saw a man laying under

the table. We thought he was drunk. I said to one feller, "There's a man laying under the crap table." He said, "Yes, he's dead. A nigger killed him last night but we ain't had no time to fool with him." They kept right on gambling with him laying under the table.

The gamblers had game songs and gambler's talk peculiarly their own. One song they sang was:

> My lover says she's broken hearted
> And that she may be
> She says I'm a drunkard
> And on a drunken spree
> I'm gonna quit gambling and save my money
> For my little family.

There were other songs popular with the gamblers such as "Wreck on the Road Somewhere," "If I Get Even I'm Gonna Get Up," "Jack's Neither; Trey's Neither Low."

The dance, or "break-down," had a more developed ritual than the other recreational activities. The two participants of the "break-down" were the fiddler and the man who called figures. An old fiddler believed that "the man who called figures was called just like a preacher." One of the dances went according to the following directions given by the caller:

1. Honor your partner
2. First gentleman and lady lead off from the right
3. And swing
4. Next lady lead out
5. Shoo Fly swing
6. Swing corners all
7. Gentlemen to the center
8. Ladies circle right
9. Form a basket
10. Break ranks, promenade to the bar

"Break ranks" and "promenade to the bar" made it necessary for the gentleman to treat the lady to refreshments. Some of the popular fiddle tunes to which they danced were: "Irish Washerwoman," "Arkansas Traveler," "Tennessee Breakdown," "Susan Jane," "Blue Eagle Jail," and "Bell Cow in the Bend." An old fiddler explained that there was not much singing at the breakdown but he remembered some of the ditties they sang:

(1)   Alabam gal
        Can't you come out tonight
        Dance in the moonlight.

(2)   Stephen went to town
        For a wagon load of peaches
        Wagon broke down
        Broke Stephen all to pieces.

(3)   Wind up your hook; wind up your line
        Fish no more 'til summer time.
        Gimme the hook; gimme the line
        And gimme the gal you call Caline
        Well, she's neat in the waist
        Pretty in the face
        That's the black gal just suit my taste.

The pioneers declared that they had a good time. They drank heavily and played strenuously but always with abandon and real enjoyment.

John Work's Untitled Manuscript

The John Work manuscript is the musical heart of the Coahoma project documentation. The transcriptions of these musical selections, while of unquestioned value, are only a portion of the treasure Professor Work has left to us. His manuscript abounds in socio/musical observations and classifications of styles and songs according to the performer's generation, gender, and degree of urbanization. He gives the material resonance beyond the musical notes.

Work's manuscript, like Jones's, offers a more clear-eyed vision of the folklorist's task in documenting the diversity that is the South. Although Work had virtually no authority in selecting who and what to record in Coahoma County, he did have the power to select which informants and subjects to emphasize in his manuscript. Sprinkled throughout the Work text are illustrations of *his* conception of a proper study of folk song. He allows Coahoma natives to articulate their thoughts about their own home in a way accessible to the reader. For example, while Lomax favors the work of the uneducated artist, Work, in addition to writing about Muddy Waters,* Honeyboy Edwards, and others, makes extensive use of quotes from a literate, articulate Clarksdale Sunday School teacher, especially in the analysis of sin and the blues. Work persists in emphasizing that Delta blacks were a diverse community.

Work's text cites recording opportunities missed, such as city church preachers and gospel soloists. Taken, these opportunities would have provided the survey a more accurate picture of religious life. An analysis of what was missed in the 1941 trip is detailed in the latter two-thirds of Appendix 2, "A Memorandum About the July Trip to Coahoma County—Functional Approach to the Study of Folklore."

Work also includes a transcription of an interview with a gambler. The gambler explicitly states that music was not an integral part of the activity; yet this knowledge doesn't stop

---

*In the recorded interview conducted by John Work in August of 1941, Muddy clearly identifies himself as, "Name McKinley Morganfield, nickname Muddy *Water*, Stovall's famous guitar picker." The photo of Muddy and Son Sims is labeled in John Work's hand, "Muddy Water." Lomax refers to Morganfield as Muddy Waters (and repeatedly misspells "Sims" as "Simms"). The first published misidentification occurs in Lomax's liner notes that accompany the 1942 Library of Congress album *Afro-American Blues and Game Songs*.

Lomax from persistently asking interview subjects, "What kind of songs do men sing when they gamble?"

Similarly, Lomax went out of his way to collect many spiritual songs. Work recounts the longstanding prevalence of the spiritual style, but notes, "In the Delta church of today, with the exception of the Holiness Church, the spirituals are fast disappearing from the service. In many of the churches they are not sung at all . . . The highly rhythmic character of the [spirituals] has become offensive to [church members]. With the introduction of the piano and the organ into the other churches, the performance of more conventional hymns and gospel-songs became eas-ier." While noteworthy to present a disappearing culture, that was not the mandate of this study. To ignore the society's changes and developments is disingenuous; it underscores Lomax's pref-erence for what he understood as the tradition of the area over a more authentic representation of the community as it was functioning in the early 1940s—the latter being the mandate of the study ("a practical working knowledge of the musical life of people," to use Lomax's words). By including the classified index of songs, which reveals the bias towards spirituals over other styles of religious songs, Work may be helping the reader understand that Lomax's prejudices "cooked the data."

After reading the correspondence of Alan's father John Lomax, biographer Nolan Porter-field wrote that, during a 1933 trip in Texas, "[John] Lomax observed that Alan was inclined to romanticize the conditions of the poor and rustic, and thus was disappointed that many of the blacks they had visited owned their farms and were relatively prosperous."[1]

"The poor and rustic" were the better part of Coahoma County's population, and between Lomax and Work, there were different ideas about how these people were to be presented. Work's perspective—as a southerner, as an educated black man—is not necessarily more valid, but it's a perspective that should certainly be heard. Like a photograph too long in a camera, Work's man-uscript is finally printed. The delay of its publication makes it poignant, but the textured detail of his picture has been fully preserved.

~

Untitled Manuscript

by John W. Work III

~

The utterances of the folk whether speech or song, present problems of considerable difficulty to the transcriber whose aim is accuracy and faithfulness to the materials to which he listens. Yet guided by this principle of accuracy, his transcriptions may be, paradoxically enough, very inaccurate. A skillful and serious transcriber upon listening to a folk singer, may record on paper a version of the song which is accurate to the last note and beat as sung. But this written version, correct as it might be, may be "the way he sang it that time."

"The way he sang it that time" may be a faulty variant of the real song. The singer's variations may comprise many errors due to a relative unfamiliarity with the original, to errors in the melody due to confusion arising out of the recording situation, or to melodic errors caused by faulty approximation of tones. The singer too might be lacking in the skills which the style of this song demands. Such a version, therefore, may have sociological value but its worth as folklore is doubtful unless an authentic version of the song is appended.

All Negro folk-singers regard the melody of their song with a free attitude. Tones are freely embellished and changed. Frequently in phrases where the rhythmic pattern is a simple one, and in strong 2/4 time, notes are lengthened, shortened, and omitted. In the course of a song repetitions of the refrain or verses are most always varied.

What then should be transcribed, is the natural question the recorder must ask himself?

The answer is not a simple one. Out of the many embellishments and variations found in the authentic song there still sounds the essential note.* The transcriber must

---

*The term "essential note" is used here in two different categories. In the first, "essential note" refers to *pitch* only and designates that note in the chromatic scale which the singer most closely approximates, and probably uses in repeated versions of the song. The second use of the term refers to a note as it appears in relation to others to form a part of a melodic pattern.

recognize this tone. Familiarity with the various song idioms helps in this. Frequent listening to the complete version of the song should aid him in noting which tones are the essential ones. The faulty version should be spotted and classified as such immediately. It should be used only as a clue to the authentic song. No attempt is made in these transcriptions to account for the variously named in-between-tones given to tonal vagaries by some folklorists who think they hear Negroes sing notes which are "neither-nor." Folk singers, singing without an instrument, are prone to *over-sing* or *under-sing* a note. But there is serious doubt that the same note is repeatedly *over sung* or *under sung* by them in subsequent renditions of the same song, a condition which must necessarily be observed if serious consideration is to be given to such tones.

In the transcription of the materials in this collection, the guiding principle has been to select that version of the song that seemed made up of the most essential notes. Where there were songs with striking variations more than one version of the particular song has been transcribed. In a few instances the entire song has been recorded. This practice has caused some of the songs to be much longer than are usually transcribed.

"Swing Low Sweet Chariot," "I Couldn't Hear Nobody Pray," "Were You There," "Free at Last," "Little David Play on Your Harp," and "I Got Shoes," so widely known throughout the South and which appear so generally in other collections, are omitted in this volume. Fragments of songs less than a verse or a refrain, likewise are not included.

For purposes of authenticity, some of the singer's errors were transcribed. In the thirteenth bar of the song "Hallelu" the first leader mistakenly shifted his rhythm which forced the chorus to shift the first syllable of their refrain "Hallelu," from an accented beat to an unaccented one. When an old lady, a more skillful singer, took over the song she sang it unerringly and maintained the proper accents.

Again in the first refrain of "I'm Goin' to Lean on the Lord" the leader repeatedly used C# which was obviously incorrect. Later in the song the essential C♮ displaced the C#. Both versions were transcribed.

Transcription of the songs by quartets, or those accompanied by guitar, is made of them just as they were performed. In no instance were these arranged by the transcriber. A reliable index of the folk style of performance could only be provided in an original version of the performance with no modification or "correction." The music of the guitar was transcribed on the piano-score instead of the guitar treble clef.

No consistent policy of writing the dialect speech of the Delta Negro Folk was followed, for the simple reason that no consistent speech practice was found among them. Much of the crude dialect of the "Uncle Remus period" was found. On the other hand many of the folk used speech which was quite "correct" and conventional. Conspicuously absent were such words regarded as typical Negro folk speech, "de," "dat," "dis," and "dem." Elisions of final G's and D's, while occurring with frequency, did not occur always. The speed of the song, and its meter, had more to do with such elisions than did any custom.

CHAPTER I

The Church

The inspiration and starting point for the most significant Negro folklore has been the church. The best known of this lore, the spirituals, for seventy years have provided both rich study-material for scholars, and musical exultation for many people far away from the rural churches where they were a part of the worship ritual. Other types of the Negro church folk expressions as well as the secular were little regarded at first as is seen from the almost exclusive treatment of the spiritual in the early treatises and articles on Negro folk song.

Today the prayer and the sermon have both come in for a large share of attention. These are yet in the study area and by their very spontaneous and ephemeral nature cannot provide, as does the spiritual, the enjoyable listening experience to people outside of the place of their creation. Some commercial firms have in the past offered phonograph records of the folk style of sermon. But their necessary brevity and the artificial environment in which they were created made them worthless except as light entertainment.

Most folklore springs from and serves a particular function in group activity. The levee-hollers, shovel-songs, or the songs of the entertaining instrumentalists might be excepted from this principle. The functions of the singing, praying, and preaching in the Negro folk-church service, however, are so definite as to become practically ritualistic. For this reason, it seems demanding that these various types of worship-expressions be studied from the standpoint of their function in the whole service rather than separately as isolated folk phenomena.

The approach to the discussion of the Negro rural church must here be restricted necessarily to its importance as a factor in the stimulation of folklore and its perpetuation. The history of this church, its role in the community, or an evaluation of it must be the task of other studies.

The area of our interest must be defined here, however, in order that a distinction of a sort can be drawn between the folk-church investigated here, and other Negro churches with greater similarity to the standard worship practices.

It is impossible to define the folk-church in any but vague terms because the criteria for determining the folk are so vague and confused. The definitions of the nineteenth century sociologists and anthropologists while applicable to nineteenth century folk are hardly descriptive of the twentieth century folk. Certainly no one would reject the definition of the folk-church as one whose congregation makes no use of the printed word and who creates its own expressions, or uses the creations of other similar congregations. But such a definition would exclude many churches where very interesting folklore is alive. If the location of the folk-church for this definition is restricted to the rural sections, many urban churches rich in distinctive singing, praying, and preaching must be excluded. The fact that the greatest of the folk-preachers pastor city churches is an indication of the weakness of this restriction. Both that definition and the designated location of the folk-church ignore the present era of gospel song with its many effective soloists, which is developing such overwhelming popularity the country over. Because the plantation church certainly conforms more closely to a workable definition of the folk-church than any other, and because the folk-worship-expression found there must be regarded as typical of those found elsewhere, this study is limited to the expressions in such churches.

Negro churches in the Delta are almost exclusively Missionary Baptist, Primitive (or Old) Baptist, and Methodist. A glimpse at their doctrinal attitudes toward church music provides reasons for the types of songs we find in the various churches.

In addition to its worship-practices of foot-washing, "close" (closed) communion, and its stern oversight of its members' daily life, the Primitive Baptist church is distinguished by its frowning attitude toward the use of instruments and printed music in the service. Its congregational singing consists exclusively of old "long-meter"* hymns frequently referred to as "Dr. Watts" and a few spirituals. No printed materials are used by the congregation. The membership of its churches is comparatively small though the churches are numerous.

The Missionary Baptists and the Methodists encourage the use of the piano and the organ whenever money can be raised for their purchase and a performer can be found. But both forbid their members performing on other musical instruments even in their homes. These churches favor formal choirs and whenever it is possible they form them. They make extensive use of their denominational hymns and sing spirituals with diminishing frequency. The Methodists only rarely sing the "Dr. Watts." No choirs, however, were found in any of the plantation churches, nor were any expected to be found.

There is an increasing use in these two churches of a new type of rhythmic gospel-song with verse strikingly similar to that of the spiritual, though more frequently varied. The most prominent figure in the composing and promotion of these songs is J. Thomas Dorsey, a Chicago musician. In many places, all songs of this type whether composed by him or not are referred to as "Dorseys." They are spread chiefly by traveling evangelists and professional gospel singers. They are rarely sung in the Old Baptist Church.

In all three churches the service pursues the same order with the exception of a few minor variations. Its program follows generally this order:

1. Song and Prayer Service (all impromptu)
2. Scripture Reading
3. Formal Prayer

---

*This term is a colloquial one adopted by the folk and is not to be confused with the same term used in standard hymnology.

4. Sermon, Evangelistic Plea, and Opening the Doors of the Church for New Members
5. Collection (Offertory)
6. Benediction

There are two important factors which distinguish this service clearly from the service of the other churches. The first of these is the vocal participation by the entire congregation throughout the service. The second is the fact that with a few interruptions, such as the reading of the scripture, the first part of the sermon, and the plea for the collection, the entire service is intoned, forming a sort of religious symphony, or more correctly, a concerto, with voices instead of instruments.

~

CHAPTER II

The Music of the Church

All the interviews with the older church members in the Delta indicate that the spiritual was almost the only music sung in the early period of the church. There were various types of spirituals which were sung for different parts of the service. Crucifixion spirituals were sung during the Sacrament. Songs both of a pleading and a warning nature were sung at revivals with the purpose of enticing, or scaring sinners into the fold. There were several ceremonials, some formal and other miscellaneous practices for which spirituals were sung. Similar though not as permanent as "shouting" was the practice of "rocking" arising out of religious excitement. The songs "Rock Daniel" and "Hallelu" stimulated this strange worship practice. "Form the Line" was sung as a signal for the Hand-of-Fellowship line.

Spirituals of a more general nature were used in the song and prayer service. Preachers often introduced their sermons with an appropriate spiritual to intensify the accord between them and the congregation. Songs with a lively rhythm were used for "taking up the collection" (lifting the offering).

In the Delta church of today, with the exception of the Holiness Church, the spirituals are fast disappearing from the service. In many of the churches they are not sung at all. In others the spirituals are used only during the "collection" and Sacrament, or as evangelistic songs during the annual revival. The Delta people call them by a name not generally used—"Halleys." The name "spiritual" was unfamiliar to many of them.

For this reason, only a small number of the spirituals which appear in this collection were recorded in the actual church service. Most of those that were recorded in the churches were sung upon the request of the recorders. Many were sung by individuals during interviews. In most of these interviews the singers were elderly persons who sang songs out of another era. It was interesting to note how many of these singers learned the songs from their mothers and grandmothers.

The fading-out of the spirituals from an active place in the folk-church, deplorable as it might be to the rest of the country, is simply explained. They are being displaced by types of songs which perform their functions more satisfactorily and more easily. The old "long-meter" hymns appeal more to the Primitive Baptists than do the spirituals because the highly rhythmic character of the latter had become offensive to them. With the introduction of the piano and the organ into the other churches, the performance of more conventional hymns and gospel-songs became easier.

The spiritual is not yet gone. Miss Alice C. Reid in her study of the Gee's Bend Community in Alabama[2] reports the spirituals as being important in the church services she attended there. In many churches in every Southern state spirituals old and new are sung with great fervor and volume, rewarding the singers with an incomparable joy.[3]

While the rhythmic character of the spirituals brought about their limited use in the Primitive Baptist Church, it proved most attractive to the Church of God, or the Holiness Church as it is more generally known. The Holiness Church has made the spiritual the core of its song-service. And what a core! It has intensified the rhythm of our dance bands in their most torrid mode. The singers' lusty voices are supplemented by hundreds of hands clapping, stamping of feet, tambourines, guitar, and a style of piano-playing which either imitates "boogie-woogie" at its "hottest"—*or started it*. Many individuals dance during the singing. This is not surprising.

From this description of the Church of God service one might receive the impression of banality and baseness there. Such an impression is not intended. A person witnessing this service becomes convinced of the utter sincerity of the worshippers and of their complete absorption in a religious spirit. Such a style of worship is clearly a revolt against the restraint of the minister-centered service. These communicants refuse to worship by proxy. Their use of present day secular rhythm in their worship while startling is probably no more than a re-echo of Martin Luther incorporating into his service the folk-tunes of his 16th century Germany. The rapid growth of the church invites consideration of its worship-principle.

This church is doing more than preserving the spirituals. It is stimulating their creation. Members are encouraged to compose spirituals. The words of these are published by the denomination in a book and distributed among the various churches. The result has been many new spirituals of unusual interest.

Of much importance to this study was the determination of the number of the spirituals heard here that belonged to this region. Such an estimate could only be an approximate one because of the easy infiltration of music from areas outside of northern Mississippi. This is unquestionably accomplished on a large scale through visiting evangelists and gospel singers, and teachers in the various schools who sang spirituals learned in the colleges they attended.[4] The easy access to Memphis, where Mississippians can learn new songs is another factor in the spread of music from the outside.

Giving consideration to these factors, two simple procedures were adopted to determine which of the spirituals were created in this section. The first was the more direct—interviews with the singers. From these interviews it can be believed that the [following] songs were created in this section recently:

Ain't No Grave Can Hold My Body Down
When I've Done the Best I Can I Wants My Crown
All My Trouble Will Be Over
I'll Be Waiting Up There
Get Right Church
All Power Is in His Hands

Older informants place in Mississippi church services at least a generation ago the following songs:

I Shall Wear the Golden Crown
Do Remember
Hold the Wind
Cryin' Holy Unto the Lord
With Angels Climbin' the Golden Stairs
Praise Him
I'm Running for My Life
Just Like Heaven to Me
My Lord's High, High
Done Taken My Lord Away
You Got to Stand Your Damnation
Low Down Your Chariot
My Soul Is a Witness
Please Don't Drive Me Away
O Sister You'll Be Called On
Chariot Jubilee
Band of Gideon
Tell Me How Long Has the Train Been Gone
Run Right to Him
There'll Be Preachin' Tonight
That's What's the Matter with the Church Today
I Know My Little Soul's Gonna Rise and Fly
You Don't Believe I'm a Child of God

Don't Grieve After Me
Sunday Morning Band
David
Daniel
Motherless Children Has a Hard Time
Rock Daniel
Sorry, Sorry For to Leave You
This Here's My Buryin' Ground
I Got a Hiding Place
Steal Away to Jesus
Calvary
He 'Rose
No Hiding Place
I'm Goin' to Lean on the Lord
I'll Fly Away
No Condemnation
I'm a Soldier
Yeh, Lord
O Let Me Ride
Form the Line
Free at Last
He Never Said a Mumblin' Word
I'm Goin' Let It Shine
Rock-a-My Soul
Got on My Trav'lin' Shoes
Glory, Glory
Glory Hallelujah
I Done Got Over
I'm Goin' Stay on the Battlefield
Lamb of God
You Got to Reap
O Lord Will You Come by Here
Let Your Heart
Katy, I Got to Go
Hallelu

as well as "Swing Low Sweet Chariot," "Were You There," and "I Couldn't Hear Nobody Pray."

The second method involved checking the songs found here with the lists appearing in published collections of Negro folksongs.[5] The following songs were not found in any of these collections:

All My Trouble Will Be Over
All Power is in His Hands
Daniel
David
Done Taken My Lord Away
Get Right Church
Hallelu
I Got a Hiding Place
I'll Fly Away
I'm Goin' Let It Shine
Motherless Children Has a Hard Time
No Condemnation
Rock Daniel
Sorry, Sorry For to Leave You
Swing Down Chariot
Low Down the Chariot
Praise Him
You Got to Stand Your Damnation
Please Don't Drive Me Away
Run Right to Him
You Don't Believe I'm a Child of God
I'm Goin' to Lean on the Lord
Yeh Lord
Form the Line
Ain't No Grave Can Hold My Body Down
When I've Done the Best I Can I Wants My Crown
Katy, I Got to Go
I'll Be Waiting up There

Most of these songs are typical. There are several, however, which seem to possess unusual beauty. Anyone listening to "David" must recognize that here is probably the finest example of the Call and Response Chant-Spiritual[6] yet published.

There is found here a type of spiritual which appears to be a new development. This is the solo-spiritual. It undeniably borrows its more sophisticated verse style and its extended musical-phrase structure from the gospel songs, without the easy performance of the latter. The congregation finding these songs too difficult to sing usually surrenders the melody and verse to a leader while it hums—or listens. The songs listed above as created recently in Mississippi are examples of this new type of spiritual. Opportunity has not been provided yet for investigation of other sections of the South to determine whether this style is widespread or merely a north Mississippi phenomenon.

Persons hearing the "long-meter" hymns sung for the first time are strangely perplexed by this singing and make varied reactions to it. Miss Reid describing it wrote: "While they were doing this (the deacons preparing the table for the Lord's Supper) the congregation sang a lengthy song which was as much of a continuous wailing and bellowing as it was musical."[7] William Alexander Percy in his book *Lanterns on the Levee* relates a meeting in a Delta Negro Church. He describes this singing as follows: "It was a hymn I had never heard, a droning monotonous thing that swelled as they repeated verse after verse, from an almost inaudible mutter to a pounding barbaric chant. . . ."[8]

The words of these songs, old long-forgotten hymn verse generally ascribed to Isaac Watts, are intoned by a leader, traditionally a man, one line at a time. The congregation then begins spinning out an unmeasured melody, totally melismatic, in which each word-syllable receives approximately the equivalent of from four to eight moderato beats, though such beats could only be hypothetical. It would be less difficult to measure Gregorian chant by beats than these long drawn-out "Dr. Watts."

The many elaborate embellishments of which the melody consists are entirely spontaneous and improvised. Each singer improvises his or her own melody in concert with the other members of the congregation who are equally individual. Abbe Niles in his *Introduction to Blues* accounts for this phenomenon as ". . . . the impulse of competitive artistic effort—in singing, of the single voice trying to distinguish itself among the rest. . . ."[9]

So varied are the individual melodies that an authentic transcription of "long-meter" singing is impossible. The song represents as many versions as there are singers. The only noticeable uniformity in this singing occurs at the cadences which usually consist of two notes. Here only do the singers agree.

The three versions of the hymn, "I Heard the Voice of Jesus Say," transcribed here, are possible because numbers two and three are solo versions, and the four women singing number one were clearly dominated by one singer. A solo version of "Dark Was the Night" was also possible to transcribe.

The Negro church undoubtedly inherited this "long-meter" singing from the white church in an era long since past. Today, as far as can be ascertained, "Dr. Watts" are sung exclusively by the Negroes. Not only have the white churches ceased singing them, but they have forgotten that they ever sang them. Interviews with Dr. Charles C. Washburn, Professor of Hymnology at Scarritt College and an authority on American church music, and Dr. George Pullen Jackson, renowned folklorist, give support to this belief.

The Reverend Thomas Walter must have been describing "long-meter" singing in the following complaint against the singing in the New England churches early in the eighteenth century. "The tunes are now miserable tortured and twisted and quavered in our churches into a horrid medley of confused and disorderly voices. Our tunes are left to the mercy of every unskilled throat to chop and alter, to twist and change according to their infinitely diverse and no less odd humors and fancies. I have myself paused twice in one note to take a breath. No two men in the congregation quaver alike or together. It sounds in the ears of a good judge like five hundred tunes roared out at the same time with perpetual interferings with one another."[10]

The Sermon

Whatever may be said regarding the character or the importance of the various functions of the individual preachers, it can be easily recognized that the folk preacher is a person of rare attainments. He is actor, orator, poet, and mystic. He has the valuable faculty of translating the stories of the Bible and Christian tenets down to the easy understanding of an unreading flock. In the high-pitched emotional excitement of the second phase of his sermon he is transformed into a seer of remarkable accuracy despite his unfailing conviction that every tragedy which befalls nation, city, countryside, or person is a visitation of God's wrath upon the wicked.

The preachers are usually large men with either big voices or mellow ones, though there are famous exceptions to this rule. Most of them are God's Trombones, but some are God's Trumpets. A big resonant voice is one of the preacher's most valuable assets. A loud, high-pitched, frantic "O Lord" at the right time will excite his flock more easily than a good thought. The *right time* is the climax of a narrative sequence which has featured spontaneously rapid acceleration, rise in pitch, and sustained crescendo—all an outgrowth of the preacher's highly emotional state.

The sermon is divided into two parts. The shorter and the first is an application of the preacher's personal philosophy to present-day problems and community situations. Here he is entirely casual, conversational, and intimate. The worldly and the enemies of the church are attacked in this part. The weapon of the preacher here is ridicule, sometimes humorous, at other times caustic and bitter. This part of the sermon, however, serves chiefly as a preamble to the main body of the sermon—a "warming up" period. Frequently the preacher punctuates his remarks with pleas for the flock to bear with him until the spirit arrives or until the Lord tells him to go 'head. A favorite apology for his halting remarks is "I'm just' layin' my foundation."

The second part begins when both the preacher and the flock are sufficiently stimulated and emotionally prepared. At this stage the intimate character of the sermon abruptly passes over into the epic. No longer is the preacher dispensing his private and personal advice but is transformed into the messenger of God. God begins to talk. The first part of the sermon was impromptu prose. It now becomes poetry. James Weldon Johnson, in *God's Trombones*, recognized this poetic character as he created his famous sermons. John and Alan Lomax have transcribed a gripping Crucifixion sermon in verse in their book *Our Singing Country*. "A," "an," "And-er," and "a ha," as rhythmic syllables frequently intersperse the lines to outline them or to supplement those which otherwise would have unsatisfactory meter.

In addition to having meter, the sermon adopts another all-important feature—intonation. From the beginning of the second part the preacher introduces a style of delivery which is a mixture of singing and speech, and assumes in places the character of a dramatic recitative. There is a definite key-center, and while the sermon is too rhapsodic to produce sustained melody, the texture consists of successive melodic fragments. They are occasionally punctuated with speech lines. These fragments have all the Negro flavor in them. The ironical fact to be observed about them is that they are exactly like the idiom in many blues, which the church attacks so scornfully. In the sermon transcribed here, the melody accompanying:

> Ev'ry brook of water done gone,
> All the grass is parched away!
> Let us divide the lan' between ourselves
> Start at the fork o' the road
> And you go one way and I'll go the other way

is easily recognized as being characteristic of Negro secular music. The melody steadily rises in pitch as the sermon progresses and the spirit becomes more intense.

There are many extravagant gestures used by the preachers. Favorite ones are marching from one end of the platform to the other with a decisive sway at either end; leaping in the air; clapping the hands; covering the ears with the hands when emitting a loud yell; rising slowly on tiptoe and extending the arms directly above the head; and "cracking the whip," that is, clapping the hands and whirling completely around. Sometimes the preacher may dramatize an incident or a situation.

The appeal of the sermon depends upon the happy combining of its poetry, its rhythm and melody, its dynamics, and the volume, the voice, and the ardor of the preacher. The importance of the actual story is only secondary. The freedom with which the stories are varied from the original without comment or objection from the flock proves this.

This style of sermon is known as the "old-time sermon" or "gravy sermon." The rural churches generally demand it while only a very few city churches will permit it. It is regrettable that this beautiful religious art form is passing from the worship scene. Even the Delta preachers are aware that the "gravy" is considered by the younger generation as old-fashioned and preached by the ignorant for the ignorant. The following incident is illustrative of this.

A few summers ago John Ross, Alan Lomax, Lewis Jones, and I journeyed deep into the Delta to witness a church service which was to end with baptizing in a river nearby. Several days before, we had secured permission from the pastor of this church to record the service. We arrived at the church before the service and set up the machines, hoping, as do all folklore collectors, to record something new and beautiful for the outlying world.

The preliminary song service was touchingly devotional and deeply felt by us all. In it were observed several variants of traditional patterns.

Then came the sermon. To our consternation and the amazement of his flock the pastor *read* a sermon on the origin of doctrine, with frequent references to the errors of translation of the original Hebraic and Greek sources. There was no shouting or moaning that afternoon, and the "amens," which were only occasionally given by his loyal but mystified members, seemed terribly strained. That minister was ashamed to let us record his preaching of a "gravy" sermon.

The following sermon, derived from the famous story of Elijah, Ahab, and Baal, found in I Kings, was preached by the Reverend C. H. Savage during a revival at Mt. Ararat church. This church is located on the King and Anderson plantation. The introductory part of the sermon is omitted.

The cadences proved difficult to transcribe accurately because in these the tone not only drops in pitch and intensity but becomes semi-speech. Inasmuch as the cadence is unique, a special symbol ∿∿∿ was selected to designate it. In no manner does this represent a slur or glide, as in most instances it is quite direct and crisp.

In the dialect it will be observed that final d's before vowels are sounded while those before consonants are elided.

SERMON

J. W. Work

7. Spoken by Obadiah
8. assure
9. idiomatic expression used by a parent to summon a child

And Ahab forgot thirsty an' he come runnin'

An' be-fo' he got to E-li-jah he said "art thou the man troublin' Israel?

You stirred up the country! You done stirred up the Lan' o' Israel!

It ain't rained fo' three years an' six months, all, all the water have gone!"

(space) And all the Prophets o' Baal joined themselves to-gether

an' went marchin' off to Mount Carmel early that mornin'.

An' the Man o' God standin' in their midst said,

"I ain't but one man here but I know my Gawd's al-right!

I put myself up a-gainst eight hundred an' fif-ty men

I know I'll come out vic-tor-i-ous, I know I'll prove Gawd to-day!

But lissen here!¹⁰ Let's get the altar-a- that's broken down-a-an' clear it off for the Lord-a-

an' don't put no fire under it-a- an' kill the bullock an' cut it in pieces-a-

an' lay it on the wood-a- an' call yo' Gawd-a- an' the Gawd that answers by fiyuh"

Let Him be God"! I saw the prophets o' Baal comin' 'roun' the altar-

10. 'idiomatic
11. fire

They got you on a contest and A-hab said you was a right Gawd,
O Baal! O Baal!
An' the Man o' Gawd walked up, E-li-jah an' said "stan' back a while-a-
stan' back a-while"!
An' commenced pickin' up stones-a- an' said
I'm gonna name one Reuben-a- I'm gonna name one Benjamin-a-
I'm gonna name one Joseph, Name one for the Twelve Sons o' Jacob,
An' set them on the al-tar an' re-pair it where it's broken down
An' slay the bullock an' cut it in pieces an' lay it on the wood
An' jes bring me four bar'ls o' water
I want it to rep-er-sent somethin' here
Ev'ry time you bring four bar'ls o' water you rep-er-sent somethin'-a-
When you bring it by four you rep-er-sent the four Gospels
Matthew, Luke, Mark an' John [12]

12. The doctrinal evidence for this part of the ceremony is not found in the source of the story.

13. pronounced as one syllable
14. idiomatic

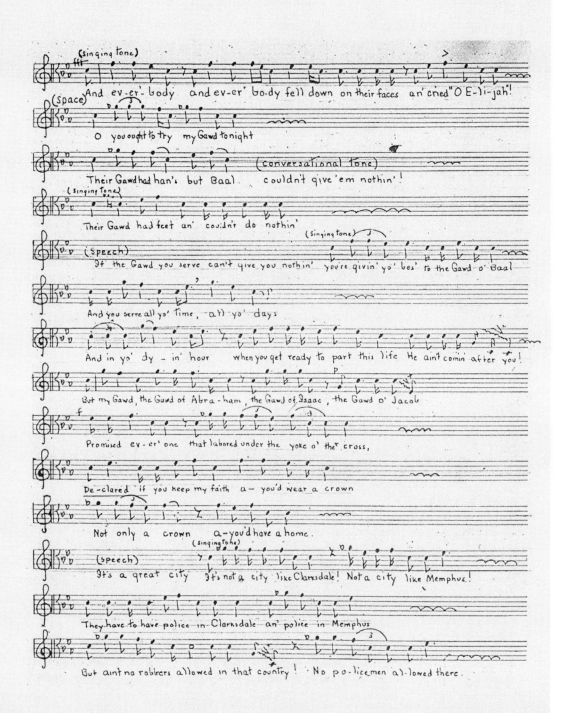

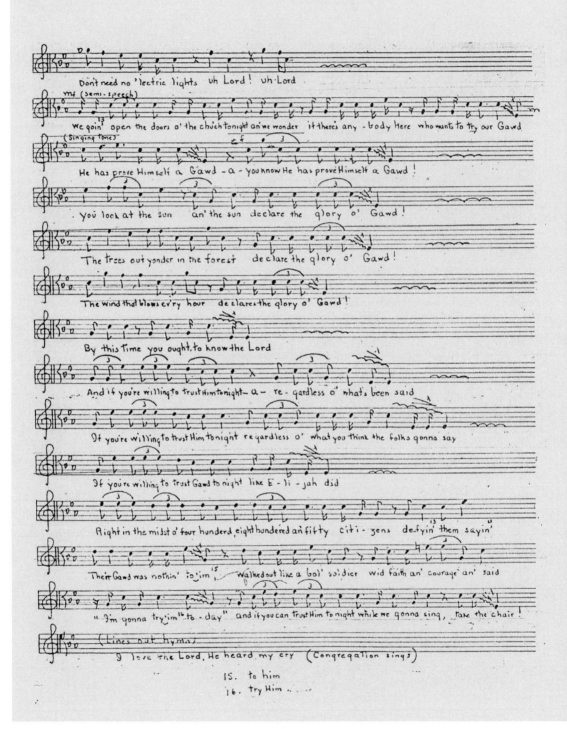

CHAPTER IV
The Folk-Quartet

Phonograph recordings and the radio programs have brought to the attention of the country over, a new source of stimulating music—the folk-quartet. This musical unit is not to be confused with or compared to the "barber-shop" quartet. While the "barber-shop" quartet emphasized harmony and "holds" on favored altered chords, and thus adopted the relatively slow tempo, the folk-quartet subordinates harmony to intricate rhythmic patterns, frequently in the form of ground motives and usually adopts a rapid, pounding tempo.

These two types of quartets are differentiated also by their songs. The "barber-shop" quartets sing usually secular songs with such well-defined melodies as "Po' Li'l Eva," "In the Evening by the Moonlight" and "Massa's in the Cold Cold Ground" or spirituals which allow opportunities for "chording."

The folk-quartet sings almost exclusively spirituals.

In both units the voices are labeled in order of their range: "tenor," "lead," "bare" (baritone) and "bass." The "barber-shop" quartet requires a tenor with a high range and good quality of voice, and a bass of low range and volume. These are the two dominant members. The "lead" and the baritone only have need of a chordal sense. Tonal quality and range demands upon them are not great.

In the folk-quartet the "lead" dominates. The other three singers are entirely subordinate to him. It is the "lead" who supplies the dazzling verses to the spirituals they sing or adds an inimitable counterpoint to the rhythmic refrain. The most famous folk-quartet is the Golden Gate Quartet, which has been broadcasting over the Columbia Broadcasting System for the past four years. They regularly supply songs through their recordings to their rural counterparts who imitate and vary them.

This quartet invests in the spiritual a complexity of both text and rhythm which would imply insuperable singing difficulties on a congregation. For this reason, these spirituals are generally limited to performances by quartet. Examples of these songs are: "You Pray On," "Holy Baby," and "Swing Down Chariot."

There are several well-known folk-quartets in this section: The Union Jubilee, Four Stars, and the Friendly Harmony Singers.

PART II

Saturday: Gambling in the Delta

Interview with a man whose favorite recreation was "Skin."

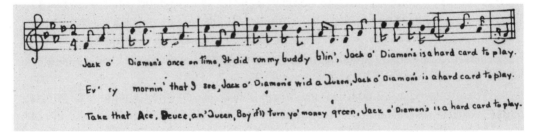

Don't no man gamble fair! If he can cheat you he will cheat you if he can. But he gonna tell you that it's a fair game. But don't no man do that. No man gambles fair. The han's always faster than a man's eye. When a man be gamblin' . . . ever'body when they sees you lucky and sees you winnin' they tries to find out how you winnin'. Everybody tryin' to find out.

If you plays green an' lucky an' makes 'em believe you's a hard workin' boy you can practically break ever-body who come along. Ever'body plays a workin'-man as a fool. Ever'body—ever'body you see. Sto'keeper, barber-shop, the tailor. Ever'body plays a workin'-man as a fool. A workin'-man has a better show for gamblin' or hustlin' than anybody else in the worl'. Why? Because—ain't nobody watchin' much!

Yo' han' is always faster than the eye. Folks may not believe that, but when you can shuffle a deck of cards an' "tote" you can have a pat han' in one han' an' show 'em the place you ain't got but two cards in that han'. That's all. You can carry a pat han' all the time. When that card comes, jes' like that, see, (he demonstrated) right over the "dead" it'll fall out!

Investigator   What kind of songs do the men sing when they gamble?

You take a man, the bigges' portion of the time when he be singin', he's a broke man! When a man gets broke, he gets hungry. Ev'ry woman he sees pretty nearly looks good to him then you know. He's settin' roun' thinkin' then, you see, about, money an' what he could a-done wid 'is money when he did have some. Long as he's got money he ain't studyin' 'about nothin' but bettin'.

You take a man where he's bettin' a quarter or fifty-cents, or somethin' like that, why ain't nothin' much to 'im. . . . But you take a man when he's gamblin' right smart o' money an' he has a right smart-like there be three, four, or five hundred dollars in the game, he can win good. But if he happens to get busted that's when he starts singin'.

You practically can always tell the broke man. He's gonna want ever'thing he sees in the house. If somebody come by sellin' a pie, he wants that. He wants a drink. He wants to talk to the women. He'll go to singin' an' hollerin'. Ever'thing gone wrong wid 'im. It's a broke man. But the man that's winnin', he ain't doin' nothin' but jes' layin' there gamblin'!

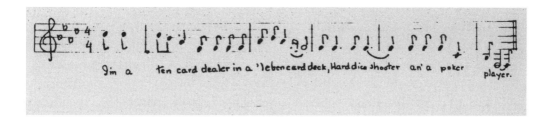

Im a   ten card dealer in a 'leben card deck, Hard dice shooter an' a poker player.

CHAPTER V
Secular Music

There is a vast amount of music which Negroes sing, work by, and dance and lis-ten to which is far removed from the influence of the church. In this category, fall the blues, worksongs, children's game songs, ballads, hollers, and social songs. Indeed it might be said that this music grows and thrives in ratio to its distance from the influence of the church. For, with the exception of the children's songs, the traditional churches have frowned for generations on this music and have condemned its makers and users to hell-fire and brimstone.

This orthodox attitude is reflected in the following statements from Delta church members gathered in interviews.

They (the church) make like they going to turn you out if you dance, and you have to beg pardon to get back. They have a group of critics and they gives you a sixty-day lay-off. All you do is tell them that you wants to beg the church's pardon for your evil ways, and that you're not going to do it no more. Of course you know you are!

A former musician said,

I learned to play the piano by ear and can play any song I hear, and more than that, I don't bar nobody. I used to play for dances but now since I done been converted I just lets my wife sin and I does nothing like that no more.

Another musician said,

Yes, I used to be a musician going around playing the guitar for lots of folks. I coulda been a rich man too playing reels and all kinds of stuff like that. But since I joined the church, I just done put all that behind. I don't even fool with none of that no more. To tell the truth, I really don't like to talk about it no more, 'cause you see it bring back too many memories.

A nineteen year old school boy said,

Yes sir! I thinks blues is wrong to sing, especially for a Christian. No folks around here who calls themselves Christians sing the blues. Dancing is all right if its just a sociable thing;* but it ain't right if its like at the juke. . . .

This same attitude was expressed three hundred miles away from the Delta in Nashville, Tennessee, by an elderly woman who when asked if she knew the song "John Henry" vigorously replied, "Shut up! Don't you mention nothing about 'John Henry' to me. Only low people sang that! Men used to work on public works and they used to holler for blocks singing those kind of songs. No! I don't want to tell you nothing about them. Those people had good voices and throwed them away. Christian folks didn't sing those kind of songs!"

In the communities where the Negro population is relatively stable and the church strong, the secular music is largely stifled. Miss Reid mentions no secular music in her study of Gee's Bend, Alabama.[11] All the music she gathered there was religious. This community as she describes it, is under the stern domination of the church which proscribes and controls as it does practically all social activities there.

In Coahoma County, Mississippi, on the other hand, where a large Negro population is eternally on the move back and forth, from plantation to plantation, from the plantation to Clarksdale—and points north, and where the church is less in control of the community life, secular music flourishes.

_____
*Round and square dancing.

Regarding the influence of the church in this Delta county the following statement secured in an interview with a very intelligent, elderly man, a Sunday School teacher in Clarksdale, reveals much:

Now I know what I'm speaking about. I done been here, and lived around here, and have seen most of it. That's not all neither. I done been all up around in the Hills.* Up there things are not like they are down here. Well, I tell you. Up in the Hills, folks don't get around as much as they do down here. The cities up there aren't large like they are down here. And the Negroes on the plantations up around in there, I don't know what they do now, but they didn't used to move around as much as they do down here. Folks get to living in a cabin on the plantation and they lives there for years and years. Everybody, all their neighbors knowed them. And the devil didn't seem to have much of a chance in the Hills.

But now you take down here, that is if you've been around any while you have been here, you can ask these folks around here as to how long they have been living in the house that they are now living in. On the whole they'll tell you around about two or three years. Mobility is very great, and the ordinary community controls that you find up in the Hills—you know what I'm talking about—well, you don't find them here. *Up in the Hills community sanctions influence almost all that you find anybody doing.*

The folks up there, as I told you, lived in one place longer than they do down here. The man, his wife, and his children feel a closer kinship to the land. A few of them own, and those who don't own still get along fair. They just been there on the land, and it's just a part of them. They have seen it for many years—when it's been good to them and when it's been bad.

I tell you, I'm getting to be kind of an old man, and when I sees things like they didn't used to be, I just can't help but get kind of concerned. No, I'm not talking about I'm against change. I can't help but want to see them change for the best. Life out here in the rural ain't near like what it used to be and don't let nobody tell you that it is.

You can see it in the children, these boys and school girls. Some of them are not interested in no lesson and are not trying to get nowhere. I just wonder if all of this is for the best.

Now I want to tell you. Not so long ago I was teaching Sunday School to a group of these boys and girls around here, and we was talking about using one's talents. You know about how God gave every man certain talents, and some used them wisely and others used them foolishly. We talked all about how various fine people had done a lot and made great advancements.

---

*The Hills is the name given to the eastern adjoining counties to contrast it with the Delta.

Then several inquisitive souls began to want to know if a person could use his talents successfully—and be a sinner? They talked about the gambler, the card shark, the policy operators, and finally they got settled down on Blues singers.

They wanted to know if it was a greater sin to let one's talents lay aside or to use one's talents in the wrong way, yet share the profits with the church. You can see what sort of things these youngsters got on their minds. Yes sir! They're getting all modern. They talked about Ella Fitzgerald who makes her living singing the blues. Some thought that singing the blues was her talent and they couldn't see how that was wrong, especially if she shared her profits with the church. Some thought it all right. Several of them jumped up and said that they didn't see how singing the blues could be any worse than some sisters sitting all up in church on Sunday and then go back the following week and talk about everybody.

You can see that they is thinking more now-a-days—at least some of them are. They hear so much more, and see so much more than they used to that you just can't say what's the world a-coming to.

No, the church ain't like what it used to be—the days of 'eye-balls a-drippin' and skulls a-bilin' . . . The preacher in those days lived right in the community, probably farmed just like anybody else. And they was sincere. There wasn't no shamming and putting-on and performing just for the dollar. These preachers that preaches out here now, they can't be as interested in the folks as the man who used to live right amongst them. They live in town, and haven't just one church but plenty of churches to preach in.

Now just take this little church up here, _____ They got a preacher, Reverend _____, and you hear some of the younger folks at the church talking about him drinking with the deacons. But the folks at the church don't seem to be able to get along without him. He lives in town, and at times, he is just about liable to show up on the first Sunday as he is not. Sometimes he goes off and preaches in other places, seems like just for the dollar.

All of these things are going on, especially in the younger generation. Long time ago, country boys mostly married country girls, and folks thought that something was wrong if they didn't. Folks used to look at city folks as outsiders. Now they go to the city so much and the city folks come out to the rural so much, that the way is not like the old. Country boys and girls that used to just live here on the plantations are now going to town. The boys marry city girls and girls marry city boys. Well, I guess all of that is just life.

Further attitudes of the Delta people are reflected in the interviews with the youth there quoted by Dr. Johnson:[12]

On lots of things the people mind the preacher. If he say somebody is all right, maybe its all right and maybe it ain't. Sometimes the folks do something the preacher don't like, but he can't do nothing about it and it's all right, 'cause so many be doing it, and maybe he be doing it too.

I have to go to church every Sunday because my father makes me but I want to leave and come home, though, for the preacher don't be sayin' much 'pears like to me.

Sometimes I want to leave church and come home, 'cause it looks like to me like the preacher don't be sayin' much. He do a lot of hollerin' and shoutin'. May be if I could understan' what he was talking about I would like church better, but I can't see what he's tryin' to say.

The Delta church, apparently aware of its weakening hold on the fealty of its younger people, in some instances had made concessions to the secular life. An example of this is the "heaven and hell" party, a strange sort of entertainment not yet encountered in other rural areas. It probably would not be countenanced in other rural sections. In addition to its being a concession to the demands of the younger people for greater secular activity, the "heaven and hell" party represents temporarily at least a practical abandonment by the church of its former rigid community sanctions.

One young woman in the Delta describes the "heaven and hell" party as follows:

Well, I'll tell you, it's costing a dime to get in. You buys a ticket, which tells you which way you'll be going—to Heaven, or to Hell. Now you can't go to both of them. You got to do what the ticket says. Well, if you gets a ticket to Heaven they serves you ice cream and cake, and you just sits around and talks, and maybe plays games. But if you gets a ticket to Hell they serves you hot cocoa and red hot spaghetti—and they dance, play cards, checks, and do most anything.

When such a party was given at _____ Church, the deacons, as a public display of disapproval, remained away. Had they withheld permission for the party, however, it would not have been given.

The secular music and pleasure activities so widespread in the Delta represent the escape from, or the indifference to, the disapproval of the church. As William Brown "picking" his guitar on a Memphis street sang: "Goin' down to the Delta where I can have my fun."

Thomas Jones, piano player, genial, and wise in the lore of Southern dance music, universally known as "Jay Bird," tells something of the secular music in Clarksdale in the twenties. The interview consisted of a few, terse, rhythmic statements accompanied by a slow soft exciting blues which never halted nor retarded.

Jay Bird	Dance halls was ev'rywhere. . . . Thirteen piano players was here. . . . Course I was the worst of all.
Interviewer	Who were some of them, Jay Bird?
Jay Bird	Well, the best of them was Eddy Hall . . . Arthur Reed . . . James Sykes . . . Milam Davis . . . Joe Love . . . That's all I can remember . . . There wasn't a note reader in the bunch . . .

Today, the dancing places are much fewer. There are no formal dance halls, and public dancing is limited to that in a few restaurants that provide dancing space. The most prominent of these are Tommy's Place located on Third and Sunflower streets, and the Dipsy Doodle on Fourth Street in Clarksdale. Young pleasure seekers, both from the plantations and the town, throng to these. On Saturday they literally swarm. Dancing, ranging from the vigorous "jitterbugging" down to more vulgar types, may be observed in these places.

Formerly the music for such dancing was largely provided by local instrumentalists who "plunked" jazz on aged upright pianos with the front board removed, or "picked" blues on guitars and mandolins. They were ably supported by harmonica players. It was very surprising—even dumbfounding that not one banjo player was found in the Delta. (The guitar seems to have replaced the banjo completely in this section as a music maker long ago.) One good fiddler, "Son" Sims, was found and recorded.

The music to which Clarksdalians now dance is furnished chiefly by the juke-boxes, which are called by the folk "Sea Birds"—a corruption of the name Seeburg, one of the makers of Nicklelodeons. The "Sea Birds" have practically eliminated the folk performers and music from the Clarksdale dancing scene. The guitarists, harmonica, and mandolin players now perform on street corners or in barber shops for pure entertainment purposes for which they collect small gratuities from appreciative passersby.

This displacement of the folk instrumentalists has had three important results, and from a certain viewpoint two of these are unfortunate ones.

The opportunity for money and acclaim no longer beckons the itinerant virtuoso who formerly stimulated and instructed the local competing players. Here is a two-pronged disaster which sees both the itinerant and the local performers dispossessed of a livelihood.

The second result of importance in this displacement is the attendant revolution in the music preferences of the Delta people. Where they previously derived great enjoyment and stimulation from their folk blues, they have been won over in a short span of years to the blatant commercial swing vended by the "Sea Birds." The blues are still there as shown by the juke-box record lists but the imprint of Tin Pan Alley has all but excluded the simpler racial beauty of the older.

The following is a list of the records offered by the juke-boxes in Tommy's Place and the Dipsy Doodle at the time the survey was being made:

After Hours
Biscuit Baking Woman
Boogie Woogies
Can't Afford to Lose My Man
Coal and Ice Man Blues
Country Boy Blues
Don't You Lie to Me
It Looks Bad for Her
Key to the Highway
Knock Me Out
Love Me
Love Me with Attention
Mattie Mae Blues
Night after Night
No Place to Go
Pine Top Boogie Woogie
Saxa Woogie
Sharp as a Tack
Set It Up and Go
She Ain't Right
She's Making a Fool Out of Me
Shot Gun Blues
Stand by Me
38 Pistol Blues
Tune Town Shuffle
When I Been Drinking

Interviews among the plantation folk revealed the extent of this influence. Their prevailing preferences of dance music included:

Before Sunrise Blues
Cotton Seed Blues
In the Mood
Pan Pan
She's a Beer Drinking Woman
Star Dust
Terra Plane Blues

Trucking
Tuxedo Junction
What You Know Joe
Yes Indeed

Phonographs and records were fairly well distributed among them. The Collins family had 85 records, 69 of which were dance records, mostly commercial blues. The McGuire family had 45 records, 36 of which were dance records.

A third effect of the popularity of the juke-box is the influence of the performance-style of the bands on the playing of the guitarists. New virtuosic melodic idioms are being introduced into their play and harmony is being enriched. These factors will be discussed and illustrated in the following chapter. But also the guitarists are increasingly acquiring their song repertory from the juke-box instead of composing their own music as formerly.

The electrification of the plantation with the possibility of transporting juke-boxes to the country dances is carrying the displacement of professional folk performers to the rural areas. This is not yet complete, as McKinley Morganfield (Muddy Water), David Edwards, and "Son" House still have a devoted following there.

A ten o'clock curfew law operating in Clarksdale sends the fun-makers scurrying out to the plantations after that time. On Saturday night this exodus from the metropolis of the Delta assumes the proportion of a huge reveling cavalcade moving out to the plantation "where they can have their fun."

∾

CHAPTER VI
The Instruments

Folk instrumental performances are practically all improvisations upon the idioms and patterns—melodic, harmonic, and rhythmic—developed by countless players for a particular instrument. They vary from the very elementary to the very intricate and complex. The variation principle works effectively upon these. Rarely are they "copied" exactly. They constantly are being modified and altered by the temperament of the players, and the incoming of new idioms and style of performance via visitors, radio, and juke-box. A typical one and one of the most widely used and varied idioms is the following:

It is interesting to note that in the interviews with them, most of the younger guitarists reveal that they improved their art and learned many of their songs from phonograph records. It is easy to recognize in some of their performances the influence of modern dance music. William Brown playing his Mississippi Blues uses as a ground-pattern the theme of Carle's Sunrise Serenade adapted freely but beautifully for his guitar.

Formerly these idioms and patterns, learned directly or indirectly from the older performers had the "folk" quality. They were chiefly rhythmic and chordal to which the voice part was a counterpoint. With the exception of the accompaniment to the ballad, these were created chiefly for dancing. "Son" House, patriarch of the Delta guitar players selects a rhythmic figure and uses it as a ground-pattern for each blues he plays.

The patterns copied from the juke-box by the younger men appear to be more melodic and virtuosic, and serve mainly as dazzling cadenzas between phrases or verses of their songs. In some instances the performers have adopted a tempo rubato in place of the strict unvarying dance rhythms of the older players. This illustrated the trend of performance from that used chiefly for dancing to the playing for entertainment mentioned in the preceding chapter. The "Watercourse Blues" as played by David Edwards is a good example of the new style.

The performance style has also become more sophisticated, not only from the point of emphasis on the virtuosic element but also from that of texture. As previously noted the older style superimposed the voice as a counterpoint over a prevailing instrumental ground-pattern. But the current style employs frequently, though not exclusively, an accompanying counterpoint to the voice. As an illustration of this style observe Muddy Water's "Late on in the Evening Blues" or Edwards' "Watercourse Blues."

A. THE GUITAR

The Delta is rich in guitar lore. It is doubtful if any section of the country can boast finer exponents of folk-guitar playing. It is very valuable to this study that there were found in this section three different, well-defined styles of guitar playing that could be classified also by the age of the performers.

In the playing of "Alec" Robertson there is seen a simple chordal strumming style. In his playing of "O My Lord" and "Clear the Line" the strumming is either chord repetition, or alternation between the root in the bass and the other members of the chord in the upper voices. Limited harmonic resources are in evidence here as Robertson only employs the tonic and dominant chord in both pieces and plays "O My Lord" entirely on the tonic. Most of the songs he played upon the guitar for recording were spirituals. This is explained by his Holiness Church background where he accompanies the services.

The playing style of Will Starks is essentially the same as Robertson's. These men are both from an older era of guitar playing. In their hands, the guitar functions exclusively as unobtrusive accompaniment with the display element entirely absent. Here it can be said "the song is the thing."

The playing of "Son" House represents the pinnacle of guitar performance. The style he employs elevates the guitar to an equal importance with the voice. In it the deeply resonant tone, the stimulating rhythm, and the fascinating patterns, as well as the thoroughly adequate harmony provide completely satisfying music. His harmony comprises in addition to the primary triads, the flatted one-seven and four-seven, an occasionally used diminished seventh, and the two-seven with a sharp. For some unexplained reason he has the unrivalled faculty of singing a tonic figure against a dominant chord on the guitar with very agreeable results. An instance of this is seen in his "I Got a Letter Blues." "Son" House belongs to the generation of Robert Johnson and "Blind Lemon" Jefferson who won the attention of the recording companies and created a mild vogue for guitar records in the twenties.

David Edwards and McKinley "Muddy Water" Morganfield, already referred to several times, are able representatives of the current virtuosic style of performance.

For over twenty years, guitar music in the Delta has been mainly blues. A detailed discussion of the blues is unnecessary in this study as they have been authoritatively defined and described in two works by W. C. Handy.[13] Some additional data on them are given here, however, to account for the variations which have taken place since Handy lived with them.

The rigid, unyielding four-bar phrase, as well as the three-phrase form described by him still prevail. But there are an increasing number of blues played by the younger men today which are in two sections. Muddy Water has two blues in this collection— "I've Never Been Satisfied" and "Late On in the Evenin'" which vary to a great extent from the traditional form. In the former, there will be observed a pattern of lines quite unlike that in any other blues in this collection.

1. Well if I feel tomorrow like I feel today
  I'm goin' pack my suitcase and make my get-a-way

Well I'm gone, gone, gone
I'm almost gone
(Interlude)
Yet I've never been satisfied
Yet I jes' can't keep from cryin'!

2.   Yeh! I know somebody sho been talkin' to you
I don't need no tellin' girl, I can watch the way you do.
Well I'm gone, gone, gone,
I'm almost gone
(Interlude)
Yet I've never been satisfied
And I jes' can't keep from cryin'.

There will be noticed in this song two refrains, each of which must be regarded irregular.

Further irregularity may be observed in the second song. There is no refrain in it but the traditional three-line form is replaced by a two-line form repeated with different melody and harmony.

1.   Well it's late on in the evenin' child, I feel like blowin' my horn
I woke up this mornin' and found my little baby gone!
Late on in the evenin' child, I feel like blowin' my horn
I woke up this mornin' and found my little baby gone.

2.   Some folks tell me the worried old blues ain't bad
Well that's the miserest feelin' I most ever had
Some folks tell me the worried old blues ain't bad
It's the miserest feelin' I most ever had.

Despite the singer's designating the songs as such, labeling them as blues might well be challenged. Reference to his "Burr Clover Blues" will prove Muddy Water's complete familiarity with the three-line form.

There are, however, three elements present in these two songs which are closely akin to the blues, so close in fact that they give the unmistakable 'blues' flavor. These undoubtedly led the performer to label the songs, "blues." The first is the before-mentioned reliance upon the four-bar phrase, the blues unit. In practically all other vocal music the length of the musical phrase is determined by the verse line. When the verse line ends, the phrase ends. It is characteristic of most folk verse that it is distributed rhythmically to extend two or four bars.

The blues phrase on the other hand is four bars long regardless of the length of the verse line which not infrequently is comprised of very few words which extend only two bars. The instrument, or instruments, with which the blues are completely synthesized with the words perform the remaining bars unaccompanied by the voice. This fact accounts for the bars of rest which appear in the vocal versions of the blues included in this collection. After three verses it is customary for the instrument, or instruments to play an entire section with the voice omitted. The playing in this interlude is much more elaborate and features more display and pounding rhythm than do those sections with singing. This interlude occurs in both the pieces under discussion.

Muddy Water's verse is clearly blues verse. The structure of the individual lines with their terse expressiveness as well as their sentiments are identical with those of the traditional blues.

The sentiment of the blues verse, again, has been discussed too completely in other treatises to warrant another description of it here.[14] One characteristic heretofore unmentioned, however, should be recognized. It is the nonsense element.

In the singing of the blues there is seen an intense, subconscious, esthetic demand that the third line—the "punch" line have a rhyming last word. The entire thought of the singer most often is expressed in this last line. The first line and its repetition may contribute to it, but more often it does not. The prime aim of the singer therefore is to provide preliminary lines with a rhyming last word for the end of the last line. Frequently these preliminary lines are "nonsense" in their relation to the last line. Here are several illustrations extracted from Delta blues:

> Brook run into the ocean, ocean run into the sea
> If I can't find my baby now, somebody goin' have to bury me.

> Minutes seem like hours, hours seem like days
> Seems like my baby would stop her low down ways.

> You know the sun is going down, I say, behind that ol' western hill
> You know I wouldn't do a thing not against my baby's will.

What relation there is between the serenity and sadness associated with the sun going down "behind that ol' western hill" and doing nothing against "my baby's will" defies discovery except in the simple incident of "hill" rhyming with "will."

The triplet is a rhythmic unit used to a great extent in the blues accompaniment, particularly in the interlude. The triplet is so predominant in many passages that it gives rise to conjecturing upon the basic rhythm of the blues as 12/8. Illustrations of this may be seen in the music idiom quoted early in the discussion and in the interlude in "Late on in the Evening Blues." It will be noted as a frequently used unit in the voice parts. But its use in the vocal part may be interpreted as prosodic rather than as an intensifying factor in the rhythm as it is when used by the instruments.

B. THE HARMONICA

The harmonica grows in favor among Negroes throughout the South. In the Delta the tinkling sound of the harmonica may be heard nightly on the streets as strolling musicians give expression to their nostalgia and blues. The harmonica is a more intimate and a more convenient companion than any other instrument. It stays tuned, ready for instant performance. It has no strings to wear or break. It is not cumbersome to carry, resting as it does unobtrusively in the master's pocket instead of swinging on his back, or dispossessing him of the use of an arm to carry it.

The music of the folk player is as often as not, a spontaneous expression of, or accompaniment to his present mood in which the listener, if there be one, has little part. This very personal music belongs to the player in the same manner that whistling or humming belong to the lonesome walker. But the harmonica probably belongs more completely to the instant mood of the lonesome traveler than other instruments.

Formerly, in the hands of the folk, the harmonica as an entertaining instrument was used almost exclusively as a solo instrument. Upon it the performer produced many extraordinary sounds. To accommodate these various sounds and figures several pieces were created, which in time became the stock repertory of folk-harmonica players everywhere. What Southerner has not heard "The Train" (usually named after the most famous passenger train of the player's particular section) or "The Fox Hunt!"

In the Delta, the harmonica today has graduated to a more respectable musical standing. It no longer is limited to its older, over-used tour-de-forces, but is now an associate of other instruments. Its chief function when used as formal entertainment is to give melodic support to the guitar and mandolin. The harmonica could not serve pleasantly in this role as accompaniment to the piano because it cannot adjust its pitch to the forever out-of-pitch condition of the pianos upon which the folk play.

This melodic support given by the harmonica to the guitar in its performance of a blues is not to be confused with the vocal melody. Instead of the ejaculatory, segmented character of the vocal melody, it is a continuous counterpoint derived entirely from the prevailing harmony and only related harmonically to the vocal melody. Occasionally the harmonica may substitute for the voice.

Some virtuosi still retain their independence from the guitar and mandolin group. These are unique entertainers who entice coins on street corners from admiring passersby. These men play spirituals and blues as well as current popular songs.

A new and unusual style of performance has been developed by them. This style consists of phrases, or segments of phrases alternately sung and played without the loss of a beat in the change. This style is not peculiar to players in the Delta, however, as it is used in other places. The well-known Sanders Terry, from Charlotte, North Carolina who has recorded much for the Library of Congress employs this style most effectively.

The most popular and possibly the most proficient harmonica player of those found in Coahoma County is Turner Junior Johnson, an elderly plantation sharecropper. Most of his songs were sung in a gruff deep bass voice. The style of playing just described with many other interesting harmonica figures may be seen in the songs recorded from his performances.

C. OTHER INSTRUMENTS

Of the remaining musical instruments traditionally used by the folk—the fiddle, mandolin, banjo, and double bass, only one fiddle and one mandolin were found played in the Delta. The fiddle was played by "Son" Sims and the mandolin by Lewis Ford. Willie Blackwell's playing of a mandolin was recorded on a Memphis street.

In the performance of these men it could be easily observed that their functions as in that of the harmonica were to support the guitar. They supplied counterpoints or rhythmic figures. Among the folk these are seldom used as solo instruments.

Only rarely are the wind instruments used in the folk instrumental combinations, the harmonica excepted of course. A trombone was used in one of the Holiness Church services but this could not be considered typical.

In _____ County in the Hills, Lewis Jones and Alan Lomax found "Sid" Hemphill, a blind ballad maker and fellow musicians using many interesting instruments. Among these were a banjo, two drums, a fife, and two sets of quills.

One of these quills had four holes while the other was a ten hole quill. These are based on the Pan's Pipe idea. Melodies only were played on these, but considerable skill was required to produce an intelligible melody on them. The chief performance difficulty in the hands of this unusual musician was the maintaining of the rhythm. Traditional folk tunes were blown on these quills. A pictured representation of a set of quills appears in Thomas W. Talley's *Negro Folk Rhymes*.[15]

∼

CHAPTER VII
*Social Songs**

There are many songs sung to the accompaniment of an instrument to which the folk dance sometime, but to which more often, they only listen in small groups. These are the social songs and ballads. The folklorist searching for these songs early becomes aware of their rarity. But while they are few when compared with the numbers of other

---

*The term "social song" as used herein, refers to the type of song which has no definite function other than light, intimate entertainment, or occasionally serving as a dance song. It is distinguished from the blues by its duplet or quatrain verse form, its moderate to moderately fast tempo, as well as its lighter and simpler mood. Musically it is akin to the ballad but its verse has little of the narrative element. Examination of the songs themselves will help to define them.

types of Negro songs they are no less distinctive or racial. It seems, that as few as they are, they are becoming fewer and when found they are usually sung by the elderly players. Snatches and fragments of these songs are remembered by a few older non-playing folk. This suggests that these songs exist only in the memory of a generation to pass.

The social songs, unlike the spirituals and some of the work songs which are sung by the group, are usually solo performances and remain largely in the exclusive performance-repertory of only a few guitar and banjo players. Aside from those that might be sung and played for dancing they serve chiefly as informal entertainment for home gatherings and occasionally for the edification of white people.

The subject matter of these songs is often trivial and in many instances nonsensical. The sociologist searching for a social message in these will be disappointed unless he is able to develop one from the implications of its almost complete absence in the verse.

Animals both of the wood and the barnyard as well as the more cantankerous insects inspire many of them. In many instances the character of the animal sung about by Negroes or told about, is similar to that popularly attached to him. Thus, the fox is crafty and sly, but in folk stories usually comes out second best in his shady schemes. But did he not do so in the fables of Aesop? The bear is usually bloodthirsty and forever chasing a man who must resort to unusual tricks, speed, or prayer to escape him. Other animals are clothed in a new character. In the Negro lore, and particularly that found in the Delta, the buzzard has replaced the owl as the animal of great wisdom and patience. This Buzzard and Hawk story as told by Turner Johnson from the Hopson plantation shows this.

> Once there was a buzzard and a hawk a-settin' up in a tree. The hawk said, "Say er Br'er Buzzard! What us goin' do for our dinner?" The buzzard looked around at the hawk and said, "I tell what we'll do,—us'll wait on the salvation o' the Lawd!"
>
> "The 'Salvation'?"
> "Yeh!"
> "The 'salvation' is too long about comin'!"
> Jes' then the hawk looked down by the side o' the fence and seed a rabbit. He sailed down at the rabbit but broke his neck on the fence.
> The buzzard flew down to the hawk and said "See 'ere! I tol' you to wait on the salvation o' the Lawd! Now I got you to eat!"

In one of Talley's Negro Folk Rhymes the buzzard is called "Jedge Buzzard."[16]

In Negro song and story "Br'er Rabbit" has been a favorite subject for generations.[17] In the Delta, however, he appears in more children's game songs than adult songs.

It is the opinion of several scholars that the widespread use of animals as subjects for songs and stories stems from African tradition. Talley accounts for this in an entirely plausible manner. He describes the deification of animals in African life and explains the transposition of the animal story of religious significance to the secular song and rhyme upon the African becoming Christianized in America.[18] Newman I. White ascribes also to the African tradition origin.[19]

The following are four animal songs found in the Delta:

The Boll Weevil
Frog Went a Courtin'
Crawfish Backin Back in the Lake
Didn't He Ramble

The more trivial personal relations which sometimes approach the ridiculous also serve as song material. These songs are believed by White to be the offspring of the older minstrel songs to which they bear a marked resemblance in phrase and in sentiment.[20] The following songs are illustrative of this:

T. P. Runnin'
Show Me the Way to Go Home
I'm a Rowdy Soul
I'll Keep My Skillet Greasy
Got on the Train
Cindy

The appearance of the radio and phonograph in rural life, as well as the spread of reading, have provided new, more convenient, and more varied forms of entertainment than that upon which the folk previously relied. The resulting broadening of interest and the sophistication which attended the incoming of mechanical entertainment and reading made the rural folk less patient with their simple, crude social songs which had already been heard by them too often. One of the chief complaints levied against the spirituals by the church folk is that they soon tire of singing the same songs, and sufficiently interesting new ones are created in too few numbers. This same reaction against the social songs certainly is more intense and has surely expedited its removal from the area of active music.

Again there is seen the usurpation of a folk cultural function formerly performed by a folk agent by outside agencies which has caused the disappearance of both the original expression and the folk agent.

CHAPTER VIII
Ballads

The Negro ballad is not so widespread among the folk as is the spiritual or the blues. Few of the folks sing them or remember more than verse fragments and titles. For this reason the search for Negro ballads resolves itself largely into a search for the ballad singer, a rarely encountered folk musician.

Charles Haffer and Will Starks,[21] two Coahoma County ballad singers, have ballad repertories which exceed those of most Negro singers elsewhere. As ballad singers, they are an interesting contrast to each other. Haffer, blind, recently moved to Greenville, is a creator-publisher of broadside-ballads which he sells throughout his section of the Delta. Starks, on the other hand, a sharecropper on the Hopson plantation until he lately moved to resume his long-time occupation as a sawmill hand, is a singer of traditional, unprinted ballads. Haffer sings his ballads without instrumental accompaniment. Starks usually strums a guitar as he sings. Another blind ballad maker, "Sid" Hemphill, living in an adjoining hill county, sings many songs of especial interest. Unfortunately, the ballads recorded from his singing are not available for this collection. Because they referred largely to persons living at present in his area, it did not seem advisable to publish those ballads here. This remarkable musician is invited to write ballads on various incidents occurring in the community by the white folk there who appreciate his talent.

The two most widely known Negro ballads, "John Henry" and "Frankie and Albert" are generally known in the Delta. Versions of the "John Henry" ballad have appeared in so many Negro folk song collections that it becomes unnecessary to include it here. "Frankie and Albert" without much expurgation is not publishable.

The five Haffer broadsides, and the eight ballads sung by Will Starks, are presented in their musical setting. The melody of the ballad is often of little more than trivial interest. And yet as will be readily heard in Starks' "Arkansas" they are not always without some charm. In contra-distinction to the spiritual in which the words are largely subordinated to the tune, the ballad employs the melody chiefly as a metrical and sustaining support for the all-important verse. For this reason the melodies are usually free of climax and have a short-range compass. In none of the melodies of the ballads sung by Starks was there discoverable any of the distinctive Negro flavor so immediately recognized in the blues and in the spirituals. In Haffer's melodies, original with him, the Negro character is pronounced. This rhapsodic character instead of the sustained phrase line, the often repeated upper minor-tonic note, and the portamenta downward leap of the fourth at accents all demonstrate this fact.

Passages in "What a Storm" are very similar to passages found in the "Elijah and Ahab" sermon by Reverend C. H. Savage, indicating common racial exhortative devices of musical expression.

A search through Professor Hudson's *Folk Songs of Mississippi*, a study of the white folklore in the state, will reveal none of the ballads sung by Will Starks, even those whose subjects are less definable racially, such as "The Blind Man," "The Fox Hunters," and "Brady and Duncan." Searching for these ballads in more general collections of American ballads[22] likewise fails to uncover them. This interesting fact clearly illustrates the elusiveness of the ballad even to an intensive search.

"Stagolee" appears in other collections of Negro songs. A comparison of Starks' version of "Stagolee" with the two given by Professor Howard W. Odum and Professor Guy B. Johnson[23] reveals some interesting variations. In the first Odum and Johnson version, Stagolee "killed the best ol' citizen," while in the second he "shot the bully." In Starks' version, he "shot thoo-an-thoo Billy Golyon," his best friend. It is easily possible that the "Bully" of the Odum and Johnson version is a corruption of "Billy" in the Starks version. In the first Odum and Johnson version no cause for the murder is given. In their second version, it was "all about dat raw hide Stetson hat." In Starks' version "Stagolee killed his best friend about a five dollar Stetson hat." Again in the Odum and Johnson version, "Stagolee" is quite penitent at the trial and pleads for mercy. Starks' Stagolee is so furious that the Judge said, "Make haste and hang 'im 'fore he kill some of us." Further, an important variation is seen in the form of the ballad with Starks' five-line form being in decided contrast to Odum and Johnson's four-line verse. In the second of the Lomax versions of the same song,[24] the story corresponds closely to that of Will Starks, although the variations in the verses are striking.

> What a Storm—Broadside composed and sung by Charles Haffer.
> I'll Be Glad to See the Sun—Religious ballad composed and sung by
> Charles Haffer. This song, though, without the narrative sequences
> which distinguish the true ballad, nevertheless, does have the
> constantly changing lines, a feature which is more akin to the ballad
> form and style than to the spiritual whose feature is recurring lines.*
> Strange Things Happening in the Land[25]—Broadside composed and sung
> by Charles Haffer.
> The Natchez Fire Disaster—Broadside composed and sung by Charles
> Haffer
> These Days Got Everybody Troubled—Broadside composed and sung by
> Charles Haffer
> Fox Hunter Song—Ballad sung by Will Starks. Learned as a boy from his
> father
> The Blind Man—Ballad sung by Will Starks. Learned on sawmill job

---

*The original manuscript reserved space between each title. Work probably intended to add comments such as these to each entry.

When You Lose Your Money—Ballad sung by Will Starks. Learned from
      Alfred Dyal, a fellow sawmill man, about 1897
Arkansaw—Ballad sung by Will Starks. Learned on sawmill job
Stagolee—Ballad sung by Will Starks. Learned on saw mill job
Brady and Duncan—Ballad sung by Will Starks. Learned on sawmill job
Rowdy Soul—Ballad sung by Will Starks. Learned from white workman
      on sawmill job
The Late War—Ballad sung by Will Starks. Learned on sawmill job

It must not be construed that every "ballet" is a ballad. Probably most of the Negro "ballets" are spirituals and gospel songs sung by traveling evangelists and singers who earned their entire income from their sales. Two of these bought from different singers on the streets of Clarksdale, follow. [See song transcriptions at the end of this section.]

CHAPTER IX

The Work Songs

Negro work songs may be divided from the standpoint of their functions, and their form, into three types. Some of them are highly rhythmic in character and are sung to coordinate the group efforts of the workmen when precision is necessary. The second type of work song is one in which the individual workman expresses to his fellow workmen, to his "captain" and to the world-at-large his immediate sentiments about his woman, his work, or the place where he is living or wants to be. This type of song is given the name "holler"* by the folk. The third type of work song is that sung by the group of men for the pure pleasure of singing together.

The rhythmic song, so fragmentarily constructed as to stimulate and direct simultaneous motions by the group of men, is the one generally referred to when the term 'work song' is used. This unique structure will be readily observed in the songs sung by Houston Bacon[26] and the "John Henry" work song. The subjects of these songs are rarely profound, or lofty as are those of the spirituals. They are almost all trivial and frequently rough and boisterous. They are rarely sad and usually show the Negro workman in his best humor. Songs of this type are not often heard on the job today.† Machines, which now dominate most important labor, and their noise have almost stifled them

---

*The term "holler" is used freely. In addition to the type of song described above, it may refer to the purely musical wordless holler emitted by young men driving teams; or it may refer to special instruction-calls to workmen or dancers.
†Convict chain-gangs are excepted.

completely. These songs like the social songs are clearly disappearing from active living folklore.

The "holler" is usually a three-line song (though often two-line) in the form of blues verse. Many of the verses of these work "hollers" are identical with those of the blues. Although in these "hollers" his sentiments are mostly introspective trivialities, the songs frequently protest the "captain's" long working hours, a practice the "captain" probably would not tolerate in direct conversation. The melody of these "hollers" differs from that of the blues in that it is much more florid and is devoid of the metrical element. Devoid of meter as it is, the "holler" is in decided contrast to the first type of work song in which the rhythmic factor is uppermost in importance. It has no group significance.

The third type of song is not so distinctive as are the other two. Sung as it is by the men for their pleasure alone, it need only have an appealing sustained tune, the type of song best suited for group singing.

The Delta is cotton country. The larger number of Negroes living there work in cotton or service those who do. The other occupations in which Negroes find work, now that levee construction is practically at an end, are negligible by comparison. The work songs of Coahoma County as a result reflect much of the Negroes' attitude toward cotton. As the various phases of cotton work—planting, chopping, and picking, as well as ginning are non-rhythmic, and the workers do not work in concert, no songs of the rhythmic type are directly connected with it. Such songs as are sung in the cotton field are most often "hollers" and an occasional spiritual.

The Delta Negro does not like cotton. To him because of its historical uncertainty in providing a dependable livelihood, it has become a symbol of hard living. Some of this attitude is seen in the following verses selected from the songs heard.

> Makin' a good cotton crop
> Is jes' like shootin' dice

> Mister Weevil, Mister Weevil what makes your bill so long?
> You done et up all my cotton and started on my younges' corn.

> I ain't gonna raise no mo' cotton
> I declare I ain't gonna try to raise no mo' corn.

∼

CHAPTER X
Children's Game Songs

Visitors to the Delta who are fortunate enough to hear them, are struck by the strange beauty of the game songs sung by the Negro children there. Hearing these songs in the distance at dusk arouses in one a feeling that is almost eerie save for the enthrallment it gives. The listener is at once aware of a musical flavor that is different from any sounds heard among city children.

Instead of the lyric prettiness of such typical Anglo-American game songs as the widely known "Go In and Out the Window" and "London Bridge Is Falling Down" most of the songs these Delta children sing are characterized by a vigorous rhapsody. In these there is a rapid, highly rhythmic alternation of parts between the leader and the group— true examples of the "Call and Responses" chant-form.[27] The singing style is ejaculatory and such melody as there is, is usually in measure-long fragments. The group usually responds with a polysyllabic word or short phrase. Thus, these songs represent the definite survival of African musical elements.

The games these children play and the songs they sing are not limited to these Call and Response songs but comprise practically all the well-known songs sung by other American children in their unregulated play periods. And so the same group of plantation children might play and sing "Who de Cat" or "Jump Mister Rabbit," and a few minutes later play "I Am a Funny Little Dutch Girl."

In addition to this last named song, the following songs which belong generally to the American play lore were recorded from the play of Delta plantation Negro children: "How Many Miles to Bethlehem," "Here We Go Looby Loo," "Mister Frog Went a Courtin'," "Go Loggy, Loggy," "Little Sally Walker," "Short'nin' Bread," "Lost My Handkerchief," "It Ain't Goin' Rain No Mo' " and "Y Girls Are High Minded."

In searching for the origins of spirituals, blues or ballads the composers are frequently found. It is interesting that in investigating the origins of the Negro game songs in the Delta, none were known. Practically all of the songs were traditional. In this connection it was found that in many instances mothers taught the games to their children and often played with them. Mrs. Bessie Stackhouse, the mother of ten children living in New Africa, a hamlet sixteen miles from Clarksdale, frequently leads the games. She sang and played several games for interviewers with much pleasure to them and to her.

Possibly the most important agency in the spread of the game songs in Mississippi is the rural school. Here recreation is informal but important. With its one, or two teachers, constantly engaged in the classwork of the several grades, recess periods are frequent and necessary. The happy solution of the problems which arise in these generally unsupervised recess periods has been the folk games.

Many of these are given to the children by the teacher. In the search for songs and

Mrs. Bessie Stackhouse with seven of her ten children

Mrs. Bessie Stackhouse, a resident of New Africa, Mississippi, was a great source of traditional game songs. Work writes, "She sang and played several games for interviewers with much pleasure to them and to her." He probably took this photograph in the summer of 1943. Courtesy of Fisk University, Franklin Library, Special Collections.

Mrs. Stackhouse playing "Humpty Stomp" with her children

Not one to focus solely on song collection, John Work was also interested in social context, performance practices, and genesis of song creation. In this photograph, probably taken during the summer of 1943, he documented Bessie Stackhouse teaching her children a dance-game—the "humpty stump." Courtesy of Fisk University, Franklin Library, Special Collections.

their origins Miss _____, teacher at the _____ school during an interview referred the investigators to _____, a book from which she selected games to be taught to her children. She admitted that the children brought more games to the play period than did she.

The spread of these game songs by their interchange among children from the various sections of the county and the various counties on the schoolyard, is highly illustrative of the growth and spread of folklore in general, a place of exchange for homogeneous folk with divergent experiences.

In the transfer of the new game learned on the schoolyard, back to the home-yard, the same errors, omissions, and additions occurred as happened when the spiritual was transferred from one church to another. The inevitable result was variants of the game and of the song. In this one county many variants of songs were discovered. The following are some of the verses with the more striking variants.

Hop Brer Rabbit

First version—by Tubby Ford Smith

> Hop Brer Rabbit in the pea vine
> I asked him where was he gwine
> Curled up his tail upon his back
> Went hoppin' on down the line.

Second version—by Mrs. E. M. Davis

> I met Brer Rabbit in the pea vine
> About a mile and a half from town
> I told Brer Rabbit I would see my gal
> Before the sun goes down
> Brer Rabbit
> > Pop yer mouth
> Brer Rabbit
> > Six cents
> Brer Rabbit
> > Three cents
> Brer Rabbit
> > Pop yer mouth.

Third version—by unidentified girl

> Met Mister Rabbit in the pea vine
> Asked him where he gwine
> He quirled his tail up on his back
> I'm huntin' for the muscadine
> Sally Walker do you bes'
> Pop yer mouth, shake yer dress!

Fourth version—by unidentified girl

> Jumped Brer Rabbit in the pea vine
> I asked him where was he gwine
> He quirled his tail up on his back
> I'm huntin' for the muscadine patch
> Keep a-kickin' Brer Rabbit!

I'll see you later
Keep a-kickin' Brer Rabbit!
I'll see you later.

Fifth version—by group of children at Friars Point

I jumped Brer Rabbit in the peanut vine
I askcd him where was he all gwine
He quirled his tail up on his back
Hopped on down to the mustard patch.
If I live to see nex' fall
I ain't goin' pick no cotton a tall.
See that house up on that hill
That's where me and my fella goin' to live
Brer Rabbit
    Pop yer mouth!
Brer Rabbit
    Do yer bes'!

Satisfied

First version—sung by group of children at Friars Point

Leader	Went to the river
Group	Satisfied*
Leader	Couldn't get across
	I paid five dollars
	For a old gray horse
	Horse wouldn't pull
	Sold him for a bull
	Bull wouldn't holler
	Sold him for a dollar
	Dollar wouldn't spin
	Bought me a hoe
	Hoe wouldn't chop
	Trade it to the shop.

———
*As a response to each line of the song the group responds without change with the word "satisfied."

Second version—led by Florence Stamps

> Leader   It takes a rockin' chair to rock
> Group   Satisfied*
> It takes a soft ball to roll
> It takes a song like this
> To satisfy my soul.

Third version—led by Annie Williams

> Leader   I ain't never been
> Group   Satisfied*
> I ain't never been
> Went down here
> To the new ground field
> Rattlesnake bit me
> On my heel
> That didn't make me
> That didn't make me
> Mamma can't make me
> Papa can't make me.

Fourth version—led by Florence Rember

> Leader   Seemo†
> Group   Satisfied*
> Seemo lady
> Seemo boy
> Seemo girl
> I got a letter
> In the bottom
> O' my trunk
> I ain't gonna read it
> Till I get drunk
> Seemo
> Seemo lady
> Seemo boy

---

*As a response to each line of the song the group responds without change with the word "satisfied."
†Probably a contraction of "see my old." This serves as a sort of a refrain.

Seemo girl
Milk in the pitcher
Butter in the bowl
Can't get a sweetheart
To save my soul
 Seemo, etc.
If I live
To see nex' fall
I ain't goin' pick
No cotton a tall
 Seemo, etc.
When I marry
Goin' marry a king
First thing he buy me
Be a diamond ring
 Seemo, etc.
When I marry
Goin' marry me a queen
First thing I buy her
Be a sewin' machine
 Seemo, etc.
When I die
Bury me deep
Put a can o' 'lasses
At my feet
An' a hoe cake in my han'
 Seemo, etc.

All Hid

First version—led by Mary Lou Brewer

Las' night, the night before
Twenty-four robbers round my door
I got up to let them in
Hit 'em in the head with a rollin' pin
All hid?
Ten ten, double ten, a hundred and fifteen
Never come sailin'
All hid?

Honey honey bee ball I can't see you
Who's all hid?
I ain't goin' count but one mo time.
That's goin' be when the sun goes down
All hid?
A fact's a fact! I tell you the fact
I lost my nickel in a buffalo track
'Way down yonder in day-break town
Billy goat buttin' the levee down
Who's all hid?

Second version—led by Queen Esther Ivory

Ten, ten, double ten, forty five, fifty
Niggers in the feed sto; I can't see them
All hid?
All ain't holler "black bird"
I ain't goin' count but one more time
That's goin' be when the sun goes down
Who's all hid?

Third version—led by Florence Rember

'Way down in Abie's quarters
Some ol' lady 'bout to lose her daughter
Who's all hid? Who's all hid?
Las' night, the night before
Twenty-four robbers round my door
I got up, let one in
Hit 'im in the head with a rollin' pin.
All hid?
I ain't goin' count but one more time
That's goin' be when the sun goes down
Who is all hid?

Fourth version—led by Ruby Hughes

One, two, three, four, five, six, seven,
Nigger in the woodpile can't count to 'leven
All hid?

Ten, ten, double ten, forty-five, fifteen
Hunter and the baker ship come a-sailin'
All hid?
Mister white man don't 'rest me
'Rest that nigger behind that tree
He stole the money, I stole none
Put 'im in the calaboose just for fun
All hid?
I ain't goin' count but one more time
That will be when the sun goes down
All hid?
All ten feet around my base ain't got no hundred.

These games are played largely by girls until they reach their mid-teens. Only very young boys as a rule participate in them. Boys have been more fortunate than girls in the inheritance of pastimes from which they may derive pleasure during idle hours. They seek those which offer more vigorous, more skillful and more individual activities. Also, in the folk life the boys are called earlier than girls to work to help with the family living. In searching for game songs it is practically useless to interview boys and men. They rarely remember any but the first line of a song.

The game-song's tradition, its widespread use, the spontaneous, easy way in which the players participate in it, its unconscious adoption by children everywhere, and its simplicity and economy of expression all combine to make it the perfect folk creation.

A comparison of the games played by the Negro children in the Delta with the twenty-four games and titles listed by Hudson[28] played by white children there showed similarity of eight titles suggesting them as belonging to a common lore. These are: "Chicken Ma Craney Crow," "Marching Round the Levee," "Little Sally Walker," "Needle's Eye," "Frog Went a Courtin'," "Green Gravel," "London Bridge," and "Looby Loo."

Although the titles of two of these songs are similar and the games are played in the same way, the verse differs greatly as the following examples show.

We're Marching Round the Levee

(white)	(Negro)
1.	1.
We're marching round the levee	We're marching round the levee, tra la la la
We're marching round the levee	We're marching round the levee,
We're marching round the levee	Hurrah for the sugar and tea.
For we have gained the day	

2.
Go forth and choose your lover

2.
Now do the lady motion, tra la la la

3.
Go out and in the window

4.
I kneel because I love you.

Needle's Eye

(white)
The needle's eye that doth supply
The thread that runs so true
There's many a beau that I've let go
Because I wanted you
With a bow so neat and a kiss so sweet
We do intend before we end
To have this couple meet.

(Negro)
O you're looking so neat
And your kisses so sweet
Needle's eye
Seconds fly
Thread that needle right
        through the eye.

There are several types of games found in the Delta. Most of them are played to the accompaniment of songs but there are many very interesting lively games that are accompanied by talking only. The talking games are no less rhythmic than those sung. These are indicated as such in the song section. Typical of the talking games are the "All Hid" games.

Most of the games recorded were ring games in which one of the players was "It" and endeavored to be released by snaring another player who when snared must take her place. Ring games are fairly common among children over the country.

The following talking-game as led by Dorothy Bawry is a good illustration of the ring game.

Group	O Bob-a-Needle
Leader	Bob-a-Needle is a runnin'
Group	O Bob-a-Needle
Leader	Goin' catch Bob-a-Needle
Group	O Bob-a-Needle
Leader	Goin' catch 'im right here
Group	O Bob-a-Needle
Leader	Better run Bob-a-Needle
Group	Better run Bob-a-Needle

Leader	O Bob-a-Needle
Group	I got Bob-a-Needle
Leader	O Bob-a-Needle
Group	Stop Bob-a-Needle

The children form a ring. Bob-a-Needle runs behind and drops an object (hand-kerchief usually) behind one of the players. As the leader sings "Bob-a-Needle is a-run-nin' " that is the signal that the object has been dropped behind a player. This player chases Bob-a-Needle around the ring and unless he catches him before he finds a place in the ring he becomes Bob-a-Needle.

Another kind of game found here is the "performance" game. In this kind of game the players perform several motions usually designated by the leader. In some instances the players imitate the motions or antics of the leader. Illustrative of this latter game is "Red Wasp Is Stingin' Me."

Another good example of the performance game is the following "Go Loggy, Loggy, Loggy" sung by Ruby Brown. [See song transcriptions following this section.]

A third type of game, not numerous, is the arch-game. In this kind of game the group form an arch with their arms to accommodate the different marching motions of the individual players. "Needle Eye" led by Rosie Shelby is a typical example of this kind of game as is the generally known "Go In and Out the Window."

The hiding games need no description.

About what do these children sing? What are the subjects of their games and songs?

The social implications of the verse are not immediately significant. The environment in which the children remotely live is occasionally reflected in their songs. References are made to the levee, to Holly Springs, to Memphis, and Arkansas. But in none of these games was there any direct mention of Clarksdale, Friars Point, New Africa or the communities where these children resided. This might be explained on the basis of the age of the songs which in many instances might be older than some of the communities.

A glimpse of the food preferences of the children is provided in a parody of the old spiritual "Come On Boys and Let's Go Hunting," and in "We're Marching Round the Levee" in which the children sing "hurrah for sugar and tea." Rural life is reflected in the frequent references to Br'er Rabbit, vegetables, cotton, shortnin' bread, the old cow, wasps, bees, pigs rootin', tater, etc. But strikingly enough, boats, mules, boll weevils, floods, and other things regarded as features of Delta life are not referred to once in the songs of the children recorded.

Strange indeed is the frequent use of death as a verse subject. Such lines as "When I die bury me deep" (Satisfied) "Your true love is dead" (Down by the Green Apple Tree), and "The old cow died in cool water" are examples of this.

The romance element has strongly flavored the games of children everywhere. The games of the Delta children are no exception to this. References to "my fella," "my sweet-heart," and "my true love" are too numerous to warrant their extraction from the verse. "A'nt Dinah's Dead," a version of "Little Sally Walker," and two other songs are omitted from this collection because of their references to sex.

The nonsense element already discussed in the guitar music is a dominant factor in the verse of these songs. Verse after verse will have lines without meaning, or are at least not understandable. Here are a few:

> A fact is a fact, I tell you the fact
> I lost my nickel in a Buffalo track
> 'Way down yonder in day break town
> Billy Goat buttin' the levee down

> Miss Rosie, Miss Rosie your true love is dead
> He wrote me a letter to turn back your head.

> My boy friend's name is Yella
> He came from Alabama
> With a big fat nose and a pickle on his toes
> And a ee–i–ee–i–o shampoo!
> Shampoo the barber,
> Blub, blub, blub
> Where'd you see him?
> Neck bone
> How's the baby?
> All right!
> And a–ee–i–ee–i–o shampoo!

These and other nonsense lines in the game songs can be easily explained. The first fact to be considered here is that the age of song has extended far beyond the memory of its subject and content which at one time may have been pertinent or grew out of an event or story.

The second consideration in the explanation of the nonsense lines lies in the pur-pose and use of the song. These songs are purely and totally recreational. Except in the instances of romance or sex-songs they carry no message. Inasmuch as the entire game, particularly the motions, depend upon the rhythm patterns, the dominating aim of the singers although not always a conscious one, appears to be to invent words and syllables to stimulate them. Why must they mean something?

The nonsense words and syllables are not new, nor are they peculiar to Negro sing-ers. "Tra, la, la," "hey nonino" in English poetry illustrate the use of nonsense syllables to supply a rhythmic need. The old American community singing standby "Ol Macdonald" with its "ee–i–ee–i–o" offers another example.

The nonsense line in the game-songs is not to be confused with that of the blues. The first one is wholly rhythmic in its function, while the latter, as previously described, provides a necessary rhyming word for the final one in the "punch line" which is quite meaningful.

APPENDIX

The background of a more intimate sort for the songs found in the Delta, and the sentiments they express is provided in the biographical sketches of a few selected singers in the Delta, appended here. To account for the spread of these songs as well as the places and people sung about, the singers were interviewed as to the extent of their travels, the musical influences in their lives, and their work. Interviews with Charles Haffer and Will Starks returned rich rewards in interpreting their varying interests in the ballad. The Reverend Ezekiel H. Price steeped in Delta lore and religious ritual was interviewed in the hope of finding an explanation of the drastic changes in church music of the Delta.

Alexander Robertson

Alexander ("Alec") Robertson was born in Tensaw Parish, Louisiana in 1867. At an early age his family moved to a plantation in Sharkey, Mississippi. There were several musicians in the section and their playing strongly fascinated him. Among them was a fiddler who encouraged him to play on his instrument. Alexander made such rapid progress in learning to play that his family and friends declared "he was born with music in him." The first pieces of music which he learned to play on the fiddle were: "Billy in the Low Ground," "Fisher's Horn Pipe," and "The Cacklin' Hen."

Robertson next learned to play a rather remarkable instrument—a forty-three string zither. Performance upon the zither gave him considerable musical prestige in the community. His attachment to the instrument was not very strong, however, as he pawned it in Helm station on a trip there and never returned to redeem it.

Robertson's family moved to a plantation in Coahoma County about 1887, where the planter, much pleased with Alexander's musical ability bought him a fine guitar. This instrument he prized very highly. A good guitar player in the neighborhood, George Wood, taught him the rudiments of guitar playing.

He soon developed such skill that he was invited to join some of the "string bands"*

---

*"String bands" usually consist of a fiddle (violin), one or two guitars, a "bull bass" fiddle (often a 'cello), sometimes a mandolin, and a piano.

in this section. Because these bands were in great demand for dances,[29] he found himself "with more money than he knew how to handle." Robertson moved to Clarksdale where eventually he organized a band of his own. The most prominent bands there at the time (about 1903), were led by William C. Handy and "Kid" Clark; these bands were larger and used in addition, brass instruments.Robertson played for a while in each of these bands. It was customary to play for white dances on week nights and for Negro dances on Saturday nights. The music they played consisted chiefly of waltzes, reels, polkas, and two steps. Robertson remembers the following line of a then popular waltz:

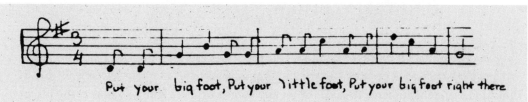

Although well acquainted with "Joe Turner" Robertson heard no real blues until Handy's era in Clarksdale. The style of playing at the time while not as extravagant and noisy as that of today's bands, bore he feels, some similarity to what is now known as "swing."

Robertson's music carried him throughout the Delta. He played on the river-boats and once played for a dance at the University of Mississippi at Oxford. He played for a while at "Pee Wee's" a famous Memphis saloon, prominently mentioned in Handy's autobiography.[30]

Today Robertson lives off the gratuities of a daughter of a former planter-employer who he calls "Missy." He now plays his guitar exclusively in the services of a Holiness church in Clarksdale, after, as he says "I played fifty-seven years for the devil."

Reverend Ezekiel H. Price

The Reverend Ezekiel H. Price was born in Union Point, Louisiana in 1882, on a farm. His family had a long tradition of preachers before him. His father was a minister in the Methodist Church, and an uncle was a famous bishop in the same denomination. With such a background, Price's entry into the ministry could be taken for granted. He dates his actual decision to enter the ministry from an experience, a vision, which came to him in 1901. As he relates it, he was accustomed to a daily religious ceremony held by his family in the very early morning which consisted of individual prayers, the recitation of Bible verses, and hymn singing. On the morning of the vision, he was lying in bed awaiting the call to prayers when into his room came several persons. They knelt and began to pray. Their prayers were said for him. After several of these, a larger and more venerable man, the leader of the visitors, pointed to him and sang the old "long-meter" hymn, "Go Preach My Word Saith the Lord." After this song, the group vanished. Price assumed his first pastorate in 1910 at Oak Grove, Mississippi. His family had moved into the Delta a few years prior to this.

Few churches in the rural areas are able to support a minister alone, and the custom has developed of a church holding its services on one Sunday only in each month, and paying the minister for this one day's preaching. The minister, thereby, is released for pastoring other churches on the remaining Sundays. He usually lives in a town and visits his charges on Friday or Saturday before preaching-day. Reverend Price, living in Clarksdale, pastors in this way four plantation churches.

When asked to account for the disappearance of the spirituals from the church service, Reverend Price blamed the younger ministers, and in many instances the "school-ministers" who have consistently preached that the spirituals, or "Halleys" as they are known in the Delta, are old-fashioned and degrading. He recalled a young preacher ridiculing the spiritual "I'm So Glad Trouble Don't Last Always" and one of its verses, and "Death come a-creepin' in my room." The "school-preacher" wants songs in the service accompanied by a piano or organ, especially gospel songs. The "Doctor Watts" are likewise under attack and Reverend Price feels certain the young men will eliminate them from the services before many more years have passed. At one service when an older minister dared line-out a "long-meter" hymn, a younger minister said quite audibly and derisively, "Where did that old man come from with that old song?"

Reverend Price is greatly concerned over the future of the Delta churches because of the rapidly increasing migration away from the section.

Charles Haffer

Charles Haffer, famous Delta ballad writer, was born in Deshea County, Arkansas in 1885. Blindness came upon him in early infancy. The family moved to the Mississippi Delta about 1900. His father being a minister, he was reared in a deeply religious atmosphere, although he did not join the church until 1904. Being able to express himself fluently, Charles began lecturing on religious topics in Sunday School while still a youth.

Haffer wrote his first song in 1909. The following interview given by him to Alan Lomax offers an interesting insight to both his creative and professional life:

Haffner	I began writing poetry, religious compositions, and song ballets in 1909.
Lomax	How did you write these songs?
Haffer	I did the dictating. Some one would write them and carry them to the press. . . . The first song I wrote was called "Stand by Me When I Cross the Jordan River." I heard a man singing that song at a convention—a'sociation. But when I went home I wrote it entirely different. It just come to me through the spirit. . . . I wrote it and some people advised me to print it. And I printed that and it made such a big song hit that I just

began from that writing compositions. . . . It went something like this:

When crossing Jordan River
Stand by me, stand by me
Jesus' breast will be my pillow
Stand by me, stand by me
Now the water's chilly and cold
The love of Jesus's in my soul
Lightnings flash and the thunders roll
Stand by me.

Through hard trials and tribulations
Stand by me, stand by me
'Mid the false accusation
Stand by me, stand by me
Troubles like a gloomy cloud
Gather thick and thunder loud
And my way seems so hard
Stand by me.

Lomax	When you got this ballad printed, did you go out on the street and sing it to the people?
Haffer	Out on the street and in churches and so forth.
Lomax	How many copies do you suppose you sold?
Haffer	Well, all around I sold about three thousand copies of that particular song.
Lomax	Did this song come to you under any particular inspiration?
Haffer	The way songs come to me—I imagine I can hear somebody singing. The tune comes to me. The tune I hear it sung in, I jes' begin singing myself in that tune and verses begin to come to me. Now it all don't come at once. I might get two or three verses wrote today. Maybe two or three days later I'll come back and write again on it. Sometimes it takes a week or a month to get the song composed. Unless it comes on—unless I'm moved by the spirit, I can't write a song. . . . All of my songs are written under inspiration. I've decided not to write any foolishness.

"Don't Drive Me Away"

A Missionary Song Taken From The Following Scriptures:
Proverbs 21:13; Matt. 18:6; Psalms 9:17; Luke 16:19-31

Composed And Published By

CHAS. HAFFER, Jr.

Noted Gospel Song Writer, Arthor, And Bible Lecturer

1503 O'HEA STREET   PHONE 990-J   GREENVILLE, MISS.

Now we all are strangers, none of us have no home.
We should'nt say hard words to each other that would cause our hearts to
    mourn
We should love one another and the Saviour's word obey
I'm a stranger, don't drive me away.
I'm a pilgrim and a stranger with nothing to call my own
Friends have deserted me and now I'm left alone.
But I mean to follow Jesus while here on earth I stay
Please dont drive me away.

--CHORUS--

Please don't drive me away, please don't drive me away.
If you drive me away, you'll need my help some day
I'm a stranger, don't drive me away.

There was a poor old beggar lying at a rich man's gate
Desired to eat his crumbs that fell from his plate.
But he laughed him to scorn, while the dogs licked his wounds.
So, p'ease don't drive me away.
When he saw the beggar, lying at his gate,
Instead of granting his request, he drove him away.
You see, he was living well; but lifted up his eyes in hell
Saying please dont drive me away.

It was then he remembered the evil he had done
In that he willfully refused to give the poor man the crumbs.
He started prayer meeting in hell, that's what the bible tells,
Saying, please don't drive me away.
When he saw Lazarus afar off in the bosom of Abraham
Enjoying the blessed favors of God, while he himself was damned
He called for him to come, with water to cool his tongue.
Saying, please don't drive me away.

His request could not be granted, though he was kindly told
How, when he was in yonder's world oppressed and dispised the poor.
He treated Lazarus mean, and now there a gulf between,
Saying, please don't drive me away.
Whosoever rebuketh my little ones, that put their trust in me,
Better have a millstone about their necks and drowned in the sea
Than to interfere with a child of God, great will be your fall.
So, please don't drive me away.

Look at our mothers and fathers, they are well stricken in age
Worn themselves out in the service of God and now they are giving away.
By their prayers and righteous living we're all enjoying today.
So, please don't drive them away.
They nursed us in our infancy, carried us in their arms
All the way through childhood, they kept us from all-harm,
Guided us every day, then taught us how to pray.
So, please don't drive them away.

They gave us education, shelter, food and clothes,
But they taught us to get salvation more precious to our souls.
Now they're old and gray, heads blossoming for the grave
Please don't drive them away.
I'm on my mission journey, on business for the King,
I must tell the story of Jesus and His wonderful praises sing.
If you drive me away, you'll need my help some day,
I'm a Christian don't drive me away.

Prices: 10c   2 for 15c   3 for 20c   4 for 26c

"TIME CHANGES EVERYTHING"

A Spiritual Song Of Praise And Condemnation Taken From The Following Scriptures:
Eccl. 3:1-8; Ps. 30:5; Dan. 5:1-8; Is 53-5 Matt. 5:14; Gal. 3:23-25

Composed And Published By
CHAS. HAFFER, Jr.

Noted Arthor, Gospel Song Writer, And Bible Lecturer

1503 O'HEA STREET   PHONE 990-J   GREENVILLE, MISS.

There was a time when our country was at peace
And we wer'nt bothering no body but were happy as could be;
but now this is changed to guns, ships, and planes,
You see, time changes everything.
Mean aggressor nations violated international laws
Trying to gain world supremacy, and plunged us into war.
We are buying bonds and stamps and going to the training camps
You see, time changes everything.

CHORUS

Time changes everything none of us knows what the future brings.
Today we may be glad; while tomorrow we'll be sad.
You see, time changes everything.

Daniel spoke about it, John, The Revelator, too
Jesus substantiated it and I know it's bound to be true.
For God can't lie and He declares man must die
You see, time changes everything.
The time has truly come when nations all must fight
And whosoever kills you will think he's doing right
They frame mischief by law and think they're serving God
You see, time changes everything.

There was once a time when we were under the law
Which were types and shadows pointing to the cross
On which the lamb was slain, to take away our shame.
But time changes everything.
Back there we offered pigeons and doves, and the blood of bullocks and cows,
But thanks to God Almighty, we don't do that now.
To us Christ is revealed, and with His stripes we are healed
You see time changes everything.

There was a time when we worshiped in temples and synagogues,
And had to go to Jerusalem to feel the presence of God.
The high priest then would pray to take our sins away,
But time changes everything.
The law being merely a shadow of better things to come.
For God so loved the world, He gave His only Son.
And if you, His word obey, He'll save you right away.
You see, time changes everything.

There was a time our people all were slaves
Were not permitted to worship God, nor enter in His praises.
Now that we are free to serve Him as we please,
You see, time changes everything.
We were not permitted to go to school, nor learn to read or write
But were forever to remain fools and never see the light;
But prayers of our fathers and mothers, broke the slavery chain
You see, time changes everything.

Some of us can remember forty years ago we rode horse drawn vehicles
Over muddy and dusty roads
Now, all of this is changed, we are riding in airplanes
You see, time changes everything.
We used to have to walk for miles to grocery stores,
And then would come back wagging with very heavy loads
Now, we can sit at home and order by the telephone;
You see, time changes everything.

Churches were not plentiful, they were few and far apart,
Faithful Christian ministers prayed for revivals to start.
They would come from all across the fields; but now they have lost their zeal
You see, time changes everything.
The woods were filled with seekers, going to their praying ground,
And they would come out telling what a Saviour they had found.
But in this modern day, they say we don't have to pray,
You see, time changes everything.

I remember the time, when we were boys and girls,
Our mothers and fathers who were Christians, lived separate from the world
A's a city on a hill, they did the Master's will,
You see, time changes everything.
The people of this generation say we back there were fools
And that to get salvation just follow the golden rule;
They say nothing about the new birth, come on and join the church
You see, time changes everything.

Now, don't forget Belshazzer, Babalyon's drunken king,
Made a great feast one night, in hopes some joy to bring,
But the writing on the wall told of his downfall
You see, time changes everything.
His knees smoted together; his countenance was changed,
He call for all the astrologers, in an attempt to read the hanrd,
It was a terrible sight, Belshazzer died that night.
You see time changes everything.

Prices: 10c   2 for 15c   3 for 20c   4 for 25c

This blind poet is very prolific. He estimates that he has written and printed more than one hundred songs. His most famous ballad "Strange Things Happening in the Land," one which has spread over a considerable area, was written in 1917. Two religious "ballets" written recently, "Time Changes Everything" and "Don't Drive Me Away" are reprinted here:

Haffer married in 1919. His wife reads books, magazines and newspapers to him daily. It is from these that he has gathered his expanded vocabulary which includes numerous words far removed from common folk usage.

His activities have not been limited to writing and singing. Once he organized a school for the blind which failed to prosper due to his inability to secure public funds for its support. In 1927 he organized a lodge, "The Ancient Order of Watchmen" which before its dissolution, he says, it paid benefits to the amount of $7000. The following printed statement, photographed from the original, indicates a new fraternal venture.

Though living in Clarksdale many years, Haffer has recently moved to Greenville, but returns to Clarksdale on Saturdays and Sundays to sell "ballets."

SOMETHING NEW
Under The Sun!

A new movement has been created, known as the United Circle of Friends, Inc. with its home office in Greenville, Mississippi. This organization offers protection to all people of African descent. There's nothing like it ever established before. It's for you and your children too. It takes from baby to Grand-paw, from just born to most gone. Now read every word of this circular so, that you can throughly familiarize yourself with our work, and the manner or method in which we do business

Now, here's how the plan works. A band of men and women of all creeds, sects and denomination regardless of age or physical handicaps have pledged themselves to befriend eachother in sickness, trouble, distress, misfortunes, calamities or whatever kind they may be as long as they are not in violation of the laws of our country.

This organization has established a relief department in which every member pays a penny a day which amounts to 90 cents per quarter, payable January, April, July and October of each year. 70 per cent of this amount is used for the purpose of paying of death claims, in other words, 70c out of every dollar that is collected is prorated among the beneficiaries of the members who die during that quarter.

Each community can organize its local circle to work in conjunction with and under the auspices of the parent body at Greenville, Miss. Each local circle shall arrange their own home ties to care for their members when they are sick and the grand circle will take care of you when you die. There is to be no red tape, no loop holes, no long questionaires or beating around the bush. All we want to know is that you are dead, and the claim will be paid as has been previously set forth.

Now you of course know, that we could not go into complete details as to our method of operation in this circular but, our constitution and by-laws will give you full information and our agents and duplues will inform you, when you have read this circular in the quietness of your own home, if you like our plan then tear off the application blank attached hereto with the required amount of $1.25 send same to the financial Secretary. Mrs. Lula Haffer; 1503 O'hea Street Greenville, Miss. and we will send to you our membership card together with full particulars for setting up your local circle in your own community.

The $1.25 paid is your joining fee. After the first quartely assesment of .90 is paid then you are in full benefit and entitled to the benefit fund. Let us hear from you.

CHARLES HAFFER, President.

Henry "Son" Sims

"Son" Sims was born in Anguilla, Mississippi in 1890. As a boy, the "string-bands" strongly attracted him. It was only natural that he should hanker to play one of the stringed instruments. The first instrument he learned to play was the guitar. There being several guitar players around to whom he could listen and from whom he could receive instruction, he eventually developed considerable skill in playing the instrument. The first pieces Sims learned to play were: "Can't Make a Dime," and "Pallet on the Floor." He afterwards became well known in the community for his playing of "Bill Bailey," "Spoonful" and "The Bully of This Town."

Two fiddlers who formerly lived in the Friars Point section, Lonnie Chapman and Rand Smith, taught him to play the fiddle which fascinated him so strongly that he forsook the guitar for it. The skill he ultimately developed upon the fiddle led him far a-field from the Delta where he has spent most of his life as a plantation worker. He has played in many of the mid-western cities and with some other players has recorded some blues for a commercial phonograph firm. There are few fiddlers now in the Delta, and phonograph records of folk fiddlers are extremely rare. As a result, Sims, not having playing models to listen to, has developed an individual style of performance. His style consists largely of bowed tremolos, trills, and counterpoints to the melodies of the instruments which he may be supporting. Although he might be expected to use it because of its rhythmic possibilities, he makes no use of the pizzicato. The fiddle in "Son" Sims hand is not a solo instrument and rarely carries the melody as is usually the fiddle's function in folk music.

Sims would like to teach some youngster to play the fiddle as he taught several to play the guitar in former days, but can interest none in it. He deplores the loss of interest in playing instruments today among the plantation youth. Recently, an admirer of his playing presented him with a new, handsome violin which is his great pride and his constant companion. Today he is a share-cropper on a Delta plantation.

McKinley "Muddy Water" Morganfield

McKinley "Muddy Water" Morganfield, one of the Delta's most popular guitarists, was born in Rolling Fork, Mississippi in 1913, but his family moved shortly after to the Stovall plantation in Coahoma County where he has since lived.

His musical career began with a harmonica, but after listening to "Son" House play the guitar, there developed within him an ambition he could not restrain to play that instrument. Under "Son" Sims' instruction and on his instrument he learned and mastered the rudiments of guitar playing. Acquiring an instrument, Muddy Water practiced endlessly. The first piece he remembers playing with any large degree of satisfaction was "How Long Blues." He copied the styles of the guitarists to whom he listened constantly on phonograph records. A particular favorite of his was Robert Johnson whose playing he studied assiduously. Many of the features of his playing were learned from Johnson's records. Most of Muddy Water's repertory has been acquired from listening to jukeboxes. But not all. He composes some of the songs he plays. These compositions of his enjoy great favor among his audiences. The more popular of them are: "Rosalie," "I've Never Been Satisfied Blues," "Late On in the Evenin' Blues," "Rambling Kid," and "Burr Clover Blues." This last one is a song of admiration for the fertility of the land on which he lives and incidentally is a blues inspired by no hard luck, disillusionment or unrequited love.

Muddy Water is in great demand as a performer among the plantation folk, both Negro and white. Sometimes he assembles other players with him into a band; but most of the time he plays solo. He explains that it is necessary to use two different repertories to accommodate the demands of white and Negro dancers.

The white dancers prefer tunes more akin to the old reels rather than the blues although the "St. Louis Blues" is a great favorite among them. Playing for a white dance

"Son" Sims   Muddy Water

John W. Work took this famous photograph of Henry Sims and McKinley Morganfield on Stovall's plantation in Coahoma county in the summer of 1943. Work and Alan Lomax made the first recordings of Morganfield—aka Muddy Waters—in 1941. Courtesy of Center for Popular Music, Middle Tennessee State University; John W. Work III Field Collection.

at the Stovall plantation on the nineteenth of June 1943, his band used the following pieces:

Corina	Darktown Strutters Ball
St. Louis Blues	Darkness on the Delta
Jingle, Jangle, Jingle	Wang Wang Blues*
Missouri Waltz	

For the colored dancers, Morganfield must play blues and music which stems from them, such as, "Number Thirteen Highway," and "I'm Goin' Down Slow"—his current favorite piece. For them he plays about one waltz a year.

Muddy Water would like to join the church but to do so would mean abandoning his guitar—a sacrifice too dear to make now.

Will Starks

Will Starks has been living in the "Bottoms"—his name for the Delta—all of his life. He was born near Sardis in 1875 on a plantation. His father was a ballad singer and fiddler and banjo player. Will early learned to play the banjo, and listening to his father, learned many songs. He next learned to play an instrument he called an "autoharp." It had twenty-eight strings. On this instrument, and on the accordion which he next learned to play, the tunes were the same as those played on the banjo—"Billy in the Low Ground," "Arkansas Traveler," and the like, as well as the then current ballads. Much later in his life he learned to play the guitar which became his favorite instrument. For many years he played for plantation dances.

When a young man, he left the plantation to work at sawmills. As one sawmill would close down, he would take work at another. When no sawmill was in operation he usually went to work on levee camp jobs. All of these jobs provided temporary living quarters for the workers. The sawmill quarters were usually shanties, while the levee quarters were frequently tents—individual tents for a man and wife, large tents called "bull pens" for groups of single men. The after-work hours in these quarters were filled with recreation varying from the milder sort to that which was more violent. The most important of these recreational pursuits, from the standpoint of the folklorist, were the informal small scale recitals, the guitar, harmonica, and fiddle players gave on the steps of their shanties, or on stools in front of their tents. The workmen, mostly itinerants, came from many different places bringing with them the songs, stories, and unique folk ways of their widely separated localities to these places of exchange.

In such surroundings, Will Starks taught and learned many ballads. All of the ballads included in this collection sung by him with the exception of the "Fox Hunters," which he learned from his father as a boy, were learned in sawmill shanties during the

---

*This is not a folk blues but a title given to a "Tin Pan Alley" popular song of a few years back.

years from about 1896 to 1920. It is extremely strange that Starks never heard "John Henry" until a few years ago and then heard it from a phonograph record.

Will Starks, upon marrying in 1920 forsook the sawmills for the plantation. He returned to sawmill work as a night watchman a year ago and lives in Clarksdale with his wife and seven children. Ironically he is today without a guitar. Though his wife is a staunch member of the Holiness church, he remains unconverted. To join the church, he says, would deprive him of too many things he would like to do. Despite his sixty-eight years he plans to become a church member sometime later.

BIBLIOGRAPHY

Ballanta (Taylor), Nicholas George Julius. *Saint Helena Island Spirituals*. New York, 1927

Campbell and Sharp: Olive Dame Campbell and Cecil J. Sharp. *English Folk-Songs from the Southern Appalachians*. New York, 1917

Cox, John Harrington. *Traditional Ballads, Mainly from West Virginia*. New York, 1939

Dett, R. Nathaniel. *Religious Folk Songs of the Negro as Sung at Hampton Institute*. Hampton, 1927

Earle, Alice Morse. *The Sabbath in Puritan New England*. Boston, 1903

Fisher, William Arms. *Seventy Negro Spirituals*. Boston, 1926

Gordon, Robert Winslow. *Folk Songs of America*. New York, 1927

Handy, William C. *Blues: An Anthology, with Introduction by Abbe Niles*. New York, 1926

_____. *Father of the Blues*. New York, 1942

Hudson, Arthur Palmer. *Folk Songs of Mississippi*. Chapel Hill, 1936

Johnson, Charles S. *Growing Up in the Black Belt*. Washington, 1941

_____. *Shadow of the Plantation*. Chicago, 1934

Jones, Alice Marie. *The Negro Sermon—A Study in the Sociology of Folk Culture*. Fisk University. MSS, 1942

Lomax, John A. and Alan. *American Ballads and Folk Songs*. New York, 1934

_____. *Our Singing Country*. New York, 1941

Odum and Johnson: Howard W. Odum and Guy B. Johnson. *The Negro and His Songs*. Chapel Hill, 1925

_____. *Negro Workaday Songs*. Chapel Hill, 1926

Parrish, Lydia. *Slave Songs of the Georgia Sea Islands*. New York, 1942

Percy, William A. *Lanterns on the Levee. Recollections of a Planter's Son*. New York, 1941

Pound, Louise. *American Ballads and Songs*. New York, 1922

Reid, Alice C. *Gee's Bend: A Rural Negro Community*. Fisk University, MSS. 1942

Sargent, Winthrop. *Jazz: Hot and Hybrid*. New York, 1938

Talley, Thomas W. *Negro Folk Rhymes*. New York, 1922

White, Newman I. *American Negro Folk Songs*. Cambridge, 1928

Work, John W. (Sr.) and Frederick J. *Folk Songs of the American Negro*. Nashville, 1907

Work, John W. *American Negro Songs*. New York, 1940

GENERAL INDEX

1. A Charge to Keep I Have
2. Ain't Goin' Be Bad Blues
3. Ain't Goin' Rain No Mo' (first version)
4. Ain't Goin' Rain No Mo' (second version)
5. All Hid (first version)
6. All Hid (second version)
7. All Hid (third version)
8. All Hid (fourth version)
9. All Hid (fifth version)
10. Ain't No Grave Can Hold My Body Down
11. All My Trouble Will Be Over
12. All Night Long
13. All Power Is in His Hands
14. Arkansas
15. Band in Gideon
16. Blind Man, The
17. Blues (Harmonica)
18. Bob-a-Needle (Talking)
19. Brady and Duncan
20. Burr Clover Blues
21. Calvary
22. Christ My Lord Comin' Soon
23. Cindy
24. Clear the Line
25. Come On Boys Let's Go Hunting
26. Cryin' Holy Unto the Lord
27. Daniel
28. Dark Was the Night
29. David
30. Didee-o
31. Didn't 'E Ramble
32. Done Taken My Lord Away
33. Don't You Grieve after Me
34. Down By the Green Apple Tree
35. Form the Line
36. Four O'Clock Blues
37. Fox Hunt
38. Get Right Church
39. Georgia Rabbit
40. Glory, Glory
41. Glory Hallelujah
42. Go In and Out the Window
43. Go Loggy, Loggy
44. Got on My Travellin' Shoes
45. Got on the Train
46. Green Gravel
47. Hallelu, Hallelu
48. Here Come Two Gents
49. He Never Said a Mumblin' Word
50. Hold the Wind
51. Holler (first version)
52. Holler (second version)
53. Holler (third version)
54. Holler (fourth version)
55. Holler (fifth version)
56. Holy Baby
57. Hop Br'er Rabbit (first version)
58. Hop Br'er Rabbit (second version)
59. Hop Br'er Rabbit (third version)
60. Hop Br'er Rabbit (fourth version)
61. I Ain't Never Been Satisfied
62. I Am a Funny Little Dutch Girl
63. I Can't Tarry
64. I Done Got Over
65. If You Want to Love a Pretty Girl
66. I Got a Bull Dog
67. I Got a Hiding Place
68. I Got a Letter
69. I Heard the Voice of Jesus Say (three versions)
70. I Know My Little Soul's Gonna Rise an' Shine
71. I'll Be Glad to See the Son
72. I'll Fly Away
73. I'm a Soldier in the Army
74. I'm a Ten Card Dealer
75. I'm Goin' Let It Shine

76. I'm Goin' Stay on the Battle Field
77. I'm Goin' to Lean on the Lord
78. I'm Runnin' for My Life
79. I'm Travellin' on the King's Highway
80. It's Hard Times
81. I Went to the Landin'
82. I Wish I Was Cap'n Ringall's Son
83. Jack o' Diamonds
84. Jes' Couldn't Rest Contented
85. Jesus' Blood Has Made Me Whole
86. Jubilee
87. Jump for Joy
88. Jump Mister Rabbit
89. Just Like Heaven to Me
90. Katy, I Got to Go
91. Keep My Skillet Greasy (first version)
92. Keep My Skillet Greasy (second version)
93. Lamb of God, The
94. Late On in the Evenin'
95. Late War, The
96. Let Your Heart
97. Levee Blues
98. Lining Track Sequence
99. Low Down Dirty Dog Blues
100. Low Down the Chariot
101. Mary Mack
102. Mississippi Blues
103. Motherless Children Has a Hard Time
104. My Lord So High
105. My Soul Is a Witness
106. Natchez Fire Disaster
107. Needle Eye
108. No Condemnation
109. Now Go on Down
110. O Lord Will You Come by Here
111. Praise Him
112. Please Don't Drive Me Away
113. Ramblin' Kid
114. Red Wasp
115. Rock-a-My Soul
116. Rock Daniel
117. Rosalie
118. Run, Run, unto Him
119. Roustabout Ain't Got No Home
120. Rowdy Soul
121. Sally Go Round the Sunshine
122. Satisfied (two versions)
123. Seemo (talking — three versions)
124. Shoo Fly
125. Shortenin' Bread
126. Shout for Joy
127. Sister You'll be Called On
128. Sittin' on Top of the World
129. Sorry, Sorry For to Leave You
130. Stagolee (first version)
131. Stagolee (second version)
132. Steal Away
133. Strange Things Happening in the Land
134. Stuball
135. Sunday Mornin' Band
136. Sweeter as the Years Go By
137. Swing Down Chariot
138. Take a Walk with Me
139. Talking Blues
140. Tell Me How Long Has the Train Been Gone
141. That's What's the Matter with the Church Today
142. There'll Be Preaching Tonight
143. These Days Got Everybody Troubled
144. This Here's My Buryin' Ground
145. This is the Hammer (John Henry)
146. This Ol' Tampin'
147. Tippisho
148. T. P. Runnin'
149. Watercourse Blues
150. We're Marching Round the Levee
151. What a Storm

CLASSIFIED INDEX

Spirituals

62. There'll Be Preaching Tonight
63. This Here's My Buryin' Ground
64. When I've Done the Best I Can
65. Yeh, Lord (Holiness)
66. You Don't Believe I'm a Child of God
67. You Got to Reap
68. You Pray On (Quartet)

Blues

1. Ain't Goin' Be Bad
2. Blues (Harmonica)
3. Burr Clover Blues
4. Four O'Clock Blues
5. I Ain't Never Been Satisfied Blues (with Guitar)
6. I Got a Letter (with Guitar)
7. Late On in the Evenin' (with Guitar)
8. Levee Blues
9. Low Down Dirty Dog Blues
10. Mississippi Blues
11. Ramblin' Kid
12. Rosalie
13. Sittin' on Top of the World (Harmonica)
14. Take a Walk with Me
15. Talking Blues
16. Watercourse Blues (with Guitar)

Ballads

1. Arkansas
2. Blind Man, The
3. Brady and Duncan
4. Fox Hunt
5. I'll Be Glad to See the Son
6. Late War, The
7. Natchez Fire Disaster, The
8. Stagolee (two versions)
9. Strange Things Happening in the Land

10. These Days Got Everybody Troubled
11. What a Storm
12. When You Lose Your Money

Work Songs

1. Hollers (five versions)
2. I Got a Bull Dog
3. I Went to the Landin'
4. I Wish I Was Cap'n Ringall's Son
5. Lining Track Sequence (Houston Bacon and Elias Boykin)
6. Roustabout Ain't Got No Home
7. Stuball
8. This is the Hammer (John Henry)
9. This Old Tampin'
10. "T P" Runnin'

Children's Game Songs

1. Ain't Goin' Rain No Mo' (two versions)
2. All Hid (five versions)
3. Bob-a-Needle (talking)
4. Come On Boys Let's Go Hunting
5. Didee-o
6. Down by the Green Apple Tree
7. Georgia Rabbit
8. Go In and Out the Window
9. Go Loggy, Loggy
10. Green Gravel
11. Here Come Two Gents
12. Hop Br'er Rabbit (four versions — talking)
13. I Am a Funny Little Dutch Girl
14. Jump for Joy
15. Jump Mister Rabbit
16. Mary Mack
17. Needle Eye
18. Now Go On Down
19. Red Wasp
20. Sally Go Round the Sunshine

21. Satisfied (two versions)
22. Seemo (talking — three versions)
23. Shoo Fly
24. Short'nin' Bread
25. Tippisho
26. We're Marching Round the Levee
27. Willie Over the Water

Social Songs
1. Cindy
2. Didn't 'E Ramble
3. Got on the Train
4. If You Want to Love a Pretty Girl

5. It's Hard Times
6. Keep My Skillet Greasy (two versions)
7. Rowdy Soul

Doctor Watts (old "long meter")
1. Dark Was the Night
2. I Heard the Voice of Jesus Say

Gambling Songs
1. I'm a Ten Card Dealer
2. Jack o' Diamonds

[Editors' note: The transcriptions that follow are reproduced from microfilm archived in the Special Collections at Fisk University's Franklin Library. The original transcriptions have been lost. The reader will notice that the quality of the reproductions varies greatly. Efforts were made to give the reader a sense of what the original transcriptions would have looked like while also achieving a satisfactory measure of readability. Some reproductions are more successful than others. An alphabetical list of transcription titles with their performers is included in the index.]

A Charge to keep I Have

Sung by the leader of the
Union Jubilee Quartet

A charge to keep I have, A charge to keep I have, A charge to keep I have, A
God to glori - fy. 1. In the be-ginning God made man, Out of the dust by
His own hand A for Adam the man was named, Placed in the garden at God's command.

2. God saw Adam alone in the shade
He put him to sleep and He made him a mate
Adam was the father of the human race
He _____ tried to hide his face
In the cool of the evening God came down
He looked for Adam and began to frown
"Tell me Adam where are you now?
You're not on your bed by the sweat of your brow."

3. You read about Samson from his birth
Stronges' man that ever lived on earth
He lived way back in ancient time
He died and went to heaven, Lord, in due time
Delilah fooled Samson, don't you know
The Holy Bible tells us so
She said to Samson down by her knees
"Tell me where yo' strength lies if you please"
Samsons wife she looked so fair
Tell her my strength lies in my hair
She shaved off his hair jes' as clean as yo' han'
Samson got as weak as any other man.

4. Ol' Satan's mad and I am glad
He missed that soul he thought he had
Satan thought he had me fust
I throwed off my chains and I'm free at last
My head got wet with the midnight dew
Mornin' star was a witness too.
Never shall forget that day
When Jesus washed my sins away
One day, one day as I was walking along
The elements opened and the love came down
I never felt such love before
It made me run from door to door.

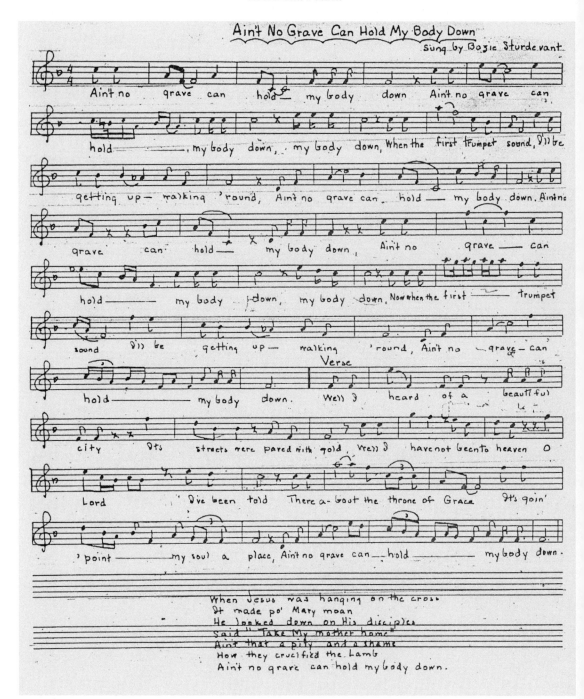

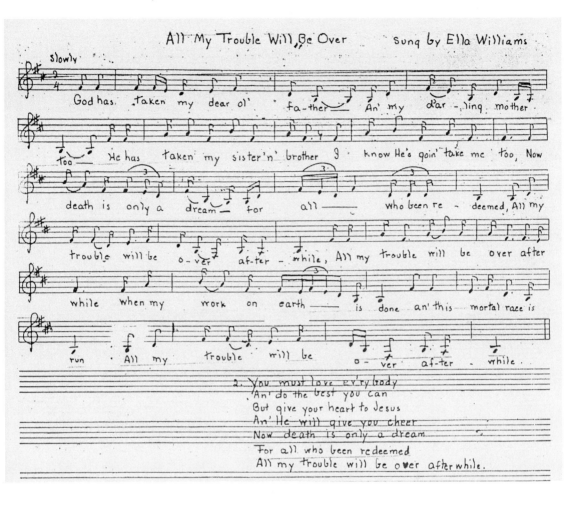

All My Trouble Will Be Over

Sung by Ella Williams

Slowly

God has taken my dear ol' fa-ther An' my dar-ling mo-ther too, He has taken my sister 'n' brother I know He's goin' take me too, Now death is only a dream for all who been re-deemed, All my trouble will be o-ver af-ter-while, All my trouble will be over after while When my work on earth is done an' this mortal race is run. All my trouble will be o-ver af-ter-while.

2. You must love ev'rybody
An' do the best you can
But give your heart to Jesus
An' He will give you cheer
Now death is only a dream
For all who been redeemed
All my trouble will be over afterwhile.

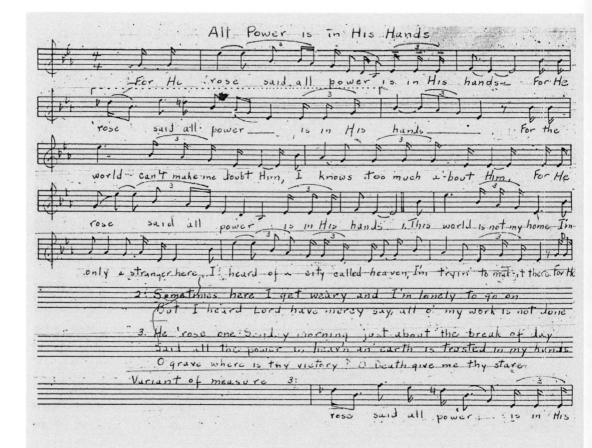

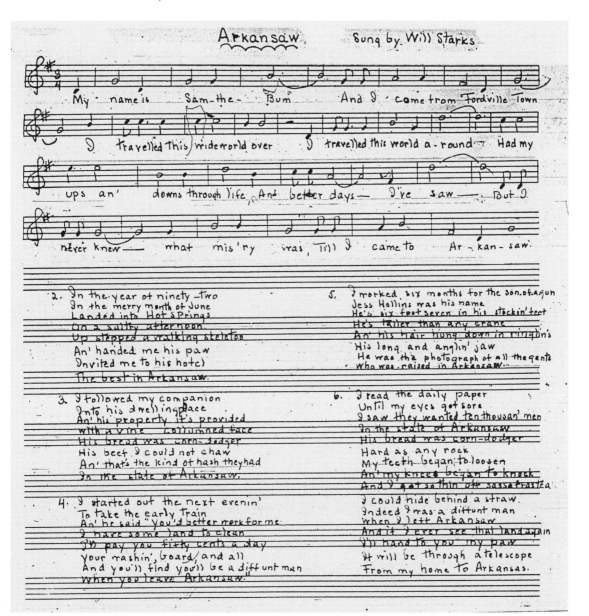

Arkansaw   Sung by Will Starks

My name is Sam-the-Bum And I come from Fordville Town
I travelled this wide world over I travelled this world a-round Had my
ups an' downs through life, And better days— I've saw— But I
never knew— what mis'ry was, Till I came to Ar-kan-saw.

2. In the year of ninety-two
In the merry month of June
Landed into Hot Springs
On a sultry afternoon
Up stepped a walking skeleton
An' handed me his paw
Invited me to his hotel
The best in Arkansaw.

3. I followed my companion
Into his dwelling place
An' his property it's provided
with a vine consumned face
His bread was corn-dodger
His beef I could not chaw
An' that's the kind of hash they had
In the state of Arkansaw.

4. I started out the next evenin'
To take the early Train
An' he said "You'd better work for me
I have some land to clean
I'll pay you fifty cents a day
Your washin', board, and all
And you'll find you'll be a diff'unt man
when you leave Arkansaw."

5. I worked six months for the son-of-a-gun
Jess Hollins was his name
He's six foot seven in his stockin' feet
He's taller than any crane
An' his hair hung down in ringlins
His long and anglin' jaw
He was the photograph of all the gents
Who was raised in Arkansaw.

6. I read the daily paper
Until my eyes got sore
I saw they wanted ten thousan' men
In the state of Arkansaw
His bread was corn-dodger
Hard as any rock
My teeth began to loosen
An' my knees began to knock
And I got so thin off sassafras tea
I could hide behind a straw.
Indeed I was a diffunt man
When I left Arkansaw
And it I ever see that land again
I'll hand to you my paw
It will be through a telescope
From my home to Arkansas.

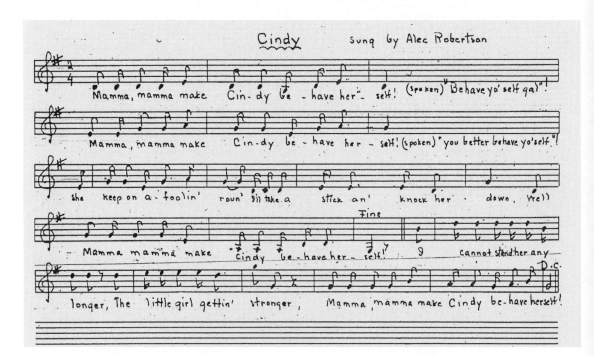

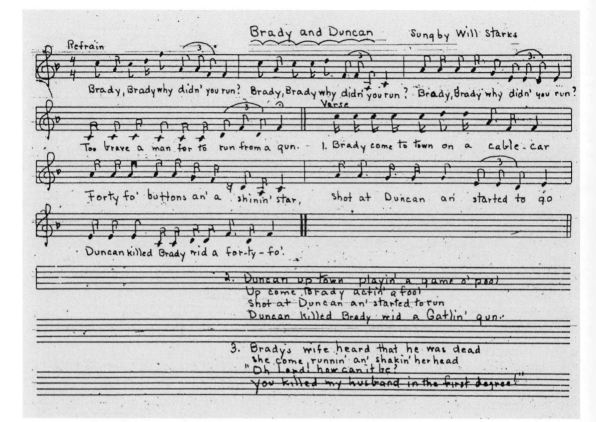

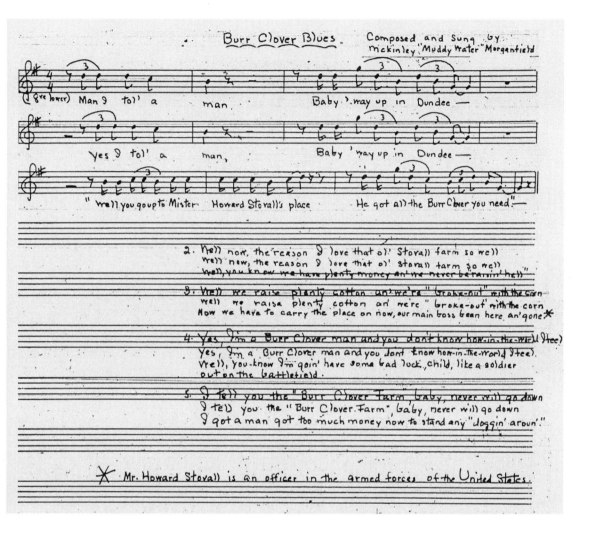

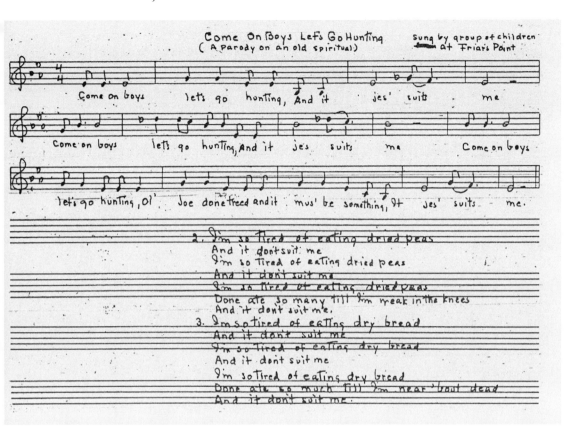

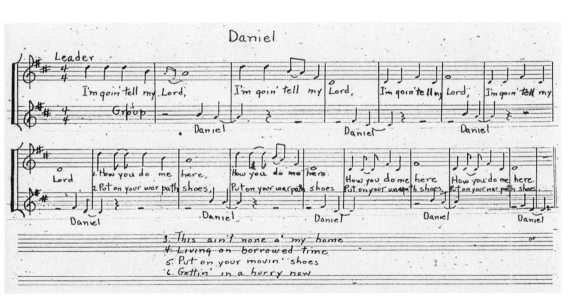

** window

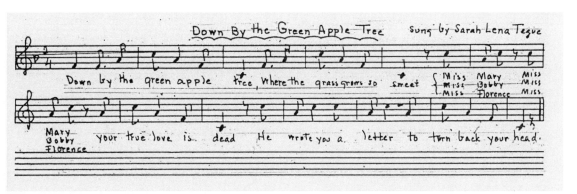

The hair on that ram's back
Growed an' teched the sky
The eagle built his nest
Hear his young 'uns cry
Didn't 'e ramble etc.

The scales that ram was weighed upon
Covered a acre o' groun'
When they rolled that ram on there
He almos' broke 'em down
Didn't 'e ramble, etc.

The man who slayed the ram
Was in danger of his life
He sent down to St. Louis
For a four-foot butcher knife
Didn't 'e ramble, etc.

The man who butchered the ram
Stood four feet in the blood
The little boy who held his feet
Got drownded in the flood.
Didn't 'e ramble, etc.

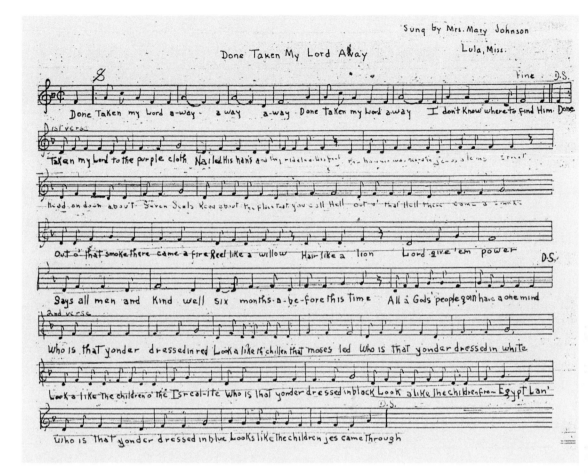

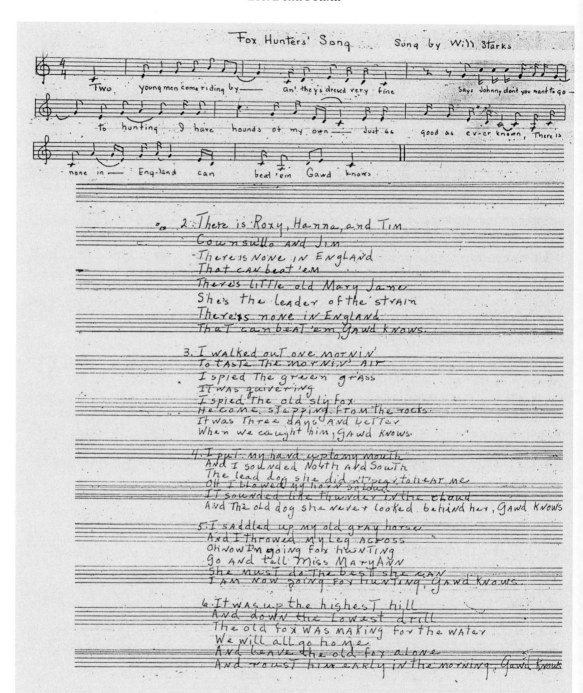

Fox Hunters' Song   Sung by Will Starks

Two young men come riding by—— an' they's dressed very fine Says Johnny don't you want to go— to hunting I have hounds of my own—— Just as good as ever known, There is none in—— England can beat 'em Gawd knows

2. There is Roxy, Hanna, and Tim
   Counsullo and Jim
   There is none in England
   That can beat 'em
   There's little old Mary Jane
   She's the leader of the strain
   There's none in England
   That can beat 'em, Gawd knows.

3. I walked out one mornin'
   To taste the mornin' air
   I spied the green grass
   It was quivering
   I spied the old sly fox
   He come stepping from the rocks
   It was three days and better
   When we caught him, Gawd knows.

4. I put my hand up to my mouth
   And I sounded North and South
   The lead dog she didn't peg to hear me
   Oh I blowed my horn so loud
   It sounded like thunder in the cloud
   And the old dog she never looked behind her, Gawd knows

5. I saddled up my old gray horse
   And I throwed my leg across
   Oh now I'm going fox hunting
   Go and tell Miss MaryAnn
   She must do the best she can
   I am now going fox hunting, Gawd knows.

6. It was up the highest hill
   And down the lowest drill
   The old fox was making for the water
   We will all go home
   And leave the old fox alone
   And roust him early in the morning, Gawd knows

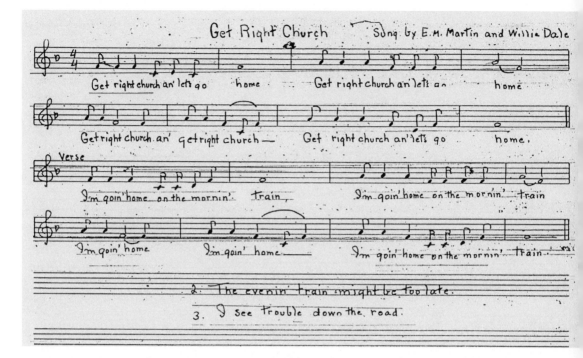

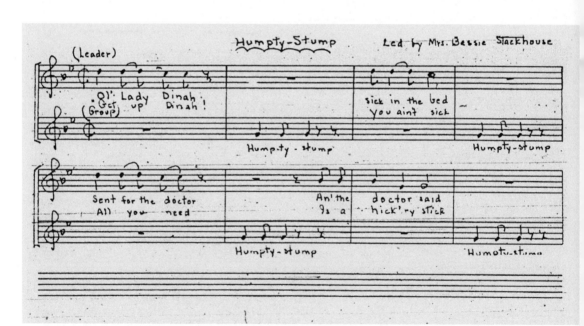

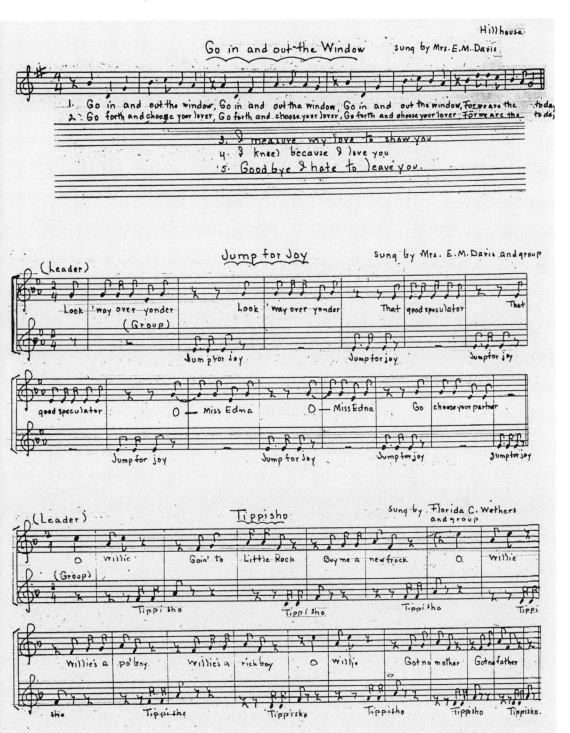

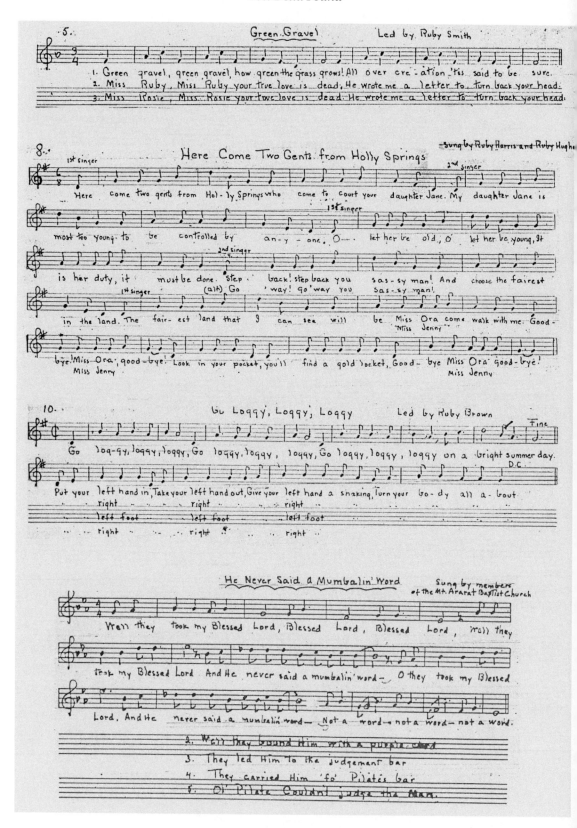

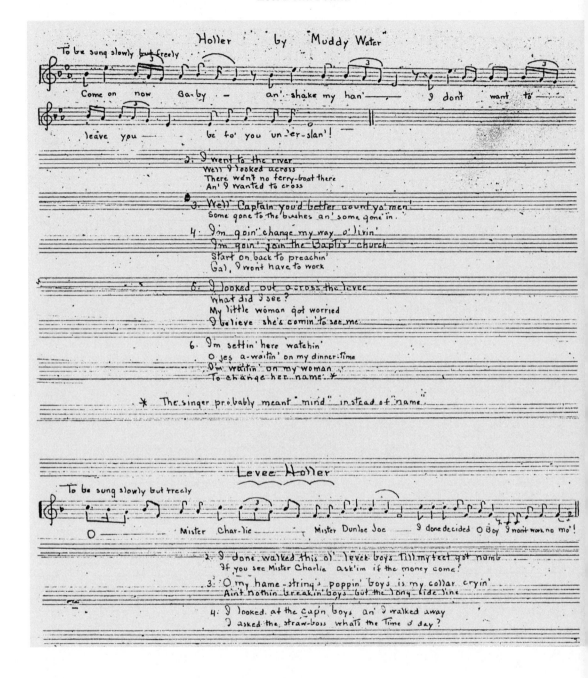

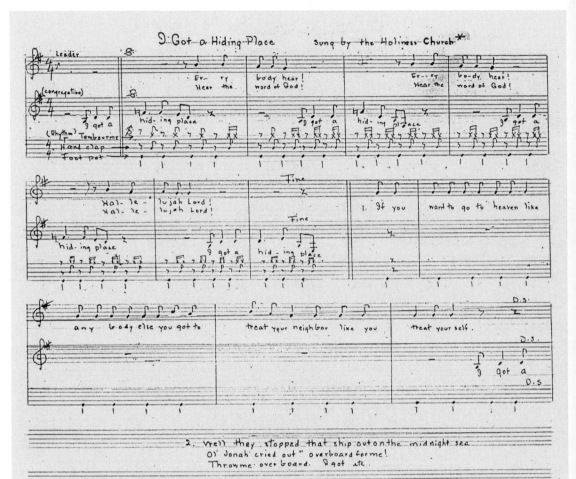

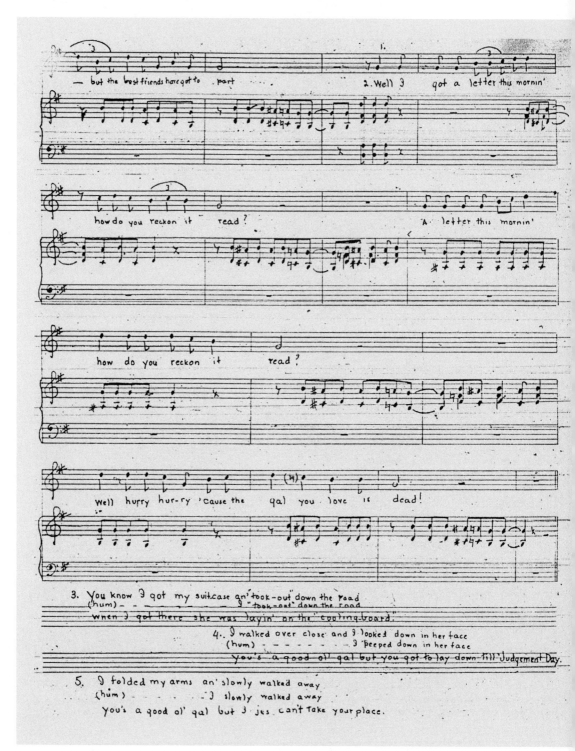

but the best friends have got to part . . . 2. Well I got a letter this mornin'

how do you reckon it read? 'A letter this mornin'

how do you reckon it read?

Well hurry hur-ry 'cause the gal you love is dead!

3. You know I got my suitcase an' took-out down the road
   (hum) - - - - - - I "took-out" down the road
   when I got there she was layin' on the "cooling-board."

4. I walked over close and I looked down in her face
   (hum) - - - - - - I peeped down in her face
   you's a good ol' gal but you got to lay down till Judgement Day.

5. I folded my arms an' slowly walked away
   (hum) - - - - I slowly walked away
   you's a good ol' gal but I jes can't take your place.

Got on the Train   Sung by Will Starks

Got on the train didn't   have no fare this   mornin'   Got on the train didn't   have no fare this

mornin'   Got on the train didn't   have no fare, you   ought to heard that con - ductor swear this mornin'!

2. He took me by the hand an' led me to the door this mornin'
   He took me by the hand an' led me to the door this mornin'
   He took me by the hand an' led me to the door
   "Don't let me catch you on this train no more" this mornin'.

3. When you see me walkin' so stiff an' stout this mornin'
   When you see me walkin' so stiff an' stout this mornin'
   When you see me walkin' so stiff an' stout
   Jes got a handout from the white folks house this mornin'.

4. Crawfish backin' back in the lake this mornin'   ✳
   Crawfish backin' back in the lake this mornin'
   Crawfish backin' back in the lake
   "I aint scared of the hen like 'tis the drake" this mornin'.

5. Hen said "Drake let's take a little dive this mornin'"
   Hen said "Drake let's take a little dive this mornin'"
   Hen said "Drake let's take a little dive
   The crawfish are over on the other side this mornin'"

6. What did the hen-duck say to the drake this mornin'?
   What did the hen-duck say to the drake this mornin'?
   What did the hen-duck say to the drake
   "There aint no crawfish in the lake this mornin'"!

✳ Although the tune and the verse cadences are the same,
obviously there are two different songs represented here. The first
song comprises verses 1—3, while verses 4—6 belong to the second song.

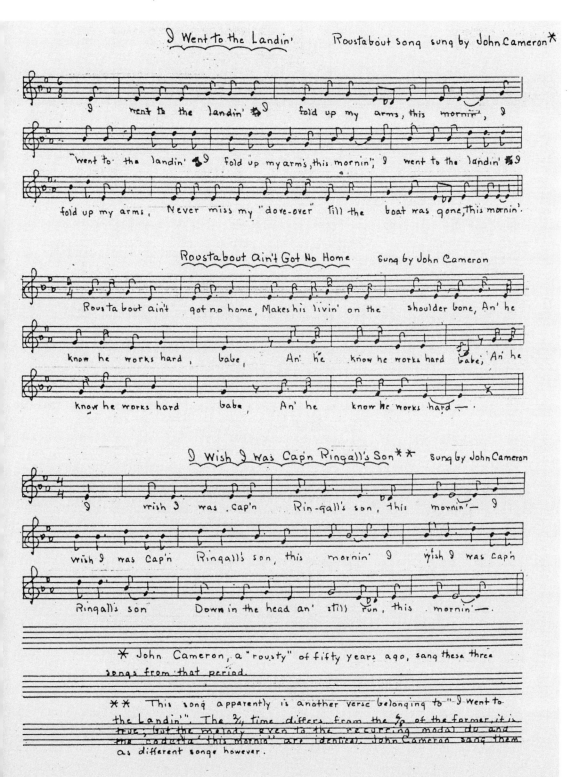

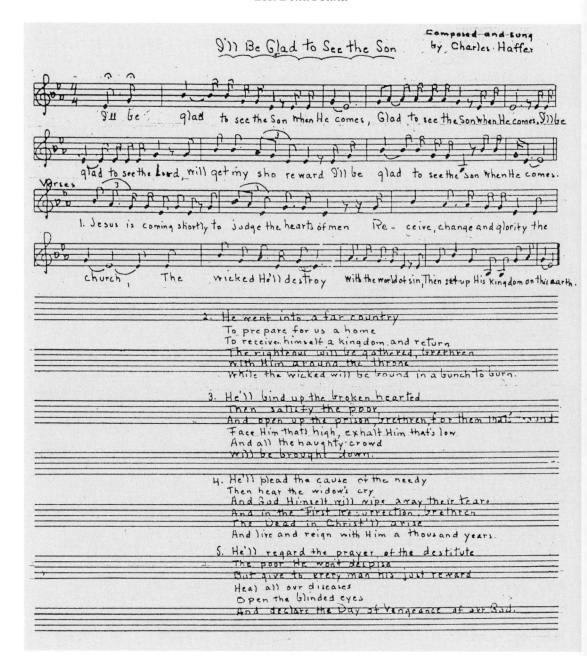

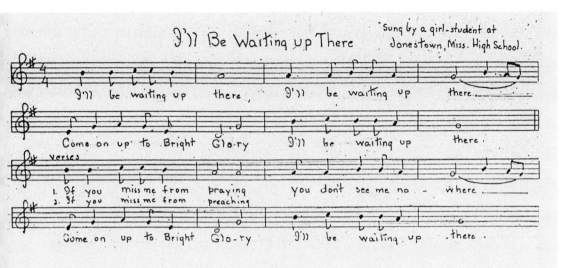

I'm Goin' to Lean on the Lord   Sung by Mrs. Rosie Threadgill

I'm goin' to lean on the Lord Lean on the Lord When my troubles rise I'm goin' to lean on the Lord 1. On the cloud my God to come, Bright flames preparin' the way, Be thunder, darkness, fire, an' storm, Lead on these dreadful days. I'm goin' to lean on the Lord Lean on the Lord When my troubles rise I'm goin' to lean on the Lord.

2. What have I gained by sinnin' Lord?
   'Twas hunger, shame, an' fear
   My father's house abounds in bread
   While we are starvin' here.

3. Here I stand here waitin'
   The blessings in my han'
   And if you come an' get them
   I'll give you the Promus Lan'.

4. I seek my Lord in weakness
   They said He couldn't be foun'
   He filled my heart with sweetness
   An' turned me all aroun'.

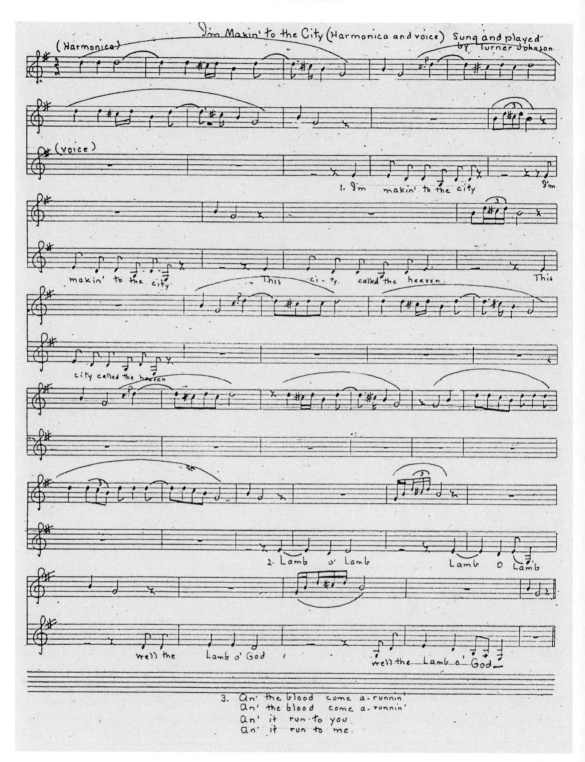

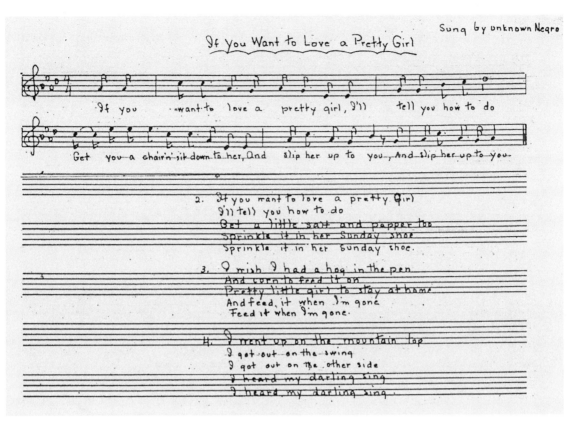

Sung by unknown Negro

If You Want to Love a Pretty Girl

If you want to love a pretty girl, I'll tell you how to do

Get you a chair'n sit down to her, And slip her up to you, And slip her up to you.

2. If you want to love a pretty Girl
I'll tell you how to do
Get a little salt and pepper too
Sprinkle it in her Sunday shoe
Sprinkle it in her Sunday shoe.

3. I wish I had a hog in the pen
And corn to feed it on
Pretty little girl to stay at home
And feed it when I'm gone
Feed it when I'm gone.

4. I went up on the mountain top
I got out on the swing
I got out on the other side
I heard my darling sing
I heard my darling sing.

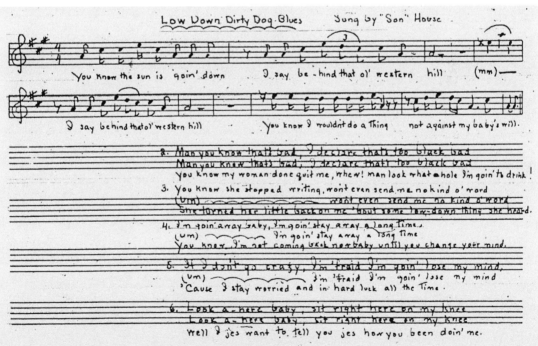

Low Down Dirty Dog Blues   Sung by "Son" House

You know the sun is goin' down   I say be-hind that ol' western hill   (mm)—

I say behind that ol' western hill   You know I wouldn't do a thing   not against my baby's will.

2. Man you know that's bad, I declare that's too black bad
Man you know that's bad, I declare that's too black bad
You know my woman done quit me, whew! man look what a hole I'm goin' to drink!

3. You know she stopped writing, won't even send me no kind o' word
(um)   won't even send me no kind o' word
She turned her little back on me 'bout some low-down thing she heard.

4. I'm goin' away baby, I'm goin' stay away a long time
(um)   I'm goin' stay away a long time
You know I'm not coming back no baby until you change yoer mind.

5. If I don't go crazy, I'm 'fraid I'm goin' lose my mind
(um)   I'm 'fraid I'm goin' lose my mind
'Cause I stay worried and in hard luck all the time.

6. Look a-here baby, sit right here on my knee
Look a-here baby, sit right here on my knee
Well I jes want to tell you jes how you been doin' me.

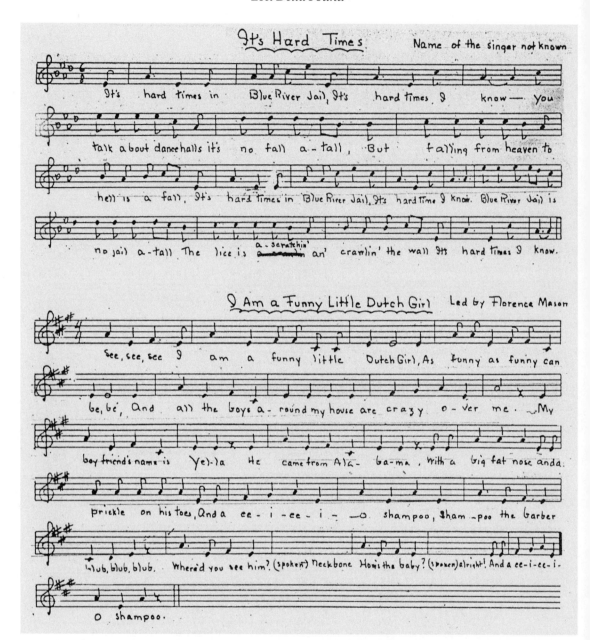

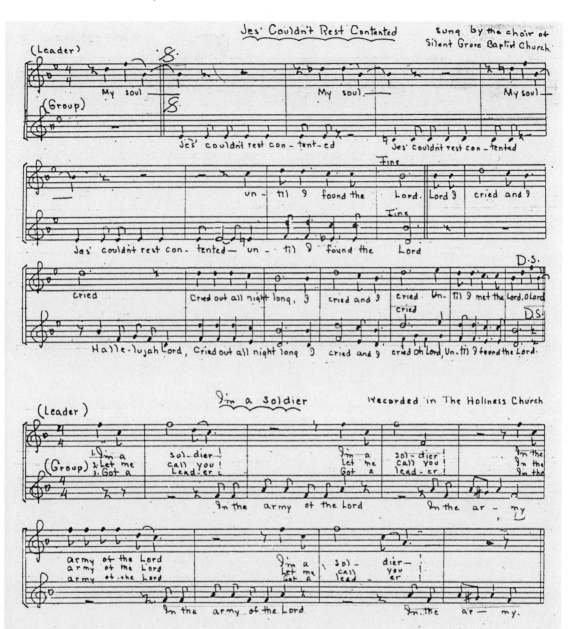

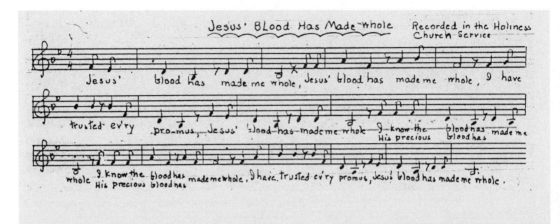

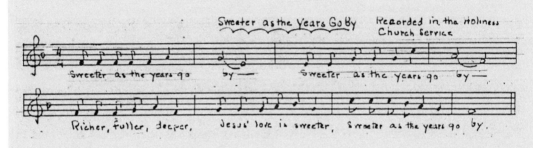

Katy I Got to Go Sung by "Alec" Robertson

Katy — I got to go, — Ka-ty — I got to go
Sadie — Sa-die —

Got to go to Judgement, I got to go, — Got to go to Judgement I got to go

This is a rare spiritual. It was used as a "rocking song" and in it the various sisters sang each other's name. Robertson remembers hearing the song fifty years ago. It is no longer sung.

Jubilee Sung by "Alec" Robertson

Charet,* Jubi—lee Charett Jubi—lee 1.Charet*is-a-comin'
2.Two white horses

Jubi-lee Charet is a-comin' Jubi-lee Charet is a-comin'
Two white horses comin' in a hurry
Come in the charet

Jubi-lee Comin' in a hurry Jubilee Charet!— Jubi-lea charet! Jubilee.
Come in the charet

* Chariot

Gonna keep My Skillet Greasy Sung by Sid Hemphill

If I can don't know when Gonna make it to my shanty if I can.

Verse

1.While the chicken in my sack an'the hounds are on my track Gonna make it to my shanty if I can.

2. These times are gettin' hard
Gonna find me a bucket o'lard
Gonna keep my skillet greasy if I can.

3. The rooster's settin' high
I'm goin' catch him on the sly
Gonna keep my skillet greasy if I can.

4. While that turkey's settin' high
Go catch you one to fry
Gonna keep my skillet greasy if I can.

5. While I'm gone to New Orleans
I'm gonna get a pot o' turnip greens
Gonna keep my pot a-boilin' if I can.

6. O the rabbit in the log
I ain't got no rabbit dog
Don't you let my rabbit get away.

* tomato

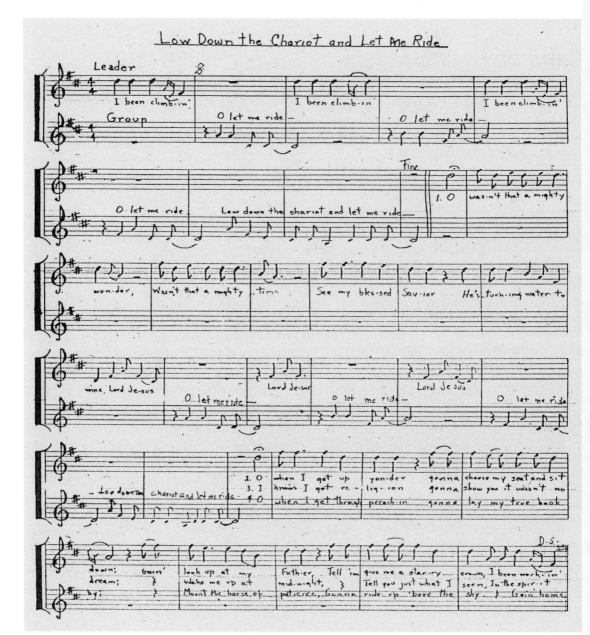

Miss Susie Anna Sue

Folk Game-Song

Arranged by John W. Work

1. Go wash your ti-ny win-dow! Miss Sue, Miss Sue, Go wash your tiny
2. Go dry your ti-ny win-dow! Miss Sue, Miss Sue, Go dry your tiny

win-dow! Miss su-sie Anna Sue.
win-dow! Miss su-sie Anna Sue.

3. Go close your tiny window, Miss Sue, Miss Sue
Go close your tiny window, Miss Susie Anna Sue.

4. Now let me see you hustle, (solo dance) Miss Sue, Miss Sue
Now let me see you hustle, Miss Susie Anna Sue.

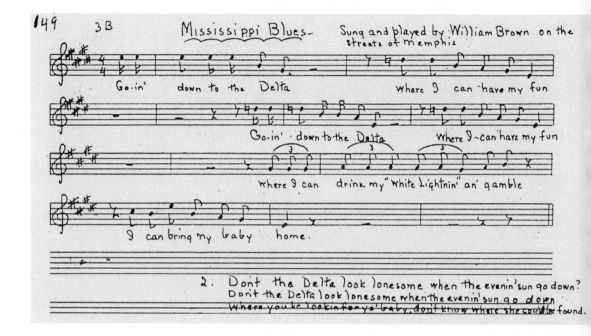

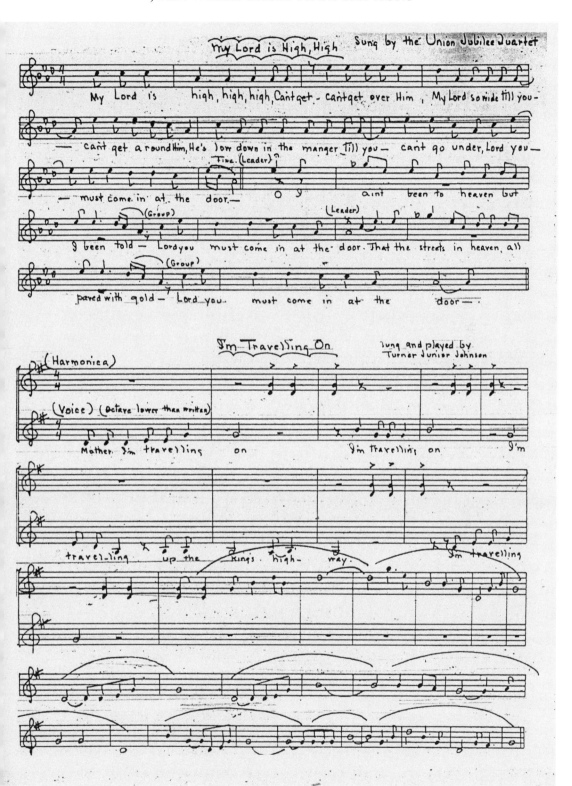

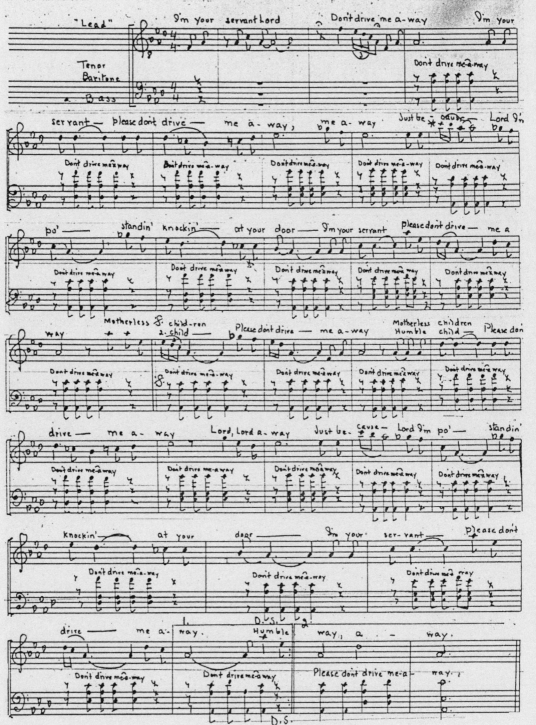

Please Don't Drive Me Away

Sung by the Union Jubilee Quartet

* Such high notes as these, and those in other songs sung by men are sung in an amazing falsetto voice.

Ramblin' Kid Blues

Composed and sung by McKinley "Muddy Water" Morganfield. Playing with "Muddy Water" were: Son Sims (Fiddle); Percy Thomas (Guitar), Louis Ford (mandolin

Well I'm a ramblin' kid   I been ramblin' all my days —   Yes I am a

ramblin' kid   I been ramblin' all my days —   Well you know my

baby wants me to stop ramblin'   For she says she'll change her ways —

1. Well now ain't no   use o' you ramblin'   When yo' baby don't want you ramblin' aroun' —

Well now ain't no   use o' you ramblin'   when yo' baby don't want you ramblin' aroun' —

Well now you know if you   keep on ramblin'   She be done drove on out o' this town. —

3. Well I aint goin' ramble, baby I aint goin' ramble no mo'
Well I aint goin' ramble, baby I aint goin' ramble no mo'
Well you know if I keep on ramblin' I'll be driftin from do' to do'

4. I'm leavin', I'm leavin', babe, child I aint goin' ramble no mo'
I'm leavin', I'm leavin' babe, child I aint goin' ramble no mo'
Well you know I been ramblin' 'roun' here, lose a woman every where I go.

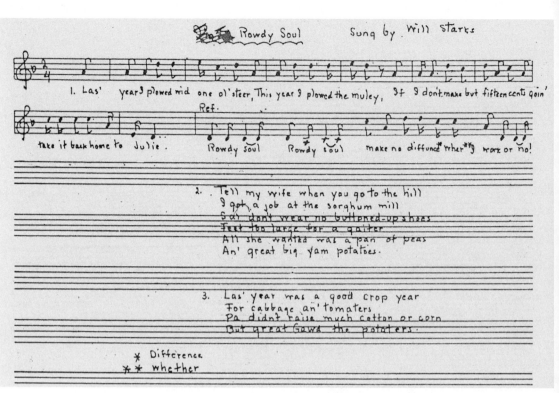

Rowdy Soul — Sung by Will Starks

1. Las' year I plowed mid one ol' steer, This year I plowed the muley, If I don't make but fifteen cents goin'
take it back home to Julie. Rowdy soul Rowdy soul make no diffunce* whether** I work or no!

Ref.

2. Tell my wife when you go to the hill
   I got a job at the sorghum mill
   Say don't wear no buttoned-up shoes
   Feet too large for a gaiter
   All she wanted was a pan of peas
   An' great big yam potatoes.

3. Las' year was a good crop year
   For cabbage an' tomaters
   Pa didn't raise much cotton or corn
   But great Gawd the potaters.

   * Difference
   ** whether

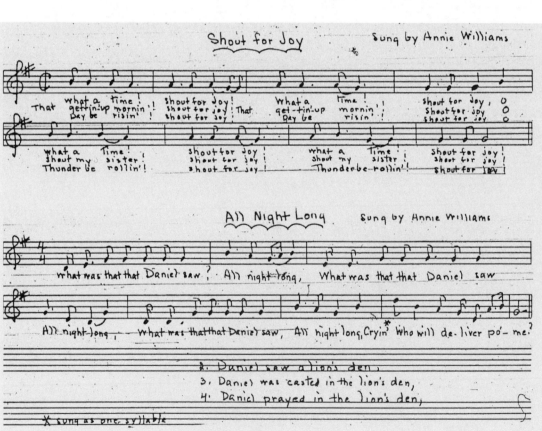

Shout for Joy — Sung by Annie Williams

That what a time! Shout for joy! That What a time! shout for joy, O
getting-up mornin'! shout for joy! get-tin'-up mornin'! Shout for joy O
Day be risin'! shout for joy Day be risin'! shout for joy O

what a time! shout for joy! what a time! shout for joy!
shout my sister! shout for joy! shout my sister! shout for joy!
Thunder be rollin'! shout for joy! Thunder be rollin'! shout for joy

All Night Long — Sung by Annie Williams

what was that that Daniel saw? All night long, What was that that Daniel saw
All night long, what was that that Daniel saw, All night long, Cryin' Who will de-liver po'* me?

2. Daniel saw a lion's den,
3. Daniel was casted in the lion's den,
4. Daniel prayed in the lion's den,

* sung as one syllable

[192]

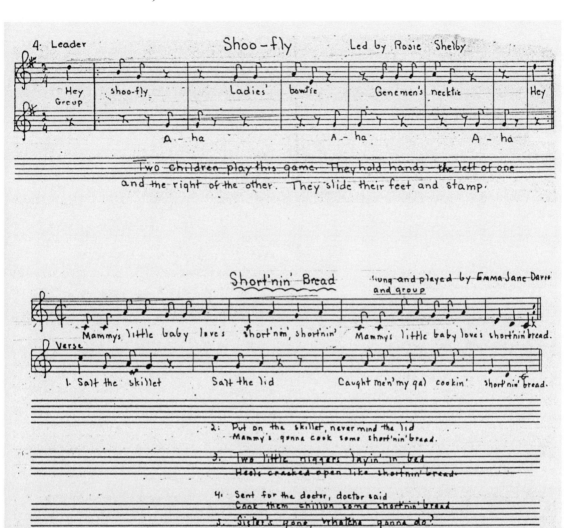

2. Stagolee had a forty-five
   He could shoot it mighty fast
   Shot thoo* and Thoo Billy Golyon
   And broke the bar room glass
   Bad man witha gun!

3. Billy Golyon asked Stagolee
   "You gointa take my life?
   I got two little chillun
   And a loving innocent wife"
   O that bad Stagolee

4. One was a girl
   One was a boy
   These two chillun
   Was his life and joy
   O that bad Stagolee!

5. I don't care nothin' 'bout your chillun
   Don't care nothin' 'bout your wife
   You done stole my Stetson hat
   And I'm goin' take yo' life."
   O That bad Stagolee

6. Stagolee asked his woman
   "Say what have you got?"
   She run her hand in her stocking leg
   And pulled out a thousand spot.
   O that bad Stagolee.

7. Stagolee was on the gallows
   He got mad and cussed
   Judge said, "Make haste and hang 'im
   'Fo He kills some of us
   O that bad Stagolee.

   * through and through

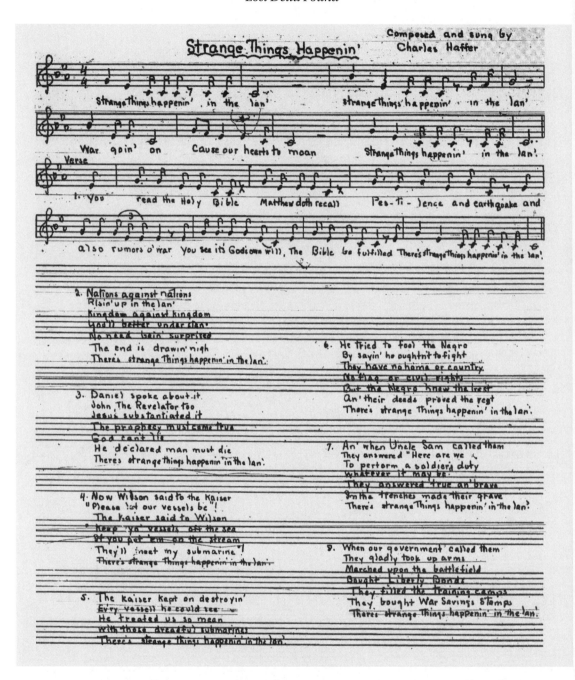

TALKING BLUES - Recited by

Went to the white folks' house to steal me a goose
White man said "You'd better turn 'im 'loose!"
I was dodgin' bullets,
Jumpin' ditches too.

I don't have to work so hard
I got a woman workin' in the white folks' yard
She killed a chicken, give me the wing
Thinks I'm workin', I ain't doin' a thing
Walkin' up and down the street
Laughin' an' talkin'
Wid other women.

Goin' home.
Put my finger in a pan o' grease
Gonna slide it cross the mantle-piece
Lookin' for cigarette butts
Chewin' tobacco
Dippin' snuff
Spittin' up side the wall.

In that hen house I was crawlin' on my knees
Thought I heard a chicken sneeze
Only a rooster saying' his prayers
Givin' out hymns to the hens up stairs.

The Late War

Sung by Will Starks

1. The reason 'Kinley was so slow 'bout sendin' men to war He was a ol' soldier Had been in war be-fo', Be-fo' the war — the late war.

2. The reason he called single men
Who wasn't afraid to die
He didn't want to send no married man
To leave his wife to cry
To the war — the late war.

3. I went over to Cuby
I went against my will
I thought over one thing a thousand times
"Supposin' I get killed"
In the war — the late war.

4. The soldiers they went runnin'
I went runnin' too
To give my feet some exercise
I had nothin' else to do
In the war — the late war.

5. Mckinley asked me why did I run
"You aint afraid to die"
I tol' him "naw! that wasn't why I run
Because I couldn't fly!
In the war — the late war.

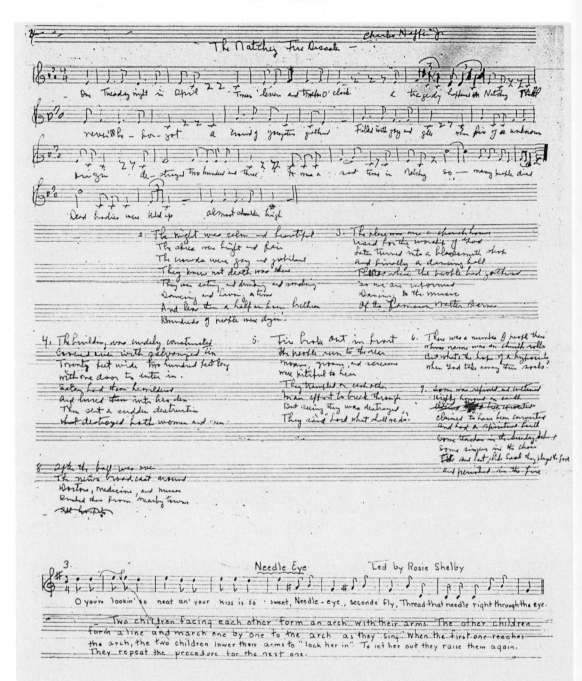

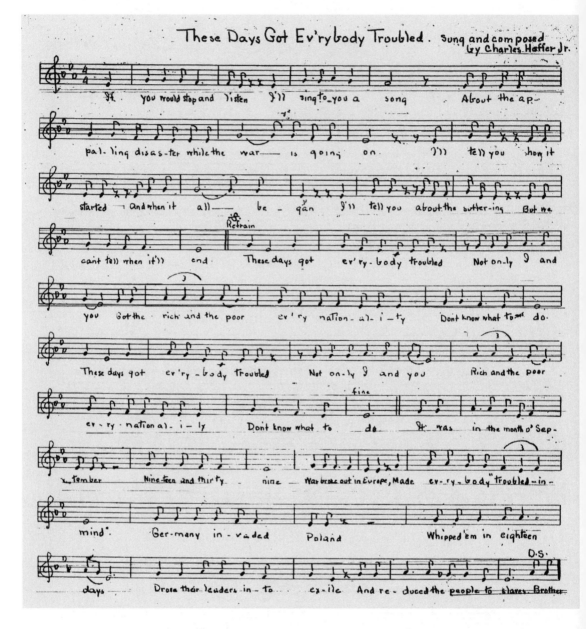

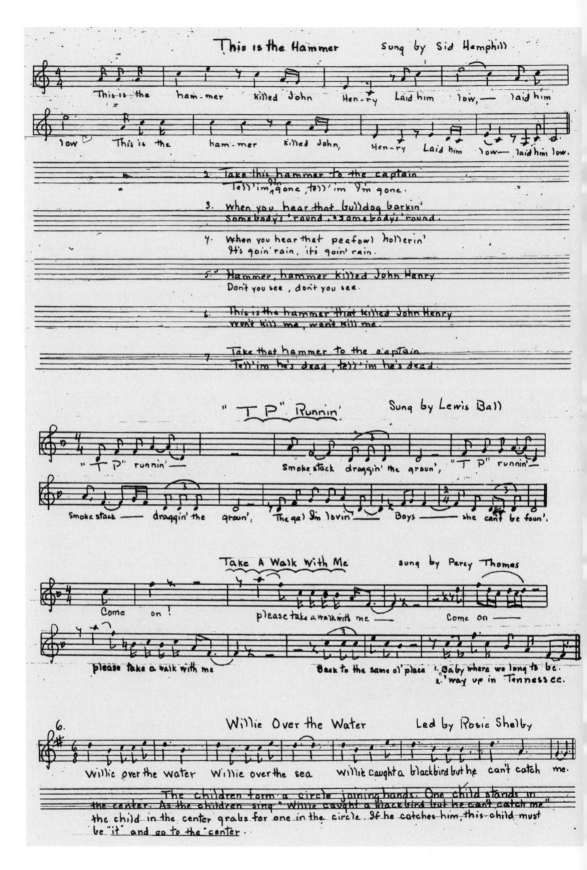

When I had money when I had money babe ... I had friends for miles a—roun' ... Now all my money gone, all my money gone ... Wo ho! all my friends cant be foun'

The following additional verses were sung by Edwards.

Section I — Baby you know I'm broke an' hungry, even aint got a lousy dime
Baby you know I'm broke an' hungry, even aint got a lousy dime
But ev'ry man gets in hard luck baby, ev'ry man gets in hard luck some Time.

Section II — Baby, that's all right, that's all right for you
Baby, that's all right, that's all right for you
Baby, That's all right now, most any ol' way you do.

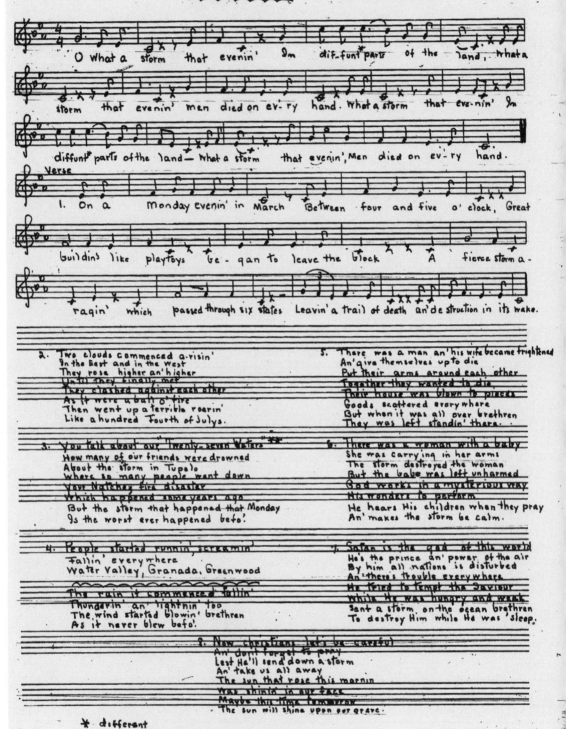

* different
** Refers to the terrible flood of 1927

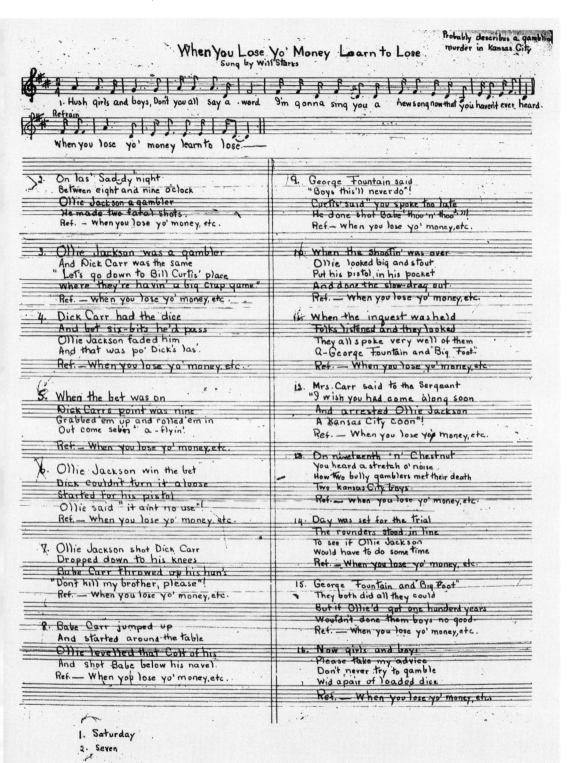

When You Lose Yo' Money Learn to Lose
Sung by Will Starks

Probably describes a gambling murder in Kansas City

1. Hush girls and boys, Don't you all say a word I'm gonna sing you a new song now that you haven't ever heard.

Refrain

When you lose yo' money learn to lose.—

2. On las' Sad-dy night
Between eight and nine o'clock
Ollie Jackson a gambler
He made two fatal shots.
Ref. — When you lose yo' money, etc.

3. Ollie Jackson was a gambler
And Dick Carr was the same
"Let's go down to Bill Curtis' place
where they're havin' a big crap game."
Ref. — When you lose yo' money, etc.

4. Dick Carr had the dice
And bet six-bits he'd pass
Ollie Jackson faded him
And that was po' Dick's las'.
Ref. — When you lose yo' money, etc.

5. When the bet was on
Dick Carr's point was nine
Grabbed 'em up and rolled 'em in
Out come seben a-flyin'.
Ref. — When you lose yo' money, etc.

6. Ollie Jackson win the bet
Dick couldn't turn it a loose
Started for his pistol
Ollie said "it ain't no use"!
Ref. — When you lose yo' money, etc.

7. Ollie Jackson shot Dick Carr
Dropped down to his knees
Babe Carr throwed up his han's
"Don't kill my brother, please"!
Ref. — When you lose yo' money, etc.

8. Babe Carr jumped up
And started around the table
Ollie levelled that Colt of his
And shot Babe below his navel.
Ref. — When you lose yo' money, etc.

9. George Fountain said
"Boys this'll never do"!
Curtis' said "you spoke too late
He done shot Babe 'thoo 'n' thoo'"!
Ref. — When you lose yo' money, etc.

10. When the shootin' was over
Ollie looked big and stout
Put his pistol in his pocket
And done the slow-drag out.
Ref. — When you lose yo' money, etc.

11. When the inquest was held
Folks listened and they looked
They all spoke very well of them
Q-George Fountain and "Big Foot".
Ref. — When you lose yo' money, etc.

12. Mrs. Carr said to tha Sergeant
"I wish you had come along soon
And arrested Ollie Jackson
A Kansas City coon"!
Ref. — When you lose yo' money, etc.

13. On nineteenth 'n' Chestnut
You heard a stretch o' noise
How two bully gamblers met their death
Two Kansas City boys.
Ref. — When you lose yo' money, etc.

14. Day was set for the trial
The rounders stood in line
To see if Ollie Jackson
Would have to do some time
Ref. — When you lose yo' money, etc.

15. George Fountain and "Big Foot"
They both did all they could
But if Ollie'd got one hundred years
Wouldn't done them boys no good.
Ref. — When you lose yo' money, etc.

16. Now girls and boys
Please take my advice
Don't never try to gamble
Wid a pair of loaded dice
Ref. — When you lose yo' money, etc.

1. Saturday
2. Seven

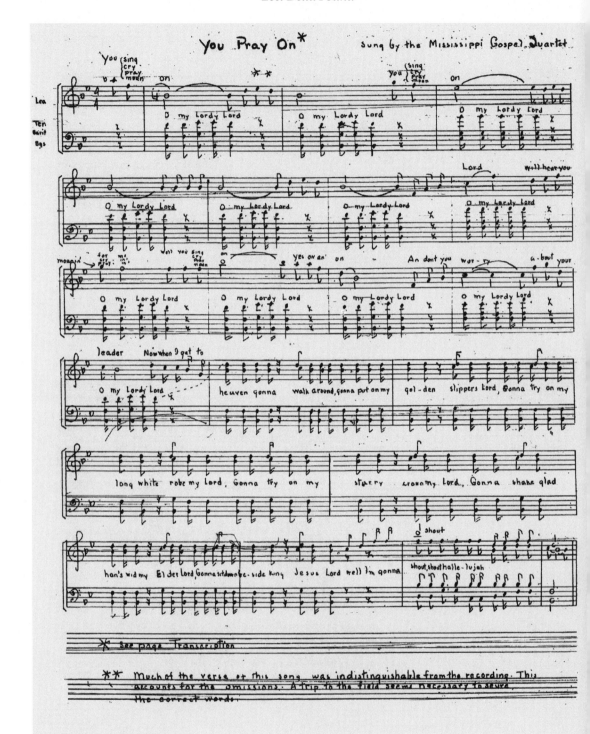

~

"Changing Negro Life in the Delta"
by Samuel C. Adams

EDITORS' INTRODUCTION

The Samuel Adams manuscript was submitted to Fisk's sociology department in 1947, ful-
filling Adams's requirements for a master's degree. Several of the years between the fieldwork and the writing were spent in service with the military.

A copy of this manuscript was discovered strewn about the floor and cabinets of Alan
Lomax's Hunter College archive; Robert Gordon collated the material and, with Bruce Nemerov
and Ms. Beth Howse, Fisk's special collections librarian, determined that the pages were part of
the Adams thesis. The original manuscript turned up at Fisk a couple years later, and their complete copy is the source for this chapter.

Adams focuses on cultural change in the Delta, the urbanization of "Negro life." He is ex-
amining a dynamic, changing culture. Written at a time when machines were performing the
labor that had always been done by hand, Adams states, "As urban influences impinge more and
more upon the traditional plantation society, other broader aspects of social life are also changing . . . The effects of the direct and indirect accessibility of plantation Negroes to urban ways
of life—resulting from the concrete highways, automobiles, locomotives, electricity, radios, and
newspapers—have been to weaken the powerful cohesive force of the folkways and mores of the
old South." His paper, he writes, "seeks to measure the effects of urbanism on the customary
modes of behavior of rural Negroes in an area where there still exist many evidences of the sway
of traditional life." (In this case, Clarksdale, a relatively small town in 1941, "was treated as the
seat of urban influence.")

In succeeding chapters, Adams illuminates church life, then secular life, and their changes.
He notes that secular society changes "far more readily and radically than the sacred." His anec-
dotal evidence of the change in society's attitude toward the church is startling; of the youngest
generation, he writes (without noting the song in reference): "The youth . . . ridicule ministers;
they picture them as 'worldly' men . . . It is reported that the children objected to the use of the
word 'nigger' in a song, so the word 'nigger' was changed to 'preacher.' "

Adams examines changes in secular life through the lens of song and story. He traces work
songs from their religious roots to their present, decidedly secular, malleable state. He then studies the source of those changes: "Specifically the victrola, the radio, the juke box, the dance halls,

[223]

the movies and the changes in technology make it possible for the plantation Negroes to have a greater access to broader worlds of experience than ever before." His evidence of such influence includes a toast entitled "Shine and the Titanic" and a song about Hitler and the devil.

Among Adams's appendixes is a sample of the questionnaire filled out with one hundred plantation families in the Coahoma study. Adams, whose task was to talk to people, also shares several anecdotes of Delta life that were too good not to include, even if they were not directly part of the body of his paper. These are detailed, informative pictures of a cultural life long gone.

~

FISK UNIVERSITY

Changing Negro Life in the Delta

A Thesis Submitted to the Faculty of
the Department of Sociology in
Partial Fulfillment of the
Requirements for the Degree
of Master of Arts

By
Samuel C. Adams Jr.
Nashville, Tennessee
June, 1947

~

ACKNOWLEDGMENTS

A very special acknowledgment is due to Dr. Jitsuichi Masuoka for his kind assistance, guidance, and insights without which this thesis could not have been completed in its present form.

Acknowledgments are due Dr. Charles S. Johnson for affording me the opportunity to study Delta Negro life and for his interest in the progress of this study. Also grateful appreciation is expressed for the interest and assistance of Dr. Edward N. Palmer.

Tribute is offered to the late Dr. Robert E. Park, who aroused and directed my curiosity in the changing Negro life on a Delta plantation.

CHAPTER I
Introduction

Negro life on the plantation is changing. The transition has been going on for nearly a century, but it has become more pronounced since the turn of the present century and, particularly after World War I. With the South becoming increasingly an integral part of the national economy, the old plantation system is rapidly collapsing.[1] As urban influences impinge more and more upon the traditional plantation society, other broader aspects of social life are also changing. Changes are in evidence everywhere in the South today and they are affecting white and Negro alike. The effects of the direct and indirect accessibility of plantation Negroes to urban ways of life—resulting from the concrete highways, automobiles, locomotives, electricity, radios, and newspapers—have been to weaken the powerful cohesive force of the folkways and mores of the old South and to increase general confusion in thought and contradictions in the behavior of the Negroes.[2] In other words, the changing South is an interesting laboratory for the student of the social sciences, especially those interested in culture change and acculturation of Negroes in the Deep South.

General treatises on social change are many[3] but realistic studies, giving a sufficient emphasis to specific and concrete factors and forces underlying alterations in cultural and social life, are relatively limited.[4] Furthermore, we are familiar with the idea of the importance of a market town as a distribution center for an area in bringing about social change and acculturation. This has been recognized, but just how important such a town can be socially as well as commercially—for a relatively isolated traditional community—requires consideration.[5] This is to be expected since the students of the social sciences are primarily interested in more or less durable and abiding changes or general social processes rather than in those changes that are short and transitory in nature.[6] But in order to understand the full import of general and cyclical trends in social change, one must study the nature of the things that are undergoing a transformation as well as forces that are acting to produce and effect changes. From the standpoint of social change, the durable and transitory alterations in social life are two aspects of a single process. So conceived, any cultural and social phenomenon can be said to allocate itself along a continuum.

With reference to change and adaptability J. Masuoka states: "social and cultural phenomena seem to allocate themselves in a kind of continuum, ranging from the most to the least readily transformable. at one end of the continuum are found those organized activities having to do with technology and secular values; while at the other are found those deep seated attitudes, beliefs, sentiments, and ideologies. It is commonplace knowledge and observation that some of these organized activities change more readily than others."[7] This general statement needs to be supplemented with empirical studies.

Regardless of size, location, simplicity, or conservatism, changes constantly take place in a society. One of the factors of greatest importance in cultural change is the dominant concern of a people or the focus of the culture. For in all cultures certain aspects of life are emphasized and the possibilities of alternatives are more readily granted a hearing, as contrasted with elements of culture taken for granted—where suggestions of change, even of relatively slight change, fall on unprepared ground and receive negative reactions. Thus, it would seem that if changes occur in the mode of life of a people, new ways of acting, thinking, and feeling precede or accompany change or acculturation. Learning is the psychological crux of acculturation in that it prepares the individual for participation in a certain way of life. For this process to occur there must be adequate motivation, drives, cues, and rewards. Thus, "one must want something, notice something, do something, and get something."[8] In short, an alteration in the environing conditions of life has its counterpart in the modification of habits, attitudes, and personalities of Negroes on the plantation.

Habits and attitudes of Negroes on the plantation are accepted as more or less different from those of the Negroes in the city. There is a difference in attitudes and conduct between a group of plantation Negroes who have been more strongly influenced by the city way of life than those who have been less affected. What does it really mean when the plantation Negro says that he does not remember old folk tales, but enjoys telling a worldly story? What does it mean when he says that he has no time to sing? What does it mean when a woman says that the burial association is better than the church? What happens to Negro folk songs and the spirituals when the influence of the "juke box" and radio are felt strongly? What happens to the "folk" culture in general when the Negro participates with zest in city life?

THE PROBLEM OF THE STUDY

The chief problem of this study consists in describing and analyzing culture and social changes that have been and are occurring in the Delta, but equally it is the concern of this study to gain insights into the processes of these changes. Thus, the study seeks to discover pertinent factors that create stability in human culture and social life as well as the necessary and sufficient conditions under which modifications in the mode of life of a people take place. This study, by investigating church activities on the one hand and singing and story telling on the other, seeks to determine as far as possible a set of conditions and factors associated with acculturation of the Delta Negroes. Stated somewhat broadly, this study seeks to determine the areas of Negro folk life that are subject to the forces of civilization or the culture of the city.[9]

The hypothesis of this study is: The greater the participation of a people in city life (which means a greater drive to learn city ways of life), the greater is the change in the traditional culture. With the changed conditions of living, there is a greater reward—both economic and social—to be had from accepting new ways than from adhering to the old ways. In this process of culture change there is a difference; some of the habits are more persistent than others and in some areas of group life social constraints and conservation are more powerful than in other areas. Thus, it would seem that the change is more pronounced in the area of less structuralized human behavior than in the institutionalized, for in this area of human activities fashions and fads have their full sway. In the case of the church, the acculturation is blocked by the vested interest groups and by more enduring group habits and sentiments.

SOURCES AND METHODS OF THE STUDY

Negro sharecroppers on the King and Anderson, a Delta plantation, were studied.[10] Clarksdale, Mississippi was treated as the seat of urban influence. The degree of participation in urban life was measured by the frequency with which the plantation Negroes visit Clarksdale; by the kind and extent of activities in which they participate while in the city; by the number of radios and automobiles that they possess; and, by changes in attitudes toward the city.

Data on folk tales, folk songs and the spirituals were obtained informally through listening in and recording what they told and sang; formally through the interviewing of one hundred individual members of the community.[11] These cooperating individuals gave information on their past and present preferences in the kinds of music, tales and stories. Data on the religious behavior of the Negro were obtained from the ministers and deacons and church members, as well as from others who have lost interest in church going. Additional data on the religious interests were secured by means of participant observation. As to the size of the families; sex, age, and marital composition; educational and economic status; and recreational and other activities of the family members studied were secured by means of family schedules.[12] In addition, by eating and sleeping on the plantation, and by participating in the community activities, the attitudes of the people were observed.

LIMITATIONS OF THE STUDY

This study, though incomplete, seeks to measure the effects of urbanism on the customary modes of behavior of rural Negroes in an area where there still exist many evidences of the sway of traditional life. In a measure this study will reveal what happens to the religious and to the folk expressive behavior of peoples when they come under the influence of city ways.

In order to provide a sufficient proof for the hypothesis of this study, a far more intensive analysis should have been made of the religious and other expressive life of the Negro. Moreover, other areas of changes, particularly the family and the school, should have been studied to show how a change in one area of life affects the other mode of life. In other words, more comparative studies should have been undertaken. As to the method of study the limitation is obvious. There should have been more quantitative analysis of the change and the case studies should have been more complete to show the dynamic aspect of the folk society in transition.

CHAPTER II

Social Change in the Delta

L ying between the Mississippi and Yazoo Rivers the Delta extends to Memphis, Tennessee in the North and to Vicksburg, Mississippi in the South.[13] It is called "the Delta" because the plain and basin are formed by the alluvial deposits of the Mississippi River. The dwelling units of large plantations, sprawling cotton fields, highways and telephone poles are the most conspicuous features of the scenery. In the Delta counties, over eighty per cent of the agricultural acreage is devoted to the production of cotton.

In 1940 the total population of the Delta was 508,022; of the total, Negroes comprised roughly 362,000 or seventy-two percent.[14] Some of the important characteristics of the present day Negro population in the Delta are: (1) that more than eighty-seven per cent of Negro males are engaged in agriculture; (2) that they are predominantly tenant farmers; and, (3) that they are largely illiterate.

CLARKSDALE

The city of Clarksdale, one of the Delta's trade and culture centers is located in the north-western section of the State of Mississippi. The city is on Federal Highway 61, and is seventy-five miles south-west of Memphis, Tennessee. The population of Clarksdale is roughly 12,000 and of this total 10,000 are Negroes. Since its incorporation in 1882, the population of the city increased steadily. The number of inhabitants in 1890 was around eight hundred, but by the turn of the century the population increased to 1,800. In 1920, there were 7,500 inhabitants; in 1930, 10,000; and in 1940, about 12,000.[15]

The paved highways connect Clarksdale with its hinterland. Here are located the business establishments, schools, and churches. Clarksdale has fifty-one food stores; twenty-two eating places; twenty general merchandise stores; twenty-four clothing stores; eleven automobile dealers and garages; eight household furniture, radio, and electrical appliance stores; five major lumber yards; nine Negro "juke joints"; and nine drug stores.[16] There are eight Negro churches but there are approximately one hundred Negro ministers; many of whom conduct religious services throughout the Delta. In addition there are two cults, namely the Saints and the Jehovah Witnesses.

The main avenues through which the plantation Negroes enter and participate in the city life of Clarksdale are Fourth, Issaquena, and Sunflower streets.

The corner of Fourth and Issaquena Streets on a Saturday Evening

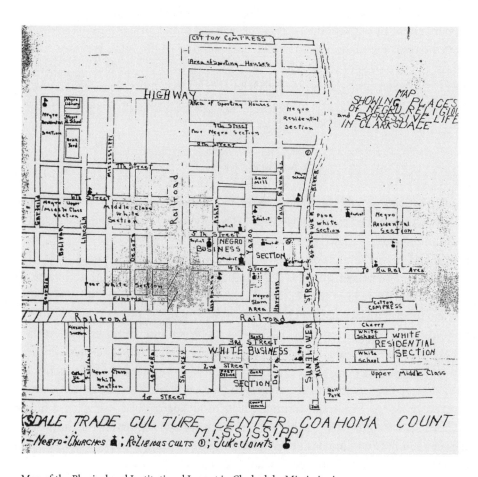

Map of the Physical and Institutional Layout in Clarksdale, Mississippi

Issaquena Street stretches two blocks. Its buildings are mostly one-story brick and frame structures. There are retail drygood and hardware stores, rooming houses, restaurants, and personal service shops. On this street the Negroes move back and forth with little intention of ever buying anything. If they buy anything at all, the purchases will be limited to a few loose cigarettes, bottles of beer, or candies. The music on the street comes chiefly from the "juke boxes" in the restaurants. The Savoy theater is the main attraction on this street.

Where Issaquena ends, Fourth Street begins. In physical appearance the buildings are dull, brick structures. This street has more Negro operated business establishments than any other street, but there are also the Jewish, Italian, and Chinese owned establishments. On this street are located the Dipsie Doodle, the Methodist and Baptist churches, Sanders Drug store, Messenger's pool room and café, the Fourth Street Cab stand, and the G. T. Thomas Block. Messenger's pool room, where Negroes and a few Mexicans play pool or listen to the "juke box" is a favorite stopping place for Negroes. As far as the plantation Negroes are concerned the Dipsie Doodle, a café and beer tavern, is probably the most frequented and popular place. On the opposite side of the Dipsie Doodle are two rather large and impressive Negro churches.

Sunflower Street is the "roughest" of all the streets. The major attraction on this street is "Tommy's Place," since this is the only place in Clarksdale where Negro youth are allowed to dance.

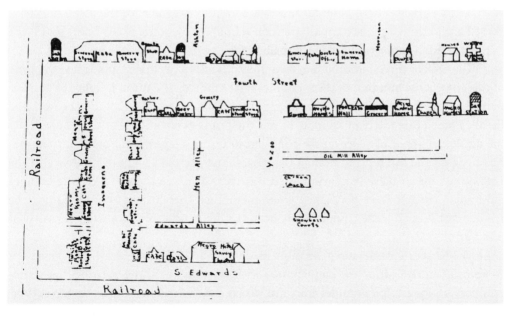

Map of Clarksdale's "Beale Streets"

THE PLANTATION

The King and Anderson plantation occupies a fifteen mile strip of Delta land contiguous to the city of Clarksdale. The U.S. highway runs through its center. Its sharecroppers are Negroes. The plantation is almost treeless, showing the intensive cotton cultivation. The black and fertile soil is beady in texture when dry and is sticky when wet. All this land is under cultivation, save the plots left for the church, the school, the gin, the commissary, and the houses.

In appearance the tenant houses are all alike; they are painted green and trimmed in white. Most of them have two rooms, but there are some with only one room. A typical house is generally bare except for the newspaper on the wall, a stove or fireplace, a table, and an old bed in the corner. Some of the houses have a separate kitchen. In sharp contrast to the tenant houses are those of the overseers. They are painted white and are surrounded by trees, lawn, and shrubbery.

The plantation store is located on the U.S. highway. Both in appearance and in stock it resembles the old "General Store." It is one of the largest buildings on the plantation.

Located about one hundred yards from the highway is the church. Its well built frame structure is painted gray with white trimmed borders. Placed on a wooden frame in the front of the church is a large bell which is used to bring the people together to inform them of deaths in the community as well as other important meetings. The interior of the church is kept neat and clean. There are Sunday School calendars on the wall, several wooden benches and a piano near the pulpit. This building has added functions; it serves as a grade school building and as a community center for the plantation people. Near the church is the agricultural high school for Negroes. It is a frame and brick structure with dormitory space for boys and girls.

There were three hundred and four Negro families on this plantation at the time of this study. One hundred of these families were studied. The mean number of persons living in these families was 3.8 persons per family. Ninety-seven out of the one hundred families stated that the plantation work was their only occupation. For the whole group the average number of years on their present jobs was 9.2 years, but only four families had been on the same plantation all their lives. The average length of residence in the community for all these Negroes studied was 10.7 years. On the average these families cultivated eighteen acres per family while the annual income was about $324.00. The median last school grade completed by heads of the families was 4.4 while for wives it was 5.9.

The King and Anderson plantation, like others in the Delta, is becoming more and more mechanized. Since the day laborers with tractors do all the plowing, the sharecroppers no longer "plow under the land" to lay fallow, or "turn it over in the spring" for planting. Flame weeders, too, are rapidly eliminating the tedious task of hoeing and chopping the crop: within a few hours an airplane sprays the cotton fields. The conse-

A Sharecropper House on the King and Anderson Plantation

quences of the mechanization are many and among them are (1) the losing fight of the sharecroppers who at present merely "watch and tend the crop," (2) the increase in the leisure time, and, (3) the increased accessibility of the Negroes on the plantation to the ways of the city people. For example, fifty families have radios and the urban newspaper is read by thirty families. The most remote section of the plantation is now accessible to the county agricultural and home demonstration agents who bring new ideas and new ways of doing things. There is also the agricultural high school where both the city and rural children come in contact: they come in contact with urban technological artifacts as well as with the teachers who are all city bred.

The plantation Negroes go to the city. Twenty-eight out of the total of one hundred families reported that some members of the families go to Clarksdale at least once in every two weeks while the remaining seventy-two families go to Clarksdale three times a week. Thirty families have automobiles. On Saturday morning the trucks sent by the merchants in Clarksdale bring the plantation Negroes into town. After the cotton picking season is over in January, the plantation Negroes have hardly anything to do till spring.

In addition to general trips to town there are special events or seasons which bring the plantation Negro to Clarksdale. The following are some of the main events:

January	New Year's Celebration
March	Afro Sons and Daughters Convention
April	4H Club Rally, Fireside Exhibits, Ham and Bacon Shows, Easter
May	Field Day (all county schools come and parade), City School Commencement

June	Christian Sunday School Conventions, Summer School Pageants
July	Methodist and Baptist Conventions, Baseball games
October	County Fair, Cotton Festival, Minstrels and Circuses
November	Thanksgiving Celebrations, Football games
December	Christmas Celebrations

Likewise an increasing number of city Negroes come to the plantation. They come to work as the day laborers, tractor drivers and cotton pickers. They come to seek pleasure in the country where the city curfew and liquor laws cannot reach them.

THE RIVER

The growth of the Delta, as of any community, is dependent upon the means of communication and transportation; in fact, so vital is this relationship that social change in the Delta can best be told in terms of the changes that have taken place in the modes of communication and transportation. The Mississippi River with its tributary, the Sunflower, lost its importance as the avenue of trade, travel, and communication at the turn of the present century. It is remembered most vividly by the old people, whose lives were organized about the river transportation and communication. The late middle aged people in the Delta associate the peak of development with the coming of the railroads, but the younger generation sees the future growth of the Delta in terms of the highways.

The first white settlers to the Delta found mounds which the Indians had thrown up to provide a refuge above the crest of the waters in flood season. Before the Civil War, there were a few small settlements, consisting of small plantation clearings along the Mississippi and its tributaries.

The early settlers migrated there in the seventies and eighties. They came from the "hills" of Mississippi, from Alabama, and a few from Georgia. at first they were slow to migrate to the Delta country because of the devastating floods which took a heavy toll of life and property; gradually they migrated in increasing numbers and found the land extremely productive.

The people who cleared the forests and cultivated the plantations in the seventies and eighties were of a hardy pioneering stock. They struggled with nature but the wild game and beasts were plentiful. They struggled with the river: they lived almost an amphibian life. They knew the water as they knew the land; they had to be skillful boatmen as well as skillful farmers.

This was the era of the river culture. The trading settlements and towns were steamboat landings. The most important trade center in the county was Friars Point at Port Royal, which was the county seat.

Harnessing the river and the railroad came about the same time. There had been some attempt at levee building before the Civil War but these inadequate earth barriers to the floods had fallen into disrepair during the war. In 1884, the Yazoo-Mississippi Delta Levee district was organized and systematic levee construction begun. Short lines of railroad were constructed in 1877 from the river to Lula, a distance of eight miles, and two years later the line was extended from Eagles Nest to Clarksdale. In 1884 a section of railroad was completed through the county as a part of the line connecting Memphis to New Orleans.

The river era was marked by the height of the plantation institutions. Much of the daily needs of the people were produced on the plantation. Labor was scarce and every effort was made to hold laborers on the plantations. The tenants made money. In the dry seasons the cotton was transported by wagon to river landings and in the wet season, when the waters rose to the point, the landings could be reached by skiff. The cotton and other products were loaded on boats. The wet season was the time also for trading.

In the Delta churches were few, widely separated and mostly of Baptist denomination. The congregations sang the "Dr. Watt" songs[17] borrowed from the white churches and modified by addition of the chanting and moaning of the long meter hymns. The old spirituals or "Hallies" were used as collection and revival songs. The church was an important institution and it had a very real meaning in community life. Affiliation with the church meant a real difference in the conduct and social attitudes of the people. The church people enjoyed recreation in which the "Rock Daniel" was a peculiar phenomenon. The "Rock Daniels"[18] were not confined to the church meeting but were acceptable to religious people at church entertainments, at quiltings, and at house parties.

The ring game was a form of recreation indulged in by both religious and non-religious people. The dances were for the non-religious and were replete with the fiddler and the dance caller who intoned the figures to be executed.

THE RAILROAD

With the coming of the railroads many changes which were already underway became more pronounced than formerly. Once more or less isolated Delta communities became more readily accessible to the big cities of Memphis on the north and New Orleans on the south. Planters, with the sense of security the levee gave, cleared and drained the swamps and lowlands and put them into cultivation. Cultivation became more intensive, the plantation lost some of its self-contained features. It became essentially a commercial enterprise and with it the percentage of laborers increased. The farm operator became more dependent on the commissary for food brought by the trains which took his cotton away. The traditional plantation order began to disappear into the commercial order.

The height of the railroad's importance marked the passage of the frontier-ways. The "bad men" and bold men became fewer. Law and order and the control of the plantation system supplanted the control of the person based on personal strength.

Moreover, Negro race consciousness began to arise in the Delta, as their lives were lived no longer completely within the small local communities. When, for example, the A.M.E. churches were organized in Reconstruction, the Masonic lodge was established at the same time. The earliest A.M.E. churches had occupied jointly buildings with the Masonic lodge. The buildings were two-story, with church on the ground floor and lodge rooms occupying the second story. The two men who organized the A.M.E. churches in this area were instrumental in starting lodges. Race consciousness expressed itself in the development of Negro businesses in the "colored sections" of the towns.

Class differences among Negroes became more pronounced in this era than formerly. On the river, there were some Negroes able to advance to owners from their lowly status of tenant. These owners remained friendly with the tenants. In the new railroad town however, a new type of Negro leadership emerged out of the situation of economic and race exploitations. Race consciousness and the notion of mutual aid were manipulated to further the individual's own aspirations. The commercial economy presented a Negro middle class to supplant the earlier "race leadership." The distinction between the wicked and the respectable became more formal and less as compulsive moral forces. The red light district came into existence in the town.

The railroad era witnessed a more or less formal expression of attitudes and feelings. To be sure, men sang their thoughts and fancies on the levee, on the railroad, and in the field, but they were confined to the spot of their making. The social song was no longer the traditional ring play and dance. There came into existence two kinds of songs which were divided into respectable and the wicked. The respectable songs were the popular written music, while the wicked songs were the blues sung in the brothels in the red light district. The spirituals were sung less and less, while the "Dr. Watts" song book, with its standardized form became increasingly popular. The "gospel" songs began to appear in the churches.

THE HIGHWAY

Highway development was slow in Mississippi, being gravel roads which were called "the good road." The main highways followed the railroads closely and they usually ran parallel. The tributary roads leading into the main thoroughfares were not well developed, and in spite of this fact in the dry season they made possible greater freedom of movement than the railroad. The early twenties saw the collapse of the cotton boom, the closing of the red light district, and trouble for the middle class. When the concrete highway came, in the thirties, it went across the country paying little attention to the location of the railroad and railroad towns. No longer was the movement of people restrained by the poor means of traveling.

The good highway meant the introduction of motor driven machinery, and the Delta economy and social structure reflected the change. Following the depression, the flat fields lent themselves to tractor cultivation, and mechanization of the southern agriculture further changed the plantation institution and social order. With this change the folk skills and folk knowledge of soil and plant and animal husbandry were supplanted more and more by scientific cultivation. The transition is not complete but the changes are in evidence in every phase of human society.

Socially, the Delta is also complicated. The complexity is shown in the variety of plantation workers and growing classes in the towns. The churches differ in form of worship from one to the other. The lodges which collapsed in the depression, struggled feebly to resurrect themselves. The burial society, which is a form of insurance, offers none of the social values which characterized the lodge. The middle class lost many of its members in the collapse of the cotton boom. Those who remain are people stripped of influence. But, there is greater standardization of human conduct wrought by the radio, the juke box, and other city-made technic-ways. Beneath these more formidable social changes the old folkways, folk tales, folk music, and the simple expressions of the illiterate people have their sway.

It is in the background of this chapter that the changing traditional plantation life needs to be studied.

~

CHAPTER III

Negro Religious Life in Transition

The Negro church is still to a large measure the center of Negro life. This institution of long standing assumes many varied functions and thus dominates, in fact, Negro life in general.

> The Negro church is much more than merely an institution of worship. The strictly religious meetings are a small part of the weekly program of the ordinary church. It tends to be a center around which a great part of the social and public life of the people revolves. It is still the center of the racial life. This is particularly the case in the villages and rural districts where the church building is the place of assembly for all public purposes. There are no club houses, theaters, parks or other places of assembly or amusement and the church serves in the place of all. It reaches all conditions of life. A large percentage of the Negroes are members; most of those not members are more or less regular in their attendance. It is the center of information for the community; it functions as a newspaper. It is a place to see friends, hear the neighborhood gossip, meet strangers, carry on flirtations and courtship . . . Funerals and weddings are held in the church.[19]

Likewise, the Negro church is one of the most important institutions of social control. It is also the socially accepted channel through which the people give formal expression to their religious emotions.

> The church is the one outstanding institution of the community over which the Negroes themselves exercise control, and because it stands so alone in administering to their own conception of their needs, its function is varied. The religious emotions of the people demand some channel of formal expression, and find it in the church. But more than this, the church is the most important center for face-to-face relations. It is in a very real sense a social institution. It provides a large measure of the recreation and relaxation from the physical stress of life. It is the agency looked to for aid when misfortune overtakes a person. It offers the medium for a community feeling, singing together, eating together, praying together, and indulging in the formal expressions of fellowship. Above this it holds out a world of escape from the hard experience of life common to all. It is the agency which holds together the subcommunities and families physically scattered over a wide area. It exercises some influence over social relations, setting up certain regulations for behavior, passing judgements which represent community opinion, censuring and penalizing improper conduct by expulsion.[20]

In short, within the church the Negro finds not only his emotional satisfaction but also the joy of free expression of religious and other emotions. Moreover, within it, he not only nurtures his plan for social living but also compensates his present hard life for the happy next world. It is, thus, a place where he feels secure;[21] where he satisfies to a large degree other fundamental wishes.

The church, as any other social institution, cannot stand alone as a bulwark against inevitable changes. Everywhere the ecological and social forces are constantly at work to bring about modification in the institutional structures and functions and this change is always in the direction of achieving some sort of satisfactory equilibrium between opposing forces. In a society the secular transition takes its place far more readily and radically than the sacred. In this process the church must take its stand. Whether the church accepts, recognizes, or denies the existence of the opposing forces, the traditional structure and function are affected. There are far more powerful and continuous forces of ecological and economic processes at work to change the institution. The fact that the Negro church has attained its present status in the community is an evidence of the fact that it has been changing in the past. If at the present, the changes seem more striking than in the past, it is because the impact of the external forces—urbanization—is far more powerful in destroying the sacred order than the forces coming within the communal living of the Negroes on the plantation.

Affected by the impact of urbanization, the Negro church is losing ground and is becoming less of the center of group life as it was in the past.

> This is to some extent a part of the general decline of religion resulting from the development of science and the spread of knowledge; the Negroes are being influenced to some extent by the spread of modern ideas. But there are other and more important reasons, chief of which is the development of new avenues of expression and amusement. In the larger towns the churches no longer have a monopoly on social resources. There is better music to be heard outside of the church. Other men are better trained than the ministers and individuals no longer turn to the churchmen for information and instruction. Places of amusement are developing, and with them the churches cannot compete. The fraternal and secret orders take much time formerly devoted to the church and they satisfy certain exhibitionist tendencies even better than the church activity. There is a growing distrust of the ministers and their motives even among the masses of the race and a growing tendency to restrict the sphere of their influence to religious affairs and so reduce the power of the church in racial life.[22]

Is this general statement also true of the Delta? In the following pages answers are given to this question on the basis of empirical investigation.

In the past, the church in the Delta was irrefutably the center of Negro life and there was a unified attitude toward the church. Religious emotions, whatever form they assumed, were part of the Negro's life and personality. So compelling was the desire to express their religious emotion, the people came together wherever they could: they assembled in the seed house, in the barns, on the levees, and in any other available buildings on the plantation. Recalling the past, one informant says:

> Way back yonder, the atmosphere of things was very low, and churches for Negroes was very few. I remembers when we used to have church. Folks didn't call it church, most everybody called it a "meeting." We used to have meetings in the seed house, and the women really did shout.[23]

At present there is a duality of attitudes toward the church and minister on the plantation and they are coming more and more to the surface. There is a growing "pervasive skepticism of the pretensiveness of the church"[24] among the Negroes on the plantation. All of these changes are clearly manifested in the declining authority of the church and the minister and, in the growing disinterested attitudes of the plantation youth toward things religious and sacred.

Statistical evidences bear this point out: Twenty out of the one hundred families reported that they belonged to no church and not all of the families on the church roll participated in the church programs actively. This seems to indicate that relatively a small number of the individuals are under the direct influence of the church. This may also mean that the disciplinary measures of the church are on the decline.

There is an ample evidence that the younger people, having acquired a greater accessibility to the city, are losing much of their interest in the church. They are largely indifferent either as to the necessity of joining the church or, if they are already members, as to the putting out of the church. Joe Batts, who is twelve years old, comments:

> My folks took me to church near 'bout every Sunday that the weather be good. Used to like getting all dressed up in my Sunday clothes to go to church.
>
> Now I don't go no more. Naw, there ain't no harm in not going. Well, we got a pretty good preacher but he ain't no better than anybody else.[25]

The attitude of the youth toward the minister may be gained from noting the numerous comments and stories floating in the community about them. These comments ridicule ministers; they picture them as "worldly" men. One story runs as follows:

> A group of boys were shooting marbles on a Sunday morning. It just happened that the preacher came by, and he told the boys that they ought to be ashamed of themselves, down there shooting marbles on a Sunday.
>
> He told them, "You ought to be praying, and trying to go to heaven."
>
> Finally the preacher decided to go, and he asked the boys, "Say, where is the Post Office?"
>
> One of the boys jumped up and said, "Man, go on about your business; here you trying to show us the way to heaven, and you don't even know how to get to the Post Office."[26]

Another story is that:

> A little boy was plowing cotton. The field that he was plowing was fenced in with a road running along the fence. He was plowing with an awful mule. It wasn't long before the preacher came along the road, and he heard the little boy cursing the mule.
>
> He said, "Son, can't you plow that mule without cursing him?"
>
> The little boy said, "Naw, and you can't either."
>
> The preacher said, "Well you get over the fence and stand where I am, and I'll show you I'll plow this mule without cursing." The preacher started plowing, calling the mule a crazy rascal. And when he came back to the end of the row, he said, "I plowed that mule and didn't cuss him."

The little boy said, "Yah, but you told so many lies about him."

Then the preacher asked him, "There ain't much between you and a fool is there?"

The little boy said, "Naw sir, nothing but a wire fence."[27]

Another story has this to say:

One night a preacher was walking across a bottom, and a bear saw him. And by the time he saw the bear, the preacher started running. He ran and ran until he got to a hill, and finally set down on a stump. Then he took his hat and went to fanning.

He said, "Whew! God was all right just as long as it was just me in that bottom, but he wasn't worth a damn in a bear fight."[28]

The words to one of the songs in this area depict the same attitude. It is reported that the children objected to the use of the word "nigger" in a song, so the word "nigger" was changed to "preacher."

Even a Christian virtue is satirized:

There was a mother who was trying to raise a God fearing child. That meant when he told a lie, she would ask, or would get him to get on his knees and ask the Lord for forgiveness. The little boy was around ten years old. One day while the mother was in the kitchen cooking, the little boy was outdoors playing.

He was looking at a collie dog, and ran into the house, saying, "Oh, mother come here, come here, come here! Here's a bear out here."

The mother ran to the door and looked. She said, "Son, you ought to be ashamed, that ain't no bear, that's a collie dog. Now you have told a story; go upstairs and get on your knees, and ask the Lord to forgive you."

The little boy went on up to his room and stayed a little while. Then he ran back down, and said, "Oh mother, God says he couldn't forgive me for that, because he thought it was a damn bear himself."[29]

There are other factors making the minister a less important person in the community. One of them is the fact that he is not an integral part of the community and, thus, the relationship between the minister and his congregation lacks the personal nature. In the past, the very fact of the preacher's presence in the community led the people to live within a certain moral bound; the people feared that he might be around. The preacher of today does not work out in the field. He is a city man and is pastor of many churches. He offers his "spiritual guidance" only once a month and he does this for a sum of money. In brief, he is no longer a symbol of subtle personal control.

Some of the Negro ministers in the Delta are aware of the demoralizing influence of the city. Others, though few in number, try to reverse the inevitable changes by stressing the value of the traditional way of life. One of them is reported to preach sermons against formal education: he points out to the congregation how much better things were in the past, "when men and women wasn't out searching for idolatry and education." Another is known to say whenever he sees an educated person walking into the church: "I may not know Greek, and I don't know no Latin, but I know the Bible." When asked by others why he makes such a remark, he replied: "Have you ever heard of people in a community arming themselves against a mad dog, well maybe I is just doing the same thing." Still another preacher is known to attack anything new. Once a county agricultural agent tried to improve the quality of the hogs within the area by new breeding, but to this the minister replied: "Blood Don't Make Meat."

In a feeble effort to stem this inevitable tide, some ministers are adapting secular means. But this causes conflict within the church. Some of the members interpret these innovations to mean a decline in the spiritual values of the church: especially is this true of the older generation. Matilda Mae Jones, fifty years old, reveals her attitudes of disgust toward the changes. She says:

> Songs they sing in church now feel like fire burning. What do I mean? Well you know how fire burns; all fast and jumpy, and leapy like. Well that's just the way these swing church songs are now. Yes sir, most churches now call themselves getting on time or something the other. Getting so some churches got people that don't pray like they used to. Praying, I'm telling you, seem to be getting out of style. Just now, they got the Lord's prayer set to notes. Long time ago people used to sing, rock, and moan. Call that "rocking Daniel;" but now they only want you to rock when you rock up to put that money down. They done put a new touch on "Give Me that Old Time Religion," and now they got it in another tune. They don't have time to bring up "hallies" like "I'm Going Home on the Morning Train, The Evening Train May Be Too Late."
>
> We have here on this plantation, a band of good folks. You kin ketch some doing more wrong than right, but that ain't supposed to be no really fall down of the church cause it suppose to put you out for dancing and cursing. Of course nowadays we send officers of the church down to places to see how members do and the officers get in more devilment than the people we send them down there to watch. But us good Christians, we don't stand for them. And we knows that they do things, yes, but undercover. People just don't go to the church like they used to. The church ain't got no "pillars." The ones it done had done left here and gone North; and they got them youngsters in there now, and it ain't no center no more. The other day, the church lasted all the day, but that wasn't with preaching and singing. They was trying to get money.[30]

Another comments:

> Yah they is having box suppers at the church, but they don't have all them old kinds of things often. And when they gives them now, it's mostly for making money and not just for no sociableness.[31]

So changed are the people's needs that even the church entertainment shows a considerable degree of urban influence. For example, during the week of October 19, 1941, "Heaven and Hell" was on everybody's mind and many people ask one another: "Are you going to the Heaven and Hell Party given by the Y.M.C.A. and Y.W.C.A. Business Club of the St. John Baptist Church?" Others merely accepted it as inevitable. Mr. John Jones, the deacon, "lives a good life and plays around with a few women every now and then," says: "All the deacons of the church are going to stay away from the party. We are going to let them younger folks, you understand, have their way."

A one room school teacher adds:

> You really ought to go. I would be going myself, but now I gets tired at things like that. Well, I'll tell you—it's costing a dime to get in. You buys a ticket, which tells you which a way you'll be going: To Heaven or to Hell. No you can't go to both of them, I guess you got to do what the ticket says. Well, if you gets a ticket to Heaven, they serves you ice cream and cake, and you just sits around, and talks and maybe play games. However if you gets a ticket to Hell, they serves you hot cocoa, and red hot spaghetti, and they dance, play cards, checks, and do most anything.[32]

The fact that more plantation families belong to the burial association than to the church may be regarded as significant. Eighty families were on the church membership roll, while eighty-six families belonged to the burial association. A sociological import lies in the fact that the burial association is a secular institution. Sue Sampson's account may be considered as an indication of the present trend.

> I really think it's better to belong to it than the church. I have to abide by the laws. Members have to be particular about one another's wives and husbands. Well you see, you can give a person laws when he's going to the church but the lodge is the thing when it comes to compelling you to stick to your laws. You're compelled to meet, and you pays your dues. You just feel compelled to do that.
>
> Now I can tell you in just about a summary way, what the lodge mean to me. The other night, a old sad looking woman pinched me, and I was so mad that I almost wanted to kill her. I just hate for anybody to pinch me. I felt like cursing and killing her. If she just hadn't been a lodge member and just a

church member to me, I probably would have, but I couldn't do a thing cause she was a member of the lodge. So I just smiled and acted kind of nice.[33]

With the increasing participation in urban life, the mental horizon of the people is slowly expanding. George Johnson, a sixty-three year old Delta plantation Negro, who has been on this plantation all of his life as a sharecropper, now has a radio. He has learned to read and expresses rather articulately the effect of literacy on traditional religious notions. He says:

There ain't nothing I can do about this unfair life here, but I got my God. My kind of God allows for all things to be right, and you can't get around that.

You know one thing, I have a different opinion of church than I used to have. I don't believe that God is a personality. I just don't. There ain't many that believe that. Most of them see God all up in the sky with the stars, way up yonder, nobody knows where. I used to see him as a grey-haired old man. Yes sir, I've learned enough to know that God is spirit, and that people is always in the presence of it. People long time ago, took things they thought rather than what they knew. I know just like Jesus knew that God is spirit. The mind is God. Man has God with him all the time. It's the mind that's God.

Yes sir, thoughts is what man has to guide him and give him the way. The mind is the part of God that man possesses. That's the best way I can see. I can sit here in this room, covered round by these walls, and with my mind I can go and can see, think, and move myself in mind from all of this. And live and not feel so oppressed. Yet in the physical, I'm still right here in this room. You can do that, now can't you. The mind is your guiding light. It's your standard and there's coming a time when the way going to be open.

Now I learned all this like I told you. I just been to the sixth grade, but I ain't stopped learning yet. Yes sir, I learned all this in a book called *The Miracle Power*. The mind is the only thing that gives you real comfort, and makes you want to do things, and tells you what's right and what's wrong. Let me tell you God is that part that is within you.

If you look at me, you might think I ain't got much sense, but I done tried hard to learn things that can be proved. There ain't no such thing as seeing a ghost. God is the Spirit. I been having some books here that explains the stars, and I know that God isn't a grey-haired old man sitting up there.[34]

This account, albeit restricted to a single case is true also of others on the plantation. He speaks of reading a book, *The Miracle Power*, revealing the fact that the plantation Negro of today is partially literate. Significant, too, is the fact that he tries to learn things that "can be proven."

Things mentioned in the foregoing pages are indicative of the changes going on in the church, minister, and religious behavior in general. They may be summarized as follows: (1) ridiculing of ministers; (2) the people do not attend church as regularly as they once did; (3) the greater emphasis upon the pecuniary and secular values than upon the spiritual life of the community; (4) increased literacy, and finally, the plantation Negro church is losing its all inclusive functions through competition with other activities within and without the community. Today the plantation Negro has many alternatives of going to places other than the plantation church.

The data seems to indicate that the religious behavior of the plantation Negro is being affected by the participation of the community in the urban way of life. In the light of the foregoing discussion we can conclude that the Negro church is changing and yet the church, because it has had a long history, resists change. Thus, it still plays an important part in the social life of the plantation Negro; not, however, to minimize the slowness with which the institution is changing. In order, therefore, to give a comprehensive picture of the Negro church in the Delta some attention must be given to the factors which resist social change.

Theories on institutional change suggest that (1) certain aspects of culture are extremely tenacious of life (habits are slow to change); (2) a mature institution is a comparatively rigid part of the social structure—especially in so far as it enhances and protects interests; (3) observation of the cultural process indicates that artifacts, the traits of a material culture, are more easily diffused and more readily assimilated than similar items of a non-material culture; trade expands and changes, on the whole, more rapidly than religion; (4) it is inherent in the nature of an institutional system to create, and in part be supported by, a complex system of vested interests.

With reference to the Negro church in the Delta, facts and observations seem to indicate that sentiments and habits are the more powerful forces in the resistance of the church to change. Especially does this seem to be true in so far as the semi-literate Negroes on the Delta plantation are concerned. The Negro church, being the oldest institution, is really a basic habit in the lives of the people, and the sentiments associated with this habit give to the church a certain fixedness. Even though the plantation youth do not seem to show much interest in being "religious" or in things sacred, even to them the church is habit, in thought if not always in action. The older people on the plantation, undeniably feel that the church is the one thing that "good folks" should attend. On the plantations, there seems to be an increasing tendency among the Negroes to veer away from the type of religious belief which served to rationalize all existing hardships—toward the type which is particularly associated with the church or with the affiliation of others in church life, because the church is in accord with other institutions and particularly with the dominant institutions.

Another factor, subsidiary to habit and sentiment, is the fact that the plantation Negro church is tolerated and approved by whites in the area. Along with whites there are certain other "vested interest" groups such as the Negro ministers, who want to continue to live as ministers and enjoy the status of professionals in the community, at the ministers conferences they talk about co-operation between Methodist and Baptist so as to regulate free competition—so that they all can have churches and members. Also there is the growing threat of the sanctified church to the previous domain of Baptist and Methodist. In addition to the ministers, there are other functionaries and office holders in the church—who gain or possess additional recognition, and are definitely interested in the existence and permanence of the church for the status it affords.

$\sim$

CHAPTER IV

Changing Folk Tales and Folk Songs

The term "folk" is useful as a heuristic concept in making an objective investigation of plantation Negro life. What is the "folk"? The folk is a group which has folk lore and folk songs. Such peoples enjoy a common stock of tradition; they are the carriers of a culture. This culture is transmitted from generation to generation and is thus preserved orally rather than by the printed page. Moreover, such a culture is local: the folk has a habitat. Within the folk group there is a narrow margin of difference as to intellectual interest and attitudes.[35]

The southern Negro is generally regarded as a folk people, especially in the rural regions because here he has a local tradition and he makes folk tales and folk songs characterized as folk expressive behavior.

Expressive behavior as used in this study implies relatively primitive, untrained, spontaneous outbursts of emotions of an individual in the group life. It includes all those emotional outbursts expressed through the channels of the cultural media of the church, folk songs, folk tales, and the more recent expression of the "blues."

This chapter seeks to describe and analyze the conditions under which folk songs and folk tales have arisen; the effect of changed conditions on the present status of folk songs and folk tales; the extent of changes in expressive behavior relative to the changed conditions; and finally to offer a principle of explanation for the changes.

THE OLD ORDER

From all indications slavery life was folk life and the slaves were folk people,[36] to be sure. Some Negroes on more or less isolated plantations of today are more of a folk people than they are city people. Living within the political boundaries of the United States, these Negroes are, nevertheless, on the margins of our culture. They are folk people, and their culture, in so far as it differs from that of the majority of us in the United States, is a folk culture. The spirituals have been, and to a very considerable extent still are, the "natural expression" of the mind and the mood of the plantation Negro.[37]

In the past, the isolated world of the plantation gave an added significance to folk expressions—folk songs and folk tales. In regards to the plantation life, one informant says:

> Yes I can remember them old times. We just farmed, went to church, went visiting, stayed around home sitting by the fireside telling them old tales, and then that was just about all.[38]

And he relates one of these tales:

> Once upon a time, there was a rabbit and a fox who raised a peanut crop together. When the end of the year came, the rabbit and the fox decided that they would gather the crop. So Brer Rabbit told Brer Fox that he would take all of the crop that had grown underground, and the fox agreed to take all that had grown on top of the ground. The rabbit housed all of his peanuts in one room, and the fox had all of his vines in another. It wasn't long before the fox's vines started to getting dry on him, and every morning Brer Fox would come over to Brer Rabbit's house, and he would hear the rabbit singing: "Mr. Fox eats the vines, and I eats the peanuts." So Brer Fox got angry, and went into the rabbit's house to take the peanuts. But when he got in, all he found was hulls. The fox got to thinking, and he told that rabbit that next year when they raised a crop, he was going to take all of the crop that was underground. The next spring came around, and they planted corn. It wasn't long before the crop ripened, and the rabbit took what was on top, and this time the fox got what was under the ground. It didn't take the fox long to see that the rabbit had messed with him again, and he was angry. Brer Rabbit began to begging mercy, saying: "Oh Mister Fox—please don't bother me, I can tell you where we can get steak for the winter." So the fox said, "Where?" The rabbit said, "Right over there in the pasture." True enough there was a big old cow laying there. The fox and the rabbit went over. After they got near the cow, they figured and they figured on how to get that cow home. Finally the rabbit told the fox, "I'm going round and jump in the cow's face, and in the meantime, you tie your tail to the cow's tail so that when the cow gets up, you haul him by your tail." So the fox said that he understood. Then the rabbit jumped in front of the cow's face, and when he did that, that old cow jumped up lickety split, running and jumping with that fox tied to his tail. Over all the noise, you could hear the fox asking the rabbit, "How can I haul this cow home, when I can't even get my feet on the ground?" The cow hauled the fox away, and Brer Rabbit didn't have to worry about the fox no more. That's how come the rabbit is so smart today.[39]

In this way of life, custom was supreme and, in the precarious world of slavery, hopes, fears, and frustrations expressed themselves in songs.

Oh the time is so hard
Oh the time is so hard
Oh mother the time is so hard
Oh Lordy the time is so hard
Oh I'm going away
Where the time ain't so hard.[40]

These songs were shared collectively and, thus they were perpetuated.[41]

Sources of expressive behavior of the Negro are to be found in the immediate world of experience—his religious and work life—on the plantation. To him the Bible stories and the "church songs" were the chief sources of his knowledge and imagination; in some measure, they became the mainsprings of his social and work songs.[42] The field hands would move back and forth, up and down rows of tall cotton stalks, chopping and hoeing in the Spring, and picking with nine foot cotton sacks on their shoulders in the Fall—singing loudly and jubilantly all along the way:

Children, I got heaven on my mind
Children, I got heaven on my mind
And it keeps me singing all the time
All the time as I walk the narrow way
You can always hear me say
Children, I got heaven on my mind.[43]

Not all the folk songs, to be sure, were religious in nature. The production of cotton was the basic activity and it had affected, as one would expect, the nature of work songs. The songs of the field hands were mostly "made up" songs. The rhythm was dependent upon the immediate conditions and activities, and the words and intonations upon the individual singer's acquaintance as well as his feeling, emotion, and temperament.

The following is one of the songs sung in the cotton field. In singing, each participant soloist held his last note until it was picked up by either the next soloist or group of singers. Singing went on for about half an hour, not always the same song but the variation of the type given below:

Old voice singing bass:
I know it was the blood.

High soprano in another part of the field:
I know it was the blood.

Thirty or more voices:
I know it was the blood
I know it was the blood
I know it was the blood for me.

Young tenor:
One day when I was lost.

Young soprano:
One day when I was lost.

All:
One day when I was lost
He died upon the cross
I know it was the blood for me.[44]

Another example of this kind of work song is as follows:

I ain't going to raise no more cotton
I declare I ain't going try to raise no more corn
I ain't gonna raise no more cotton
I declare I ain't going to try to raise no more corn.

If a mule was running away with the world
Woe-ee-ee Lord, I'd let him go.[45]

Moreover, in the early days of the Delta plantations, the rampages of the Mississippi River occupied a great deal of the time and attention of the plantation Negro. While they worked to build the levees, the Negroes sang. "Them floods came, and they'd sing when the work was going on. The big boss wouldn't be there, but the walking boss would. Most time they sang about the walking boss, and everything round about, even making up songs about the mules."[46] This old informant continued: "The people lived in tents, and the levee camp looked like a village, miles long. Sometime one person be singing one thing and pass by somebody else, and if it fitted how the other fellow was feeling or thinking he would pick it up; just like he be walking along—quit talking and start singing."[47] And, he gave the following as an example:

Low-rainey and May
Hagar and Jane
Went out in the collar

And broke the iron bound hame
Now ain't that something.[48]

Other examples of the levee songs may be added here:

When I was working for Idaho
I had to walk everywhere I go
Now I'm working for George McVain
He give me a dollar
And I can ride the train.[49]

If I miss the long table (dinner table)
Up the road
I'm gone
If you don't believe I'm ducking
Count the days I'm gone.[50]

If Talley don't pay you
Charley Session will
I worked for Ben Talley
He won't pay
Went to Charley Session
He's the same damn way.[51]

The singing games also occupied an important part in folk expressive life, especially among the younger generation of the plantation Negroes. The words to some of these games are as follows:

Mr. Rabbit jump
Mr. Rabbit hops
Mr. Rabbit bit my tops
Now go on rabbit
Satisfy, satisfy, oh satisfy.[52]

Put on the skillet
Never mind the lid
Mamma going to make some shortening bread

Two little babies laying to the bed
One playing sick and other playing dead

Mamma love, papa love, sister love, brother love,
I do love shortening bread.[53]

THE CHANGING CONDITIONS

The abolition of slavery profoundly disturbed the traditional plantation Negro life: it brought about changes in land tenure, i.e., the relation of the laborer to the soil. The Negro had been a slave; with emancipation he became a sharecropper.[54] Moreover, many plantation Negroes were able, for the first time, to come into intimate contact with the city way of life, making the plantation no longer an isolated society.[55] And yet, a great number of Negroes once accommodated; the old way of life did not lose at once the sway of the old tradition. Broadly speaking, the older generation lived in the past, but there was a change affected by a new scheme of things. They sang the old hymns, but not with the same conviction. The younger generation, especially the ambitious, newly educated, "city wise" individuals, refused to sing the old songs. They desired to put all memories of slavery and the past behind. The result: the folk songs were either not created or, if created, they lacked the quality of the "natural expression" of slavery songs.[56] Each year the number of folk songs created diminished; the older forms of expression lost its function, disappeared, and is now replaced by music and story of a different sort.[57]

A set of conditions conducive to the development and the maintenance of folk tales, spirituals, and work songs is rapidly changing. These changing conditions exist in the continuum from the folk society to urban society. The change is definitely in the direction from illiterates to literates; from dependence upon rumor to newspapers and to other forms of printed matter, the popular magazine, and pamphlets, as well as to the moving picture; and from traditional folk songs, folk tales—animal tales and spontaneous group singing to popular songs and worldly stories.[58]

The present facts concerning the plantation Negro in the Delta seem to indicate that they are ceasing to be a folk people. They have at their command means whereby they can participate in the things falling beyond the world of plantations—the men by working in the sawmill, compresses, on the roads; the women by working as domestics. But, by far more significant are such as the going to the town of Clarksdale on Saturday and there to dance, gamble, or participate in other activities; in addition, there are radios, victrolas, and juke boxes to pick up popular songs. Through them the world of the outside comes to plantation Negroes.

Specifically the victrola, the radio, the juke box, the dance halls, the movies and the changes in technology make it possible for plantation Negroes to have a greater access to broader worlds of experience than ever before and this change reflects itself in their present day expressive life. In other words, there is a definite departure from the traditional folk life and the movement is definitely in the direction of the secular and the worldly. For one thing, the mechanical music box, commonly called the "Sea Bird" or "juke box" in this area, has almost completely displaced the old time guitar and "box pickers."

The Negroes on the King and Anderson plantation are acquiring formal schooling (the median last grades completed for family heads was 4.4 and for wives 5.9) and with it, they are becoming self conscious and losing to some extent their spontaneity in expression.[59]

The literacy of the plantation Negro is having its influence on the present day songs and stories of the plantation: it may indicate in a measure how the expressive forms of behavior disappear. Literacy enforces reflection and reflection makes the writer self conscious which in turn destroys the "natural spontaneity," the essence of folk creative activities. Since folk songs and folk tales are the literature of an illiterate people, one of the effects of the introduction of reading and writing among the Delta plantation Negroes is to destroy social psychological motivation for spontaneous songs and tales.[60]

The "gang singing" is rapidly disappearing. On one occasion when an old cotton picker was asked whether or not the people sang as they worked, he laughed as he repeated the question to others. In fact he yelled it out across the field. They all seemed to be amused by the question. "Ain't got no time for no singing," he ended. Moreover, the influence of mechanization is to make man "not want to sing." A young informant emphatically states:

There ain't nothing about a tractor that makes a man want to sing. The thing keeps so much noise, and you so far away from the other folks. There ain't a thing to do but sit up there and drive.[61]

Mechanization means the end of gang work, but there is a further effect. It changes the content of songs as shown in the following:

Friend, I'm married unto Jesus
And we's never have been apart
I have a telephone in my bosom
I can ring him up from my heart
I can get him on the air (radio)
Down on my knees in prayer
I don't know what I'd do without the Lord.[62]

Then, too, the relations of people are becoming less intimate and personal than formerly. The people are, as one informant says, "less sociable like"; with this change the original and spontaneous expressions are no longer transmitted as adequately as in the past.

Well there ain't much I can be telling you 'bout no songs and stories, but I can tell you this. When I was coming up people show did sing more than they does now. Folks was just more sociable like then, than they is now. There has been times when us kids used to get together all in the house, boys and gals, and we'd see which one of us could tell the biggest story. All of us just studying and thinking whilst we sitting there, lying, and singing, and telling them old riddles. But now these kids round here don't do nothing like that. Most of them go in the shows and around in town there in Clarksdale. Old folks do 'bout the same thing too, cause most of the time, that's what I does.[63]

One of the consequences of the city life is the decline of the customary controls on the one hand and the increase in the authority of the sheriff on the other hand. This secular authority is incorporated in a song.

> They was to try my case by four o'clock
> They tried my case before Lot
> They sent me to the farm and $25.00 fine
> I told Lot to kiss my behind
> Hard times, po' boy
> Hard times, po' boy
>
> Old Capt. Quinn I most all forgot
> He's the meanest old white man we had in the lot
> For $5.00 he'd run you right well
> For $25.00 he'd run you to hell
> Hard times, po' boy
> Hard times, po' boy
>
> When I was lying in Clarksdale jail
> I seen a louse as long as a rail
> Cut off his head nine feet from his tail
> And still he was long as a ten foot rail
> Hard times, po' boy
> Hard times, po' boy
>
> Old E. M. Eager, I most all forgot
> He was the meanest white man we had on the lot
> He'd put you on the farm without no bond
> And you bound to work on Eager's farm
> Hard times, po' boy
> Hard times, po' boy

They wakes me up about four o'clock
They gim' me a piece of bread as hard as a rock
And a piece of meat as thin as a knife
That is a poor supper for prisoners at night
Hard times, po' boy
Hard times, po' boy

Every six months the accessioner comes round
To see how we is faring on this old farm
He wears a suit of navy blue
For 99 years the shackles on you
Hard times, po' boy
Hard times, po' boy[64]

The tales which flourish today on the plantation are mainly the worldly stories. These stories have their place in the new scheme of living, peculiar to the young generation. For instance, John Jones, age 22, says:

These tales I'm about to tell you now, the old folks very seldom tells. To hear this kind you got to go around where there's a lot of young folks. They get to gambling and going on, and everybody be drinking. We don't tell these stories to everybody, cause we wouldn't let them in to hear. They only let them in that they wants. They gets in a room, start to drinking. One fellow tells one that he done heard and somebody else tells about another one. It'll go on that way all night long, then maybe the next night instead of going to the same place, go over to the "Gator" and have different follows there, and I tells the ones I heard; then they do the same and you can learn a lot of them that way. I guess I know around seventy or eighty. Here's one of the best: it is known as "Shine and the Titanic."

Give me your 'tention good people, and I'll tell you about the great Titanic and every fucker that was in it. On the 18th of May was a hell of a day. I received a letter from the old home town, that the big mother fucker was sinking down. The Captain and the Judge were up on the deck having a few words. Captain said, "Stand back judge lets have a few blows, because here comes Shine from down below." Shine said, "Captain, Captain, I can't get no steam. The water's running in my fire box by the great big streams." Captain said, "Shine old boy, that couldn't be so. For I have 144 pumps to keep the water out of the fireman's door."

Just then, Shine looked over the water as far as he could see. Fish in the ocean was saying, "Bring your black self to me." The Captain said, "Shine old boy, if you jump over-board you will surely drown. Shine, you will surely drown." Shine said, "I'd rather jump overboard than going round and round and to be on this big mother fucker and she's sinking down." Just then Shine jumped overboard and began to swim. The devil in hell turned over and grinned, said, "Shine old boy, you a long time coming but you welcome here." Shine looked over his shoulder and laughed and said, "Mr. Devil, you got to do some swimming to catch my black ass."

Just then a thousand white folks plopped up on the deck, and said, "Shine old boy, come to save me. I'll make you richer than a Shine can be." Shine says, "There's fish in the ocean, there's whales in the sea; hop your white asses overboard and swim like me." Just then the Captain's daughter plopped up on the deck with her slippers in her hand and her petticoat around her neck, had nipples on her tits as big as a plum, hairs on her cock make a dead man come. You could tell she was pregnant by the shape of her belly; her ass was shaking like a plate of jelly. She says, "Shine old boy, come save po' me. I'll give you anything your eyes can see." But Shine said, "Your petticoat look low and your words may be true, but there's women on the shore that's got better booty than you."

Just then Shine swam to the New York shore, where they was betting a dollar and a dollar more.[65]

In all probability this story and others like it are not indigenous: these stories reflect a considerable urban influence. The fact that on the plantation the stories about Hitler and other international characters exist, shows clearly that the plantation is no longer an isolated world. The plantation Negroes are becoming increasingly aware of world affairs.

> Hitler called the devil up on the telephone one day,
> The girl at central listened to all they had to say,
> "Hello," she heard Hitler say, "Is old man Satan at home?
> Just tell him it's the dictator who wants him on the phone."
>
> The devil said, "Howdy," and Hitler, "How are you?"
> "What can I do," the Devil said, "dear old pal of mine?
> It seems you don't need any help—you're doing mighty fine."
>
> "Yes, I was doing very good until a while ago,
> When a man named Roosevelt wired me to go more slow.
> He said to me, 'Dear Hitler, we don't want to be unkind.
> But you have raised hell enough, so you'd better change your mind.'

"I thought his lease-lend bill was bluff, and he could never get it through,
But he soon put me on the spot, when he showed what he could do,
Now that's why I called you, Satan—I need advice from you.
For I know that you will tell me just what I ought to do."

"My dear Hitler, there's not much left to tell,
For Uncle Sam will make it hotter than I can here in hell,
I have been a mean old devil, but not as half as mean as you
So the minute that you get here the job is yours to do."

"I'll be ready for your coming, and I'll keep the fires all bright,
And I'll have your room all ready when Sam begins to fight.
For I can see your days are numbered, and there's nothing left to tell.
So hang up your phone, get your hat, and meet me here in Hell."[66]

Some of the literature of the present day plantation Negro exists in the form of ballads. These ballads recount a tragic event relative to the lives of individuals in the community or may be a re-interpretation of an outside occurrence in terms of the local experience. Examples of these ballads are as follows:

Have you ever heard the song of Mary Steward?
On Saturday evening about two o'clock
Had to go to the ball to see that man
Buck Bliss throwed up
Will People knowed
He jumped behind Mary Steward
And she caught the load.[67]

The next ballad "Frankie and Albert" or "Frankie and Johnny" has been of national fame. However, the particular account provided in this area may represent a departure from the original version.

Frankie went down to the corner store
She called for a glass of beer
She asked the bar room tender, has he seen old Albert here
He is my man.

I ain't going tell you no story
And I ain't going to tell you no lie
Albert left here just a hour a go

With a woman called Alice Brice
He is your man, but he done you wrong

Frankie went down to the dancing hall
Found old Albert there
He was setting down in some cheap girl's lap
He show was buying some beer
He is my man, but he done me wrong

Albert, Frankie is calling
Albert said, I don't care
If you don't come to this woman you love
They will haul you away from here
He is my man, but he done me wrong

Frankie shot at Albert
She hit him some four or five times
She looked beyond the smoke of her gun
And she saw old Albert Flinging
He is her man, but he done her wrong

Albert got to his mother's house just about 12 o'clock
He said, open the door dear mother
All of your son is shot
I am your son and the youngest one
Albert's mother, she come to the door screaming and crying
She said, look here what that woman done to this darling son of mine
He is my son and the youngest one

Albert's mother sent for the doctor
And Albert layed across the bed
He said, All those bullets in my back
They show is pains me so
I am your son and the youngest one

Turn me over mother, over and over slow
All those bullets in my back
They show is pains me so
So I am your son and the youngest one

Albert's two sisters come running, screaming, and crying
Mother, the doctor told me one hour ago
Brother Albert's dying
He is your son and the youngest one

Rubber tire with buggy
Carry him away with a hack
They carry old Albert to a new graveyard
And see, they ain't brought him back
He was her man, but he is dead and gone

The sheriff 'rested old Frankie
And carried her 'gainst the courthouse wall
You might heard Frankie say
Judge he done me wrong

The judge come down off the stand
Had done plead little Frankie's case
He said Frankie you are free
Go and kill you another man
Albert was your man, but he is dead and gone
He was her man, but he done her wrong

Frankie went down to the graveyard
She fell down on her knees
Speak to me dear Albert and give my heart some ease
You was my man, but you dead and gone

Frankie went to the depot
To catch the evening train
She thought about what harm she done
And she slammed out her brains
Albert was her man, but now they both is dead and gone.[68]

The spirituals can no longer be said to be "the natural expression of the mind and the mood of the plantation Negro" of today, for the "natural idiom of the Negro proletarian, the blues" is used to express the plantation Negro's mood of the present. In the past the plantation Negro sang of "the Pearly Gates and Dem Golden Slippers" as a compensation for the hard life of this world, but now he expresses the realities of today by singing:

I'm just a po' cold nigger
Me and the white man and the boll weevil
All living off of cotton
The white man and the boll weevil
All getting fat
And here's po' me
I ain't got a dime
I'm just a po' cold nigger

Done worked all the summer
Done worked all the fall
And here comes Christmas
And I ain't got nothing at all
I'm just a po' cold nigger.[69]

With an increased participation in the urban way of life, the element of loneliness creeps into the plantation man's moods; and the "Blues" are the natural expressions of the urbanized Negro. The following blues composed by a plantation man reveal secular influence:

I wonder why the bald eager eager eagle
Keeps flying around my door
I wonder why the bald eager eagle
Keeps flying around my door
Everytime he fly round my door
I take the blues and hang my head and cry

I'm going to take the blues some day
And catch that long freight train
And ride my blues away
I wonder why my baby
She won't ever write to me
I guess because she live so far
Take $25.00 to send me a postal card

Bye bye baby
Maybe you'll be back home some day
Then I'll sing my blues away.[70]

Roll me over baby
Like you roll your flour dough

Roll me, roll me baby
Till I come back some more
Roll me baby
Like you roll your wagon wheel
Roll me in the morning
Roll me late at night
I want you to roll me baby
Like you roll your flour dough
Roll me baby
Till you drive my blues away.[71]

I ain't going raise no more cotton
I declare I ain't going try to raise no more corn
I ain't going raise no more cotton
I declare I ain't going try to raise no more corn

If a mule was running away with the world
Woe-ee-ee Lord, I'd let him go
I wouldn't tell a mule to "Get up" if he was setting in my lap
I wouldn't tell him to "Whoa" if it would hurt my old grand pap
All night long, hollering Whoa, Gee, Get Up—in my sleep.[72]

Moreover, the blues are now sung by boys and girls as they pick cotton.

Love me baby, love me
Love me baby, love me
If you don't love me baby
I'll throw myself in the sea
Where the fish and whales can fuss over me

Love me daddy, love me
Love me daddy, love me
If you don't love me daddy
I'll shimmy on the mountain top
Where everybody can fuss over me.[73]

The plantation Negro knows that "he has a place" in the city. He seems to delight in telling stories or reciting poems that show the Negro "besting the white man," as well as ridiculing the white woman.

I took a gal to the ball the other night
We hadn't got far before we got in a fight
The cop said, "Move on," but we didn't budge
Next morning, I had to say—Good morning judge.

The cop said, "Judge, this coon is a fad"
Then I pulled a thousand dollars out of my money bag
Put on my coat, and started toward the door
All the darkies in the court room began to roar
"I wonder what is that coon's game
The way he spends his money, why it's a shame
Is he from Klondike or from Maine, is what I want to know
He has got me a little worried, I must admit
The yellow gals will make a terrible hit
And I wonder, what is that coon's game?"

All the darkies held a meeting with a great delight
All the darkies went to court the next morning soon
To see what they did with that mysterious coon
The judge said, "One hundred dollars," and the darkies dropped dead
When I pulled out a roll of money as big as your head
I put on my kid gloves, and started for the door
Every darky in the court room began to roar
"I wonder what is that coon's game?"[74]

Even the ring plays and singing games of the youth are changing. In the past the words to one ring play were:

Turn to the East
Turn to the West
Turn to the one you love the best.

But its present version is:

Shake it to the East
Shake it to the West
Give it to the young man you love the best.[75]

Another popular ring play is called "Satisfied." Any number of adolescents may partici-pate in it at one time: they join hands going around in a circular fashion, singing and clapping their hands. The words to "Satisfied" are urban in content.

> See more little girl, satisfied
> Would you be mine, satisfied
> Have nothing to do, satisfied
> But to wash and iron, satisfied
>
> I got a man, satisfied
> And a sweetheart too, satisfied
> My man don't love me, satisfied
> But my sweetheart do, satisfied
>
> See and hear that train, satisfied
> Coming around that bend, satisfied
> Loaded down, satisfied
> With the Memphis men, satisfied
> See more little girl, satisfied
>
> Hello dude, satisfied
> Where you going, satisfied
> Going angling, satisfied
> Wedding dress, satisfied
> Big dog of chitterlings, satisfied
>
> If I live, satisfied
> Get to be twenty one, satisfied
> Going to marry me, satisfied
> Some woman's son, satisfied
>
> Little girl, little girl, satisfied
> Come and go with me, satisfied
> I'm going to town, satisfied
> To buy me some rope, satisfied
> Going to beat my man, satisfied
> To a buggy load, satisfied
>
> I got a letter, satisfied
> In the bottom of my trunk, satisfied

I ain't going to read it, satisfied
Till I get drunk, satisfied.[76]

Another consequence of urbanism on the Delta Negro life is the growing race consciousness and this growing race consciousness affects social and work songs and other folk expressive life. On this point Dr. R. E. Park said:

The Negro is now, to an extent that was never before true, awake. The Negro race, for good or for ill, is coming out of its isolation, and entering a world where it is exposed to all the contagious influences of modern life. The unrest which is fermenting in every part of the world, has gotten finally under the skin of the Negro . . . The disposition of the Negro in America to-day . . . no matter how slightly tinged with African blood, is to accept the racial designation that America has thrust upon him and identify himself with the people whose traditions, status, and ambitions he shares.[77]

The following poem exhibits this growing race consciousness on the part of the Delta Negroes:

Think something of yourself you crazy dunce
No matter if you was a slave once
Every nation done been a slave once
They didn't draw up and act a dunce
Think because you a nigger
You just can't get no bigger
But you always be on the bottom shelf
If you don't learn to think something of yourself

You think because you black
You got to always stay on the back
But you always be on the bottom shelf
If you don't learn to think something of yourself

You think cause your hair is knotty
You got to stay behind everybody
But you always be on the bottom shelf
If you don't learn to think something of yourself

Look at Booker T. Washington
And all them other great mens

They got on the top shelf
Why? Because they thought something of themselves
But you always going to be on the bottom shelf
If you don't think something of yourself

Don't feel yourself so embarrassed
Always be ready to reply
No matter what the other fellow say
Then you'll be on the top shelf
If you learn to think something of yourself.[78]

With the rise of race consciousness among Negroes, songs not only became less expressive and spontaneous, but the songs seem to have some purpose other than mere expression. Some of the purposes may be to ridicule whites, or to make subtle protest against the bulwark of racial segregation. The following songs may be indicative of subtle protests.

Captain's got a dungeon
Thinks he's bad
I'm gonna take that dungeon
Beat the captain's ass.[79]

White folks in the dining room
Fussing over turnip greens
Niggers in the kitchen
Fussing over cabbage greens.[80]

White folks ride from town to town
Niggers move from corn field to corn field.[81]

Captain is it dinner time
Give me my dinner, or
Give me my hold back time.[82]

And even more so, from some of the reasons given for preferring Negro music one can see clearly the growing race consciousness. It should be noted that these subjects have a little idea as to Negro music, but the fact that they conceive of certain music as being "Negro music" is an important expression of race consciousness; racial identity and loyalty. Some interview comments[83] reveal this point: "I don't like white music at all, it ain't nothing but trash."; "Nigger music anytime. Ain't no question. It's just the best.";

"Always will like Negro music, because that's my race and they can beat white singing any day."; "Negroes have a better voice for music. And too, they is my own color." One plantation youngster who constantly frequents the movies of Clarksdale says:

> I just like it best cause I can't get nothing out of what no white man do; but boy I get a thrill out of what the colored do. Because that's one thing they can do better'n white folks.

Jim Madison, a plantation sharecropper, who operates a secret bootlegging whiskey still on the plantation says:

> When I hear nigger music, I can say that's some of my color doing that. Sometimes I have the radio on and hear whites and turn it off.

Sue Flowers, one of the active members of the plantation church, comments:

> I like Negro music the best. Heard that before I ever heard any other, and I'm used to it and can enjoy it the best. It seems to me like praising God through my own color, and I loves my color and I'll go further to praise them than whites.

Sadie Sampson, one of the younger women of the plantation community, who feels that it is better to belong to the burial association than the church, says in regard to music:

> Negroes making music are of the same nature as my own, and to me they are the best in the world. No whites can sing to suit me. When a nigger sings, he sing with more emotion. Ain't nothing no white man do sincere.

THE EXTENT OF CHANGE

Today when a plantation Negro sings he is more likely to sing a popular song than a spiritual or folk song. Of the kinds of songs known by Negro sharecroppers on the King and Anderson plantation approximately forty-six per cent are popular songs. Of the total of two hundred and sixty, only eighteen per cent of the songs were spirituals; more than half of the songs were other than religious; and, the largest single category among popular songs was the blues.[84]

The sociologist may discover in these blues and other secular expressions the general outlook on life and attitudes on the present nature of relationships of the Delta plantation Negro. These secular songs record the reactions of the folk Negro to the outer world of the city. They reflect his disappointments, disillusionments, and yearnings for sympathetic understanding, intimacy, and full association and identification with the urban forms of life to the extent that he was integrated in the folk society. There are hardly any aspects of urban life or areas of contact that one cannot find touched upon in the songs and tales that they sing and tell today.[85]

Although both the younger and older generations are familiar with popular songs, the former is far more acquainted with them than the latter. The titles of favorite songs provided by the older generation are as follows:

Popular Songs

Good Morning Mister Blue Jay
Down by the Old Mill Stream
My Country Tis of Thee
Home Sweet Home
God Bless America
Yes Indeed
Jumping Jive
I Don't Want to Set the World on Fire
He's 1A in the Army
You Are My Sunshine
Daisy May
My Girlish Days
Walking by the River
Lets Dream This One Out
In the Shade of the Old Apple Tree
In the Mood
Good Morning to You
Lift Every Voice and Sing
Star Spangled Banner
Tuxedo Junction
Old Black Joe
Swanee River
I Want a Girl
Stardust

Hymns

I'm Going to Rest with Jesus
Lord When I've Done the Best I Can
I'm Sending Up My Timber
The Day of Jubilee
How Sweet the Name of Jesus Sounds
Come Ye That Love the Lord

The Old Rugged Cross
Have a Little Talk with Jesus
I've Heard of a Land
There's a Happy Land of Promise
Precious Memory
On Jordan's Stormy Banks
Just a Closer Walk with Thee
What a Friend We Have in Jesus
My Faith Looks Up to Thee
God Be with You Till We Meet Again
Forgive Me Lord
Silent Night
Father I Stretch My Hand to Thee
I'm Living for Jesus
Nearer My God to Thee
Somebody Touched Me
Near the Cross
In the Cross of Christ I Glory
Glory, Glory, Hallelujah
There's Rest for the Weary

Spirituals

O the Time Is So Hard
Little David Play on Your Harp
Steal Away
I've Heard of a Land Called Heaven
Wade in the Water Children
Go Down Moses
Swing Low Sweet Chariot
Bye and Bye
I'll Fly Away
Going to Put on My Travelling Shoes
Lord Stand by Me
Amen

Before This Time Another Year
Give Me That Old Time Religion
I Couldn't Hear Nobody Pray
Everytime I Feel the Spirit
Nobody Knows the Trouble I See
Keep Your Hand on the Plow, Hold On

Blues
Bumble Bee Blues
Confessing the Blues
St. Louis Blues
Walking the Floor Over You
In the Dark

Going to Chicago
Chauffeur Blues
Highway Blues
Sweet Home Chicago
How Long Blues
Lonesome Blues
Weary Blues

Lullabys
Hush Little Baby Don't You Cry

Work Songs
Working on the Levee

Of the favorite songs of the older generation nearly twenty-nine percent were popular songs (songs definitely other than church or religious songs); thirty-two per cent, hymns; twenty-two per cent, spirituals (together fifty-four per cent); fourteen per cent, blues; and two per cent lullabys and work songs.

In contrast to this the younger generation listed more than twice the number of blues as given by the older generation. Thirty per cent as favorites, and thirty-eight per cent popular songs; eight per cent, hymns; twenty-two per cent, spirituals; and two per cent work songs. This is illustrated in the following listing:

Popular Songs
Carolina Moon
Carry Me Back to Old Virginia
Coming through the Rye
Darkness on the Delta
Drink to Me Only with Thine Eyes
Girl of My Dreams
Going Home
Honey Suckle Rose
I Love You Truly
Is It True What They Say About Dixie
Kiss Me Again
Lazy Bones
Lost in a Fog
Minnie the Moocher
My Blue Heaven

My Old Kentucky Home
My Wild Irish Rose
Negro National Anthem
Nobody's Baby Now
The Object of My Affection
Old Black Joe
Old Spinning Wheel
O Susannah
Rainbow Round My Shoulder
She'll Be Coming Round the Mountain
Sitting on Top of the World
Stormy Weather
Sunny Boy
Sweet Sue
The Man I Love
Sweet Jennie Lee

The Johnson Gals
When You and I Were Young Maggie
Yesterday

Hymns
Amazing Grace
Bless Be the Tie That Binds
Father I Stretch My Hand to Thee
How I Love Jesus
I'm Sending Up My Timber
My Jesus I Love Thee
The Old Ship of Zion

Spirituals
Ain't Going to Study War No More
Come Along Little Children
Death's Black Train Is Coming
Done Got Religion at Last
Go Down Moses
I'm Going Home on the Morning Train
I Shall Not Be Moved
If I Could Hear My Mother Pray Again
In That Great Gitting-Up Morning
Listen to the Lambs
Mary Martha, in the Garden
Nobody Knows the Trouble I See
O Mary Don't You Weep
O Didn't It Rain
O Freedom
Roll Jordan Roll
Standing in the Need of Prayer
Steal Away
There's a Great Camp Meeting
Wade in the Water

Blues
Banny Rooster Blues
Basin Street Blues
Beale Street Blues
Biscuit Baking Woman
Black Gal Blues
Black Snake Blues
Careless Love
Digging My Potatoes
Evil Woman Blues
Fur Trapper Blues
Going to Move to Kansas City
Hell Broke Loose in Georgia
Highway 61 Blues
How Long Blues
Livery Stable Blues
Mean Mistreater Blues
Milk Cow Blues
Railroad Blues
Railroad Rag
Rattlesnake Blues
Salty Dog Blues
St. Louis Blues
Sugar Mamma Blues
Talking Blues
Tin Can Alley Blues
T. B. Blues
Walking Blues

Work Songs
Water Boy
Working on the Railroad

Other evidences of the changes may be gained from the following list of favorite dance pieces on the plantation. It is important to note that none of these favorite dance pieces are the traditional and local music. They show clearly the influence of movies, juke boxes, and radios.

Basin Street Blues

Boogie Woogie Piggy

Blue Champagne

Biscuit Baking Woman

Chattanooga Choo Choo

Confessing the Blues

Daddy

Flatfoot Floogie

Fur Trapper Blues

Going to Chicago

Here I Go Again

I Don't Want to Set the World on Fire

I Want a Big Fat Mamma

It All Comes Back to Me

Mamma Don't Tear My Clothes

Moonlight Serenade

One O'Clock Jump

Slide Mr. Trombone

Stop Pretending

Sugar Mamma

Yes Indeed

And, too, the favorite radio musicians were: The Golden Gate Quartet, Cab Calloway, Artie Shaw, Benny Goodman, Count Basie, Duke Ellington, Glenn Miller, Tommy Dorsey, Gene Autrey, Roy Acuff and his Smoky Mountain Boys, Memphis Minnie, Sister Rosetta Tharpe, Lanny Ross, and Mary Lou Williams.

Even though worldly expressions are supplanting the old, there is an opposition by the older people toward the inevitable transition. This phenomenon is shown by the replies of ninety-six of the one hundred heads of Negro sharecropper families on the King and Anderson plantation. Of the total, twenty-four individuals felt that "no kind of song" was wrong to sing; seventy-two said that it was wrong to sing blues, jazz, or popular songs; and of the last group, ten stated specifically that no Christian should sing the blues. Moreover, as these people come to use new cultural traits, they develop inevitably a new sense of appreciation for them; while the basis of appreciation expands as the powerful influence of imitation and fashion are more strongly felt than formerly.

Some cultural traits diffuse very slowly, but such things as news, rumor, and songs seem to diffuse with uncanny rapidity; "instances have been reported," writes Dixon, "where a new song has spread completely across a continent in a single year."[86] If such is the case even in preliterate societies how much more true it would be in modern society.

We may infer safely from the foregoing discussion that as Clarksdale grew as the trade and culture center, it supplanted the dominance of the old plantation. In the city of Clarksdale, opportunities for the plantation Negro to participate in the urban way of life have increased. Other factors, such as the development of the highway, the coming of the radio, the automobile, the movie, the juke box and juke joints, furthered the contact opportunity for Negroes on the plantation.

PRINCIPLE OF EXPLANATION

The basis for the spontaneous expression of plantation folk was the primary and isolated group life as well as the restraints imposed upon the Negro slaves by the plantation institution. This primary group life has been destroyed by the historical factor of emancipation and more powerful forces of urbanization and mechanization. With these changes the folk expressions of the plantation Negroes have been affected: spontaneity of expression is rapidly supplanted by conscious expressions. In comparison with the transition in the religious life as already noted in Chapter III, these more spontaneous and natural expressions are being affected far more dramatically as plantation Negroes participate widely in the way of the city. How may this change be best explained?

Professor R. B. Dixon offers a useful framework for the understanding of what has and is occurring to the folk life. He says, "diffusion . . . depends primarily, on the triad of opportunity, need, and appreciation; if one of these is lacking, the diffusion is unlikely to take place."[87] He is speaking basically of secondary diffusion: culture traits are diffused by other means than primary contacts. In modern society, much of the diffusion is of this type. Today the radio, newspapers, telegraph, movies, highways, automobiles, railroads—make the opportunity for diffusion greater than ever before. The needs are also expanding with alteration in group life. The needs are further augmented as Negroes come to town to buy or to work, or just come with the interest in "seeing." The movies bring ideas of world events and also awareness of the fads and fashion of the outer-world. The radio, the juke box, and other city things come to be more and more daily necessities of the plantation Negro in so far as "having a good time" is concerned. And even more important is the fact that plantation Negroes come in greater numbers to Clarksdale and with this their needs increase. With the increase in needs and the resulting satisfaction of these needs, there is a concomitant phenomenon of appreciation. The fact that so many of the worldly things are embodied in the songs and stories the Negroes now sing and tell indicates a growing sense of appreciation. Then, too, the plantation Negroes, even though they may be in very dire economic circumstance, have large collections of jazz records together with victrolas or radios; all this bespeaks of their worldly interests and appreciation. The fact that the "juke joints" are now a part of the cotton field, or that the church now gives "Heaven and Hell parties," indicates that the city is not too far away in their daily experience.

To sum up: the extent that urban forms of expression have been diffused to the Delta—that they have supplanted much of the folk songs and folk tales—may well speak of the impact of the city upon traditional life of the Negro. It may be further stated that the urban culture had the opportunity to spread, came to be needed, and is now appreciated. This diffusion has gone on without the interference of conservative elements, since both the folk songs and folk tales were less structuralized or less formalized aspects of Negro life on the plantation.

SAMUEL C. ADAMS

CHAPTER V

The Conclusion

It has been stated in the hypothesis of this study that: The greater the participation of a people in city life (which means a greater drive to learn city ways of life), the greater is the change in the traditional culture. With the changed conditions of living, there is a greater reward—both economic and social—to be had from accepting new ways than from adhering to the old ways. However, in this process of culture change there is a difference; some of the habits are more persistent than others and in some areas of group life social constraints and conservatism are more powerful than in other areas. Thus, it would seem that the change is more pronounced in the area of less structuralized human behavior than in the institutionalized, for in this area of human activities fashions and fads have their full sway. In the case of the institutionalized area of the culture, the acculturation is blocked by the vested interest groups and by more enduring group habits and sentiments.

In an effort to test the validity of this hypothesis one hundred Negro sharecroppers on the King and Anderson, a Delta plantation community, were studied. Clarksdale, Mississippi, the trade and culture center of the Delta, was treated as the seat of urban influence. Specifically, the frequency of visits to Clarksdale, the kind and extent of activities entered into, the number of radios and automobiles possessed, indicated changes in attitude toward the city and were regarded as measures of the degree of participation in the urban life.

Church activity, for this study, represented the institutionalized area of the culture; while folk tales and folk songs—the area of less structuralized human behavior. Data on the religious behavior of the Negro were obtained from ministers, deacons, the churches, the non-churched, and by participant observation. Data on folk tales and folk songs were obtained through informal listening and recording of songs and tales; by interviewing the older and younger generations of the community. These cooperating individuals gave information on their past and present preferences in the kinds of music, tales, and stories. By the use of family schedules; by living on the plantation and participating in community activities; socio-economic data on families and some idea of existing attitudes and values were obtained.

The data indicates, that with the U.S. highway running through its center; with the increasing use of technic ways—the plantation is not isolated, being not only accessible to the city—but the plantation Negro has access, participates, and experiences the city way of life found in and radiating out of Clarksdale. Also, city Negroes come to the plantation as day laborers, to seek pleasure and to escape the curfew and liquor laws of the city. Thus, innumerable processes are at work in the lives of the Delta Negroes. These processes are not unique but are a part of those ongoing processes of social change attributable to urbanization.

Social change in the Delta can best be told in terms of the changes that have taken place in the modes of communication and transportation. In the Delta, the changes in the modes of communication and transportation relative to social change seem to have progressed through three eras. First the era of the river culture—which marked the height of the plantation institutions. The plantation, for the most part, was the unit through which most of the needs of the people were produced. For the Negro this was largely an isolated world. The church had an important place and real meaning in community life. The spirituals, folk songs and folk tales were common forms of expression. Second, the era of the railroad is characterized by lesser isolation, more intensive cultivation, evidences of beginning Negro race consciousness, the distinction between worlds of respectability and wickedness, the tendency toward the substitution of spontaneous traditional forms of expression (spirituals) to standardized forms (songs from hymnals). Third, the era of the highway meant that no longer was the movement of people restrained by poor means of travelling, motor driven machinery was introduced, alternatives to going to church existed, the radio, the juke box, and other city-made technic ways came to be important in the lives of the plantation Negro. Thus, the area of opportunity for participation in city life increased.

With the participation in urban life new patterns of meanings and standards emerge. For one thing, the Negro church is losing its traditional functions. The changes going on in the church, minister, and religious behavior of the plantation Negro is indicated by: ridiculing of ministers; declining rates of attendance; greater emphasis upon pecuniary and secular values than upon the spiritual life of the community; and, the substitution of other activities for the past all inclusive functions of the church. And yet, owing to the fact that the church, which has been and still is to large degree the central institution in Negro life, there are certain factors of institutional inertia. Vested interests, the rigidity of sentiments and habits, social and cultural sanctions of its institutional role, all tend to resist changes, thus causing the change to be slow and not complete.

The spontaneous expressions, the Negro folk tales and folk songs, are less structuralized than the church. They are therefore disappearing and are rapidly being supplanted by city forms of expressions. The radio, newspapers, movies, highways, automobiles, railroads—along with the fact that the basis for diffusion—opportunity, need, and appreciation—existed within the culture life of the plantation Negro offers a principle of explanation to account for the changes. The extent that urban forms of expression have been diffused to the Delta; that they have supplanted much of the folk songs and folk tales, may well speak of the impact of the city upon the traditional life of the Negro. Today when a plantation Negro sings he is more likely to sing a popular song than a spiritual or folk song. In short, in this area of the culture, the changes seem to be more complete.

Although this study is in no way complete, the findings of this study give an added validity to the general theory of social change. To sum up: the findings of this study indicate that changes are occurring in the lives of the Delta Negroes; that these changes are associated positively with the increased participation in the ways of the city; that the increasing prestige of the city offers greater rewards by identification with it, thus, underlying much of the present attitudes toward change; that these changes are more complete in the non-structuralized culture of the folk songs and folk tales than in the formalized institutionalized behavior of the Negro church.

BIBLIOGRAPHY

Bossard, J. H. S. *Social Change and Social Problems* (New York: Harper & Bros., 1938)

Caldwell, E., and White, M. *You Have Seen Their Faces* (New York: The Viking Press, 1937)

Dixon, R. B. *The Building of Cultures* (New York: Charles Scribner's Sons, 1928)

Dollard, J. *Caste and Class In a Southern Town* (New Haven: Yale University Press, 1937)

Federal Writers Project. *Mississippi* (New York: The Viking Press, 1938)

Frazier, E. F. *The Negro Family in the United States* (Chicago: The University of Chicago Press, 1939)

Hallowell, A. I. "Sociopsychological Aspects of Acculturation," in R. Linton (ed.), *The Science of Man in the World Crisis* (New York: Columbia University Press, 1945)

Johnson, C. S. *Growing Up In The Black Belt* (Washington: American Council on Education, 1942)

Johnson, C. S. *The Negro in American Civilization* (New York: Henry Holt and Co., 1930)

Johnson, C. S. *Shadow of the Plantation* (Chicago: The University of Chicago Press, 1934)

Johnson, C. S., and Associates. *Statistical Atlas for Southern Counties* (Chapel Hill: The University of North Carolina Press, 1941)

Johnson, C. S., Embree, E. R., and Alexander, W. W. *The Collapse of Cotton Tenancy* (Chapel Hill: The University of North Carolina Press, 1935)

Kolb, J. H., and de S. Brunner, E. *A Study of Rural Society* (New York: Houghton Mifflin Co., 1940)

Lee, G. W. *Beale Street* (New York: Ballou Co., 1934)

Lundberg, G. A. *Social Research* (New York: Longmans, Green and Co., 1942)

Malinowski, B. *The Dynamics of Culture Change* (New Haven: Yale University Press, 1945)

Masuoka, J. "Social Change and Progress in Race Relations in the South," *Social Forces* (Forthcoming Issue)

Ogburn, W. F. *American Society in Wartime* (Chicago: The University of Chicago Press, 1943)

Ogburn, W. F. "Social Change," *Ency. of Soc. Sciences*, III.

Olmsted, F. L. *A Journey in the Seaboard Slave States* (New York: G. P. Putnam's Sons, 1904)

Park, R. E. "Negro Race Consciousness as Reflected in Race Literature," *American Review*, I, No. 5 (1923), 505–516.

Park, R. E. "Reflections on Communication and Culture," *The American Journal of Sociology*, XLIV (September, 1938), 204–205.

Puckett, N. N. *Folk Beliefs of the Southern Negro* (Chapel Hill: The University of North Carolina Press, 1926)

Redfield, R. *Folk Culture in Yucatan* (Chicago: The University of Chicago Press, 1941)

Redfield, R. *Tepoztlan, A Mexican Village* (Chicago: The University of Chicago Press, 1930)

Reid, Alice C. "Gee's Bend," *M. A. Thesis* (Nashville: Fisk University, 1941)

Reuter, E. B. *The American Race Problem* (New York: Thomas Y. Crowell Company, 1938)

Stanley, H. M. *My Dark Companions and Their Strange Stories* (New York: Charles Scribner's Sons, 1893)

West, J. *Plainville, U.S.A.* (New York: Columbia University Press, 1945)

Wirth, L. "Urbanism As a Way of Life," *American Journal of Sociology*, XLIV, No. 1, (1938), 1–24.

Wirth, L. "The Urban Society and Civilization," *American Journal of Sociology*, XLV, No. 5, (1940), 743–755.

Work, J. W. *American Negro Songs* (New York: Howell, Soskins & Co., 1940)

APPENDIX A

Family Schedule and General Musical Questionnaire
(Folk Culture Study)

Schedule No.	_____
Date	_____
Investigator	_____

Name of head
of Family _____ Post Office
Address _____ Community _____

Name of each person in Household	Relation-ship to head of Household	Sex	Age	Marital Condition	School grade Completed	Attending	Name of School
1.							
2.							
3.							
4.							
5.							
6.							
7.							
8.							

Members of family living away from home	Present Address
1.	
2.	
3.	
4.	

Economic Status

Occupation	Place of Employment	Weekly wage or yearly Income	Length of time on Present job	Other occupations followed
1.				
2.				
3.				
4.				

Do you own a home: _____ Own a farm? _____ Amount of rent paid _____

If ownership is encumbered how much is the mortgage? _____

Housing

No. of Rooms _____ Do you own an automobile? ____ make _____ model _____

Construction _____ Do you own a radio? _____ piano? _____ victrola _____

State of Repair _____ organ? _____ Other musical instrument? _____

Painted _____

For Farm Families

Tenure _____ No. of acres cultivated _____ Work stock owned _____

What does the farm produce for family consumption? fowls _____ meat _____

milk _____ vegetables _____ fruit _____ other _____

Community Status

Place of birth _____ How long have you lived in this community? _____

How long in Coahoma County? _____

Places family has lived outside the county _____

	Organizations to which members of the family belong		Recreation of members of family	
Name of Organization	Members of Family Belonging	Kind of Recreation	Location of Recreation Center	Frequency of Visits to Center

1. _____

2. _____

3. _____

How often do you go to Clarksdale? _____ For what purposes do you go there?_____ How often do you go to Memphis? _____ Other places outside the community visited _____ Events responsible for visits _____ Do you hold any offices in church, organizations, or clubs? _____ What? _____

Musical Questionnaire

What kind of music do you like best? _____ Why? _____

What kind of instrument or instruments do you like the best? _____

What are your favorite songs? _____

What kinds of songs do you know? _____

Do you like to dance? _____ If not, why? _____

What are your favorite dance pieces? _____

What songs do you think are wrong to sing _____

Who is your favorite musician? (local or radio) _____

Which do you prefer, Negro or white music and why? _____

_____

APPENDIX B
Conflict and Adjustment

Wherever social changes occur there are problems of conflict and adjustment. This aspect of the changing Negro life in the Delta was not treated in the body of the thesis for it was not the problem of study. However, incidental to the gathering of data on the changing church and folk expression certain attitudes of the informants revealed conflicts and adjustments. The incompleteness of the data prevents systematic organization, thus, the attitudes are presented as individual accounts.

ATTITUDES TOWARDS THE JUKE HOUSE

Within the body of the thesis numerous references are made to the juke box and to the juke house (dance house where the mechanical music box provides the music). The attitudes of the people toward it, ranging from disgust to approval, reveal conflicting values in the community.

One informant said in disgust:

> They got a juke right up there at the church. The juke's right there, and the church's right there. I think it's a disgrace, that's what I think. Yes sir, I think blues is wrong to sing, especially for a Christian. No folks round here who calls themselves Christians should sing the blues.

Another has accepted the juke as inevitable and says:

> Well son, lots of folks think it's very degrading. We got two kinds of houses out here where the folks goes. One of them houses is the church house, and the other is a juke house, and the members of the church house—they encourages that sort of thing by coming to it. Now for me, I don't see no harm in it. That juke house been down here since 1939, and they does the same thing at one place as they does the other; at the juke house and the church house alike. They drink whiskey, they drink beer, they swear, and they gamble at the church—and they gamble at the juke. You knows good and well that thing couldn't of stayed and been going there in that cotton field if some of the folks hadn't been going there. And let me tell you, the church peoples most of the time makes the crowd up at the juke. They is suppose to put you out of church if a professing Christian goes to that kind of a place, but fellow let me tell you, quickest thing to do to get put out of the church round here, is to not pay the

money. Now the first thing God say was to love one another and you can do anything and go anywhere you wants just so you do good. Jesus himself went everywhere.

ATTITUDE TOWARD TOWN AND MORALITY

When I was a girl I didn't go into town and stay out all of the night. Mothers just not raising their girls right; allowing girls to smoke cigarettes, ride automobiles, drink, and do everything. And the church don't say nothing about it. These younger folks calling themselves having a good time. They drinks whiskey, they gambles, and they goes to town. Hasn't always been that way. The folks long time ago used to have spelling bees and things to go to right here in the community, but since that town done got to be what it is, spelling bees and that sort of things is too slow.

What we got to do now is git us something of our own, but with all this new day—folks just going. I guess we all just people though. Now folks used to go to the plantation store for everything. It still has everything just like it used to. It still has everything from tacks for shoes when you living to caskets for you when you dead. Peoples goes to town don't have no need to go. Some folks say they goes to town cause you need a friend in more than one place. People living on a farm rather go to town than anything. They want to go to town to raise all kind of devilment. And you know there ain't very much right in our cities now. There used to be special places to raise the devil, now the whole city. They got a class now that oughta be called the New Rising Devil Class.

ATTITUDE TOWARD THE PLANTATION YOUTH
AND THE INFLUENCE OF MOVIES

Lots of these youngsters just act like they in a flock. Most of these youngsters go to the show. And some parents don't mind and don't care; have whole lots of families where the child is the head rather than the parents. Yes folks now a day just talking about the child got to have his pleasure. They think there ain't no harm at just looking at the picture, nor if they is dancing and cutting up, or straddle the fence.

Yes, I goes to town practically all the time, but let me tell you, I seldom goes there with anything worth any count on my mind. Now and then I shows myself round in town, but most of the time I goes to the pitcher shows. I like to see the cowboys, and them colored peoples that they show from Chicago. They's really a kill.

THE CONFLICT AND ADJUSTMENT OF A PLANTATION BOY
WHO WENT TO MEMPHIS

Well I tell you, I didn't like Memphis. There was too many folks just sitting around. Just sitting and not hitting a lick. I didn't like that. It ain't like what I used to be seeing. They gotta live, and they going to live off the poor folks who was slaving. I just could not get used to that; kind of frightened me. But I tell you this, I likes Memphis this way. There ain't as much prejudice. You don't have to merry bow as low there to the white man as you does in Mississippi. You work for wages there. You go at a time, and you quit at a time. I couldn't take Memphis for long though. It was too big for me, too many folks knew more'n I did and I went back home.

When I got back, I knew all about machinery and things like that; so they got me to driving a tractor on the plantation. They got many Negroes driving them things now. But let me tell you, I was different than them other fellows down there. That old agent up there make them drive night and day. I ain't going to drive no man's tractor past no five o'clock, and I wouldn't start before seven-thirty. Would just lay up in bed with my big black self, and just don't work 'fore no seven-thirty.

The agent come out to me one morning and say, "Boy, where in the hell do you think you are? Down here, don't you know a nigger works from 'kin' to 'kaint'?" I told him, show—he knowed I done live down here, and what he think he mean by 'kin to kaint.' So he come sneering back, telling me that I was supposed to do like he say. I just told him that I wasn't one of them 'kin to kaint' niggers. I told him that when I worked for the man that owned these plantation—in the city, I went to work at 7:30 and quit 5:30 and now that I'm down here on his place, I'm doing the same thing. And I told him that I was spose to get $2.50 a day. He couldn't say nothing much, cause he knowed that I knowed the head man. Other niggers was so surprised that I was making money. One time, he tried to get me anyway, but I messed him all the time. Ha, Ha; I remember one time, early in the morning he come down to the shack. Knocked on the door, yelling "nigger, why ain't you in the field. It's past 7:30." I yell back,—man you wrong, it ain't no 7:30. He pulls out his watch saying, "Looky here, it's past 7:30." I say, naw man—at 7:30 I be's in your field, not a minute later. I pulls out my watch, it say six something. So he say come on lets go up here to the store and see. I go jumped up in his car, and we goes up to a store that has an electric clock and he sees mine's right. I guess he knowed all the time.

ATTITUDE TOWARD THE ENLIGHTENMENT OF THE NEGRO:
AND HOPES FOR CHILD

The town, the radio, newspapers, awareness of their plight, and the larger worlds of experience create within some plantation people a more ambitious perspective in so far as race consciousness, education, and hope for the future. One informant says,

> Us colored folks just now really getting the light. The farm bureaus give information concerning raising our own food stuff, hogs, cows, and talking about the "living at home plan." And another thing they come out and give pitcher shows at the church, and come to your house and can your meat for you in tin cans. Now the colored person got a chance. The daylight just been turned on. What we got to do now is git us something of our own.

The plantation people are becoming increasingly interested in the education of their children. "I learned long time ago the 'vantage of education. I ain't got but one child; that's the main reason I ain't got no more, cause I'm going to see her in school. Naw sir, I don't even include her in my crop. I wants her to make the 12th grade and I'se taking out insurance for her to go off to college."

ATTITUDES OF CONFLICT AND ADJUSTMENT
IN RACE RELATIONS ON THE PLANTATION

Much of the traditional forms of relationships between whites and the plantation Negro still remain, but there are evidences of changes at the present.

A departure from the traditional paternalism of the plantation system is revealed in the following account: "Old man Anderson ain't as bad as they say, but you know he ain't going to vivy up [sic] and give you something for nothing. Anyways the best way to handle him is to be around him as least as possible. That's the way he gets most folks. Yah he'll give you money on a car and let you take up most nigh all the food stuff you need, and even that you don't need. Now me, I don't get nothing from him, that way I ain't got no account at his store. Even at that he had me counted up for $420.00—says it was for seed and planting and things like that, and they airplane sprays your crop. I guess maybe he's right, it might done cost him that much. Now supposing I had gotten food, meat, money for a car, and things like that—well that white man woulda been owning me. That's just the way most of these folks round here is. My notion is to take as least from the white man as I can—that way when he get through taking from me, as I knows he is show to do; there's something left for me, but if I takes from him (food, etc.) when he starts taking from me, he just takes it all."

Conflicts are recurrent and the habits are in clash with the customary ways of behavior. One informant relates an incident. "I remembers one time when I couldn't even leave this place. Well it come about once when I was cropping here and was doing pretty good. Had me three head of mules and most near the makings of 'bout fifty bales of cotton in the field. I was driving my car across the lot. An agent there come over and up and tell me that I looks like I'm trying to run over him. He kept on talking about a little old nigger getting to buy a car. And he shoved me through the window of my car, and kept cursing. Man, I didn't say a word, just reach down by the seat in the car getting that old 32–20 of mine. My cousin who was sitting there by me, started yelling, "Oh Lordy, oh Lordy! Please don't." That white man got so scared he ran. The news that a nigger had run a white man with a gun just spread like hell, and I started figuring I had better get out. That night the old man over the plantation came up and told me that I better not think of getting away because no nigger had better not be thinking he could do nothing and get away. Told me to stop telling other folks that I pulled a gun on a white man. He told me also that if any Negroes asked me about it, 'tell them that it was a lie.'

This change in attitude is also observed in other areas of activities. The following incident is indicative of a departure from the traditional pattern of race relations on the plantation: a white agent yelled up to a Negro on the cotton wagon, "Come on boy— spruce 'em up. You ain't doing a damn thing. Looks like I got to come up there and beat your ass 'fore you going to do anything." The Negro answered, with a slightly emphatic drawl, "Listen here white man, you got that wrong. You ain't going to beat nobody."

~

APPENDIX C

Interview with Ola Perkins

Ola Perkins, age thirty-five, Negro sharecropper on the King and Anderson plantation, is quite a pathetic looking creature—all blind in one eye and barely squinting out of the other. She is brown skin in color, weighs about one hundred twenty-five pounds, and is almost sixty-three inches tall. at the time of the interview she was dressed like "Joseph's Coat" in the sense that her attire was made up of many colors. On her head, and pulled down all around her ears, was a yellow, blue, and green cap with a yellow tassel on top. Her legs were clothed by some reddish purple stockings. Her skirt was black and her vest jacket was tan. Her mouth had only a few snuff colored teeth which were quite in keeping with her general appearance of unkemptness.

The Perkins' home is located about a mile and a half back off the highway that runs through the King and Anderson plantation, and is mainly surrounded by acres and acres of dying cotton and corn stalks. The house, painted grass green and trimmed in a cream colored white, is of the two room "shot'gun" house style. One can stand in the muddy dirt in the front of the house, when the door is opened, and see the adjoining cotton field in the back. The house has no windows.

The Perkins family is a plantation family. Ola Perkins is the contractual head of the family. The crop and all the business transactions for the family are carried on by her. When asked concerning this, she said:

> Yes sir, I is the head of this here family, and my second man is living here with me and my daughter, but me is the one that's the head. The crop is in my name and the settlement comes to me.

When asked whether or not she and her "man" were married, her reply was:

> Sir, what's that you trying to talk about here. Cose we is married. The preacher and my children stood right here and witnessed it. What you wants to really know is how is it's me that's head. Well, that man that's my husband and I got married when my first husband died, and he had done run away from a plantation over yonder where he was owing them a great crop bill. And see, if they catches up with him and he was the head of the family, he would have to pay them out of what I done made. So just to be stopping anything like that, I just go on and makes myself the head. He can owes all he wants, but this a way there's one thing show—he won't be paying for nothing with my sweat.

Most of Mrs. Perkins' children by her first husband are married and live near her on the King and Anderson plantation. The girls married when they were about twelve or thirteen years of age. When asked why so many of her girls married young, and as to why she let them do so, she said:

> Well sir, some of them just wanted to and that one down the road who wasn't bare over twelve years this here day, she birthed that boy's baby and now she's gone. Then there ain't much no need for no large house of childrens now days cause before you could work them, but now most out here they gots tractors that does the plowing. And nobody just don't got no need for no big head of children.

When asked concerning what music she liked best, her reply was:

> Now that's one thing I seldom does, and that's think about music and songs and stuff like that. But I guess I likes any kind just so it ain't blues cause I'm a Christian and I just don't follow nothing like that. I'm just a Christian following like my ma taught me. Naw sir, I never was much of a songster. Most of

mine, I does it in church and seldom does it then. My folks never practiced us on no songs. The ways these folks doing their childrens now, they just ain't raising like they ought'n be. Long time in my time folk didn't low no children out after sundown. Now times—seems like they don't low you in after sundown, and they is certainly going to sing the blues.

∽

APPENDIX D

Interview with Albert Williams Jr.

If intelligence is something that can be displayed externally, expressed in general carriage, manner of speech, and in awareness of human courtesies, one may say that the seventeen year old student at the Coahoma County Training School on the King and Anderson plantation is quite an intelligent lad. He was dressed in brown tweed slacks, blue shirt and tie, suspenders, and a pair of tan shoes; much neater than the majority of the boys in the school. He is around five feet eight inches in height and weighs probably one hundred four pounds. The interview comments, largely conversational in character, were as follows:

> Yes sir, I know a lot about this area and the people. Made survey for the government. They had first given it to whites and the colored folks wouldn't tell them nothing. You see the government wanted to know about living conditions, homes and things like that.

From this point, he began to tell about some of the Negroes in Clarksdale:

> Well, there's some Negroes that got quite a bit. Take G. T. Thomas has quite a bit of property, more than any other Negro in town. He's really the richest Negro in town. T. J. Huddleston got something too, but not as much as Thomas—cause he has quite a number of incomes; the burial association, property, plantation, restaurant—in fact that whole block where the burial association is belongs to him.

The interviewer wondered as to what was the white reaction to a Negro owning so much in a place like Clarksdale. The interviewee explained this by saying:

> Negroes around our part sometimes set themselves aside. Thomas is all right. Recall a big confusion about something and he took over for the common class. Naturally some of the colored folks like that and the jealous ones didn't.

You get some pretty fair-minded white folks; they don't pay no attention much to what nobody has unless you like some Negro woman come up in town all dressed up in a fine car and the white folks stop and look.

They tells me that Thomas started off paddling fish and all the white folks knew him then and they know what he's got now cause he goes to the bank. They know what he has. A man by the name of Procman looks after Thomas' business. He does right by the white folks and they let him have. You know one thing, Negroes do dress and white folks don't like that. Used to be old Syrian policeman who just don't like to see Negroes dressed up or nothing like that. He wasn't nothing though.

The population of Clarksdale is around about 13,000 and about half or more are Negroes. We found out that on the average, there's about seven Negroes living in a house. Government had homes inspected to see if they were any good. Some of these people rent for $2.50; you get three rooms, small back and front yard, electric lights if you put them in yourself and most have toilets outdoors, and some of them use oil and have grates. For a real good house, if a white man rents it he can get anywhere from $30.00 to $50.00 a month if he has all the housing conveniences. Then take a Negro—for the same house couldn't rent it for over $15.00.

When it comes to working in service, they do just about the same here as they do elsewhere—wash, iron, cook, and that's what some of them do. For all the work you got to do, what they pay you is no money. Lots of times you got to even pay car-fare out of what they give you. If white people ain't out "playing society" they come and get you. I'm telling you what I know. Frankly, some of these Negroes really get a bad deal. Negroes could really do better but there's no co-operation. But if Negroes got together and wouldn't go to work for these white people for such low wages, they would be better off. However, if somebody around here said that, before he could get it out of his mouth, the white man knows about it.

They got a few light kids around. Most of them nice. Kids don't let their color go to their heads. As far as I know, I think they are very nice. For one while around here you could really see that white folks are funny folks. One day a boy by the name of Woodrow Campbell, a dark young fellow was walking down the street with some light Negro girls. A policeman called him up and told him not to be seen again, and to stop. And the Wards, that's who the girls were, had to have the boy stop visiting. Well the Wards' father was white and their mother is part white, but the kids go for colored around here, and when they is away I've heard they sometimes goes for white. Their father died not so long ago. The mother has a plantation in Jonestown; don't guess white folks care. Their father came home every evening to his family. The Negroes talked, yet if anything was given the Wards was invited.

Well I tell you, up until recently, so many colored women living with white men that it was really something and the part about it some of them consider themselves high class women. You can believe this or not, lady name Dora, everyone of her children had a different father. When she would have them, she would send them off to St. Louis; then get her another white man and get some more good living. But since Gregg Rice took up to cleaning up the country, this stuff had to stop. Still quite a number of Negroes and Chinese marry. You know about the China girl that went to the University of Chicago—she goes with a colored boy. Lot of people around here don't like her. Once her father wanted her to do something and her mother wanted her to do something else and she jumped up and told them, especially her mother, "I'm not a nigger and I'm not a Chinaman, I'm just a mixture." People heard about it and cause she sassed her mother, people didn't like her.

I used to work in one of the leading white stores in town, Max Landon and Company. Started as porter, after a while they would let me go in the cash drawer, that's one thing that Negroes seldom do. The owners were Jews and pretty nice people. I really had a chance to learn a lot about types of people. Used to wait on whites that didn't mind. I could usually tell the kind that wouldn't mind. You'll find that the white people that you work for are all right just as long as you with them, but if the table's turned, you got to know where to put your foot and where not to put it. Lots of times people asking me things.

GENERAL MUSICAL QUESTIONNAIRE

Well I tell you, I like classics, semi-classics, and swing. For the different occasions I think the music should be appropriate. If it's dance; should have dance music. If it's a program; should have program music. I like the piano and the organ best, but I can't play neither. My favorite songs are: The Negro National Anthem, Star Dust, Send Out the Light, To a Wild Rose, I'll Fly Away, Carmina, The Rosary, Deep River, Steal Away. I don't know no work song other than "I been working on the railroad all the live long day." When it comes to the blues, I just don't like them unless its something like the "St. Louis."

There's one little old song I doubt if you know that kids around here sing when they is playing nothing special.

> Oh, the bull dog on the bank
> Told the bull frog in the pond
> You big old water fool
> Singing tra, la, la, la

That's really pretty when harmonized.

Yes, I think dancing is all right in the proper place and at the proper time—like at socials. I don't got much use for no night clubs like other boys and girls around here that go to "Paradise Hall."

When it comes to what I want sung at my funeral, I haven't thought nothing about it, but one of my favorite songs is, "Oh Precious Lord," and I think that would be appropriate for the occasion. Like I told you, I don't think there's no songs that's just out and out wrong to sing but there's a time and place for everything.

(Which do you prefer, Negro or white music and why?) Negro all the time. Well, because it's a gift that seemingly no other race has, and I think that every man should praise the ground he stands on. If you have the gift, you should praise the best.

∾

APPENDIX E

Interview with Joe Cal

Joe Cal's present family is an all male family on the King and Anderson plantation; when asked concerning this he said:

Well, you see, I'se been with more'n one woman, and that last one I was with— she didn't want to act no right, so even if she wanted to she had to get out. And I hadn't been with her no more'n a year. In fact she ain't hardly been up here from Texas longer than a year. Oh yeah we was married, but now we's separated. She live right up there. She got out and took her 'bout six kids, that was already hers and made her a crop of her own, and took care of them children. Man that woman can really work; can pick four or five hundred pounds of cotton a day.

To tell you the truth, there ain't but two kinds of folks that ain't slaves in this here man's land and that's the white man and the nigger woman. It used to be just the white man, cause I remembers when there was no separating like there is now. A woman couldn't just get up and go once she done left home and been married to a man. If she got in her head anything like that, her folks would just pack her right back on up and bring her to her man. But now a days they is practically all free. They can do most they wants to do. Leave when-so-ever they get ready, run round with white men, and most everything. Same thing go for the white man, but the poor nigger man and the white woman, they is the ones that's catching it. They'll lynch a nigger for fooling with a white woman and run the white woman out for fooling with a nigger; but the white man and a colored woman can get together any old time.

One time I pulls a gun on a white agent and was wanting to get away from here, but old man Anderson told me I better not think 'bout no getting away. Well I just figured that things was getting bad, so I went up and told a bad, gun toting, shooting, white man 'bout how things was, and he sent old King and Anderson word that he was sending his trucks down and he wasn't expecting them to come back empty. Then old Roy King got in touch with me and told me that I could leave if I paid him $75.00 for every acre of land. I told that bad white man what they said, and he went to see them. And Mr. King told him that I was a good working nigger, and he just didn't want me to be getting away, and at the same time let me know I couldn't get way with no raising no gun at no white man. Well things cooled down and I went on and stayed.

There's one thing 'bout down here, most the colored folks know that they can't do nothing and you find very few of them that will do anything. Now takes me, I'll take most anything off a white man excepting him hitting me. Most niggers even take that. I remembers once, not so long ago, down there on Issaquena Street up there near Fourth, there was a colored man walking down the street reading and not watching where he was going, and he kind of accidentally fell over a little white girl playing on the sidewalk. Colored folks was round everywhere. A white man, whose little girl it was, he jumped out of his car yelling, "You damn black son of bitch, why can't you see where you going— round here falling all straddle my little girl. I got a mind to beat your head off." Oh he was ranting and cursing and carrying on. All them colored folks was just standing there looking. The man didn't fall over that gal 'tentionally and he was pleading and begging that white man not to beat him. Talking 'bout, "No sir boss, I didn't mean no harm." And the white man's wife, who was sitting there in the car, told him to come on and let that nigger go. He left, and there was three more white mens coming down the street who didn't have nothing to do with anything. They grabbed that poor colored boy and was ganging up and beating him scandalous. Nobody tried to help him, but there was one colored follow who come up and he said right out loud, "Wish somebody would try to beat me that way." Them three white men turned the other nigger loose and told him—"Nigger you show is going to get your wish." And they started towards him, but that po' boy was a fighting black man. He fought and fought and was beating them white fellows up so bad that they was begging for him to quit, but he just wouldn't. Somebody called the police and that boy wouldn't stop fighting until the sheriff hit him right on the head with one of them blackjacks. Some folks say that they was going to hang that nigger, but I for one knows they didn't.

When asked concerning things that he did for amusement, he said:

Well son, I ain't fit for as much fun as I used to be fitten for. I'm getting kind of old now and things done kind of changed. I just can't keep up there with them youngsters. Now you take them boys of mine, they can tell you 'bout having a time. Now when I was a boy, I was a fella for you, but even then folks didn't do like they does now. Well I tell you, show I danced. Used to be me that used to be the head figure caller at all the parties. Folks danced more sociable like then than they does now. When I was a boy, old time ago—everybody join a circle, the fiddler and guitar and box man be playing for day and night. I'd be up on a box, yelling as loud as I could, just calling them figures like—Two and two, hand in hand, turn your lady loose, hands up sixteen, circle right, when you get home—boy I can't remember all that stuff. You see son, I'm a Christian like man, and I just don't like to talk about all them old bad things. Here you come here talking to me about dancing and old tales. You ought'n to be done doing that. (When he said this, all the children started laughing, and his brother said, "Come on Joe, tell him something, you may be somebody's Christian, but he should come around here and hear you sometime.")

He said:

You boys makes me feel kind of shame. I knows lots of them old tales and songs, and when I'm by myself I sings them, but I just don't like to do that kind of stuff among folks that ain't like me. And some of them stories is bad, bad— but I knows and tells them. I'm just going to tell you one. Have you heard about Casey Jones? Well here it is. (As he told this tale, all the members of the family stood around, laughed, and corrected him when he made an error.)

> On one Sunday morning
>   it look like rain
> Round the curve
>   come a passenger train
> On the bump was Casey Jones
> Two locomotives
>   and they bound to bump
>
> Casey Jones was a son-of-a-bitch
> And run his engine on an open switch
> The boiler busted
> The whistle split
> The fireman fotted

And Casey shitted

When I make a hundred
I make a hundred and a half
Going back to Memphis
To sit on my black ass

In the way of songs, there was one that was made up by a man on this plantation a long time ago. It's about Mary Steward a real woman who got shot. I
knows it's the truth cause I was there. Now she wasn't nobody famous, just
somebody that everybody round here knowed. And this man what wrote it
was good for fiddling with words. Have you ever heard the song of Mary Steward? Well this is it.

One Saturday evening about two o'clock
Had to go to the ball to see that brown a man
Buck Bliss throwed up
Will People knowed
He jumped behind Mary Steward
And she caught the load

She ran inside the house
And leant up side the door
The blood a dreaning all over the floor

They took little Mary fore her mother's door
She hollered, Oh Lord the bullet pain me so
They took little Mary to the Doctor's house
Took two or three women to lay po' Mary out
The Doctor cut and bobbed her arm off short
Now little Mary can laff and talk.

APPENDIX 1

A Spark in Natchez

by Robert Gordon and Bruce Nemerov

Natchez, Mississippi, is on the Mississippi River, about 200 miles northwest of New Orleans. It's a swampy area, but evenings in April can still be pleasant. When the owner of the Rhythm Club booked Walter Barnes and his Royal Creolians Orchestra for April 23, 1940, he'd booked a big engagement. Barnes, based in Chicago, was a popular bandleader, especially in the South where he was one of the first to tour heavily.

At the Rhythm Club, the owner's concern was gate-crashers, those who would sneak in to the popular show without paying. As a preventative measure, he had all the windows in the club boarded shut. (By some accounts, these windows were covered when the club opened in 1938.) The club, 200 feet long and "entirely sheathed," according to a deputy sheriff[1] at the scene of the carnage, "in corrugated tin," had a large ventilating fan, which would present something of a breeze to those inside the building.[2]

A fire began accidentally when a match spark intended for a cigarette ignited the Spanish moss decorating the rafters. Elevator operator Ernest Wright witnessed the inferno, arriving at the club after getting off work at midnight. According to the wire story:

> Wright said he saw two girls come out of the women's room near the front of the building, and heard one of them say: "Now you did it. You set the place on fire."
>
> "I looked up but didn't see anything for a minute," Wright said. "Then I saw a blinding sheet of flame. In a minute the whole place was on fire."

"Then," according to an account in the *Pittsburgh Courier*, "there was a hissing roar like a heavy gust of wind blowing through a forest and the entire inside of the building appeared to be filled with flame and smoke."[3] The club's only exit was also its entrance, an "ordinary-sized" door at the front.[4] When the screaming broke out, patrons at the far end thought a fight had started. "But within a minute," according to the survivors, the flames flashed through the moss down the entire length of the hall and enveloped the dancers."[5] (Some speculate that the moss was drenched in paraffin to ward off mosquitoes.) Bandleader Barnes, attempting to keep people calm, kept the band playing. The tune was "Marie."

"The only calm person in the building was Mr. Barnes, the orchestra leader," said survivor Frank Christmas.[6] "After quieting members of his orchestra, Barnes urged them to keep on playing while he attempted to get the attention of the milling, yelling, hysterical throng that was crowding the building's only exit. I think Mr. Barnes knew the danger he was in but believed that if he could prevent the crowd from piling up around the door, which incidentally opened inward, he could fix it so most of the people could get out.

"But that crowd was beyond human control. The whole band, had it wished to, could have saved itself. The bandstand was near the door, and they could have reached the exit before many of the people who were in other parts of the hall. But they didn't choose the coward's role. They were like a brave captain and his crew and went to their death with their ship."

Dancers trapped within pressed against the bandstand wall. A few ran through the flames and survived. Julius Hawkins, who was near the door, described the anguish: "Inside, everyone was trying to get out and crushed each other as the fire was burning them. All were crying and yelling and after a while I could smell the burning meat."[7]

"When the smell got so bad, I had to leave, couldn't take it no more," vocalist Dwight "Gatemouth" Moore told *Living Blues* (May/June 1989). Moore, who has since become a Reverend, had been the band's featured singer the previous year; he was visiting on the band's bus with a female fan when tragedy struck. "Two [of the band members] got out. Everyone else burned up, bandleader and everybody. The drummer and the bass got a hammer and knocked out—see, they had wire [over] the windows. They only had one door to get in. They were able to knock the wire loose, back where the drummer was, and got out."[8]

Rescuers faced the gruesome sight of seared bodies heaped upon each other as high as the windows; the town coroner described them "piled up like cordwood." In its account the next morning, the *Natchez Democrat* wrote, "Under the masses of the dead could be seen signs of life. The dead were pulled away and, from under, several who were partly suffocated and partly burned were taken out and rushed to the Natchez Hospital."

The deputy sheriff postulated that the building's tin exterior "formed an oven in which the dancers were baked." Quoted in the wire story, he continued: "All indications are that the fire started near the door and spread quickly in the moss, which had been hanging for several years. A ventilating fan in the rear may have sucked the fire upon the helpless dancers who were huddled near the bandstand in the rear.

"When I got there, moans were heard under the mass of flesh and we dug among the bodies to bring them out and take them to hospitals. It was gruesome work."

The wailing in Natchez continued long after the fire was extinguished. "The unearthly cry of those who were burning to death could be heard for blocks even before the fire alarm had been sounded," wrote the *Natchez Democrat*. Neighbors rushed to the scene, joined by families. Into the morning, "work was devoted to getting the dead bodies out of the building while on the outside the shrieking and crying of relatives of those believed to be in the building made the blood of all who were nearby run cold."[9] Every doctor in the city administered to the survivors; many worked thirty-six hours straight. The hospitals were overwhelmed and had to send home many patients in severe condition. WPA laborers were employed to dig graves. The Red Cross sent three relief workers from Washington. "That was most every family in Natchez," said a witness, Josephine Clemons Bell.[10] "Very few black families didn't have somebody in that fire."

Nashville Banner front page, April 24, 1940.

APPENDIX 2

A Memorandum about the July Trip to Coahoma County Functional Approach to the Study of Folklore*

I. The following pertinent material is available in the field work notes and interviews of Mr. Young and Mr. Adams:

1. There has been adequate documentation of the preference pattern in relation to musical instruments. The piano ranks first and the guitar second, for most of the informants. A very religious person will include the organ in the first or second place and a young person interested in dancing includes the saxophone in first or second place.

2. The five or six most favored songs of a group of approximately 100 individuals is available. This material correlates well with the secular-sacred preference pattern of these individuals, described below. No effort was made to document the titles obtained.

3. The secular-sacred preference pattern comes clear in the 100 interviews. Age of the informant is the most important factor in urban and rural residences. The main pattern seems to be:

   Sixteen to thirty—Blues frankly liked. Dancing indulged in and defended. Modern city jazz preferred as dance music. Spirituals and hymns occupy a second place as songs for more serious occasions.
   Thirty to fifty—Blues are generally disapproved of rather more by women than men. Religious music given first rank. Attitude towards dancing varies between "I can't do modern steps" and "it is wrong."
   Over fifty—Secular music is the devil's work. Dancing is a sin, etc.

4. Numerous song texts noted rather inaccurately.
5. A few good personality portraits by Mr. Adams.
6. Much good material on the change of attitude toward personal and churchly conduct in the last 50 years.

---

* This memorandum was probably written by John Work; less likely by Alan Lomax. From internal evidence, it was written after July, 1942.

7. Good material on the importance of the folk medicine practiced by midwives and grannies.
8. A few paraphrased folk tales.
9. Lists of popular phonograph records with no bibliographical data.

II. Lewis Jones' reports give us a good portrait of Mr. Mangrum, an important middle class Negro, interested in music; general community activity during the cotton picking season; sources of information about secular musicians and secular music.

III. Last summer the following material was recorded with full documentation:

1. A very ordinary and unexciting Baptist revival service.
2. A group of old fashioned "hally spirituals" sung by the older people of this same Baptist Church.
3. Song singing by this same group.
4. A Holiness Church service in the northern part of the county.
5. The songs of a blues fiddler and a blues guitar player.

To complete our picture of the musical life of the county from the functional point of view we need the following materials:

I. From non "folk group"
    A. (1) Attitudes of whites towards Negro folk music
       (2) Accounts of white residents of the history of Negro musical life in the community.
       (3) General musical activity of the whites.
    B. This same material from the Negro middle class especially those persons concerned with cultural activity in the county.

II. Printed and recorded music available
    (1) Accurate bibliographical data on song books, sheet music, etc. in the area. Accurate data on records in the juke boxes and private homes.
    (2) Study of the use and absorption of this material by the folk group. Attitude of the folk toward written music, song sheets, song books, records, etc.

III. The Church
    (1) Distribution of the population by denomination.
    (2) Definition of the musical activity of each denomination, one rural and one urban sample.
    (3) Historical background of each denomination and its musical activity in the

community.

(4) Interviews with singing deacons, ministers, choir leaders, church pianists, etc.

    a.   What music is best, why?

    b.   Musical training

    c.   What music do congregations like the best?

    d.   How is music specifically used in various parts of the service?

    e.   Attitudes of various denominations toward shouting? spirituals? long meter hymns? dancing in the church?

    f.   History of musical life of the church from the oldest people—60 to 80.

    g.   Recorded studies of sample services—quartets, choirs, singing leaders, etc. Emphasis on construction of harmony in group singing.

    h.   Shape note singing groups. The complete repertory of hymns and spirituals recorded as samples of singing style.

    i.   Recordings of samples from all repertoires of all sorts of individuals. Comments of audience noted.

IV. Children's Music

(1) Interviews, questionnaires filled out for leaders of children's songs.

(2) Definition of the repertoire. Texts taken. Dances described. Questions—why is it good, better? Dance or song dominant? What do words mean? Sample records made. Photographs.

(3) Intensive interviews with one or two of the most talented children.

(4) Discussion of history of children's games with older informants.

(5) Attitude of teachers toward the games and children's songs.

(6) What are the teachers trying to do in their program of school music? What are their standards? Their criticism of their standards?

V. Cross section study in the rural area

(1) Intensive recorded interviews with a number of the individuals interviewed by Adams and Young.

(2) Intensive recorded interviews with 10 people of between 60 and 80 on the history of folk song in the county.

(3) See section on the Church

(4) See section on Non-folk Groups

(5) See section on Children's music

(6) See section on Secular music.

VI. Secular Music

    A.   The Dance

        (1) Descriptions of Saturday night dances. Sample records.

(2) Descriptions of various kinds of parties.
(3) Intensive recorded interviews with active secular musicians. Taste of musician. Taste of audience.
(4) Intensive recorded interviews with the old time secular musicians. Parties, dances, serenades. History of instruments used in the area.
(5) The repertoire—texts and titles—correlated historically.

B. The Job
(1) The work song repertoire. Why? Who? Where? When? How did it make you feel? Work easier or not? Whites encourage it or not?
(2) Visit to the chain gang. Visit to the Parchman. [The Mississippi state penitentiary in Sunflower County, just south of Coahoma County.]

C. Bawdy Songs, Criminal Songs, etc.
(1) The bawdy repertoire
(2) Attitudes towards it
(3) Gambling songs and chants
(4) Jail songs
(5) Ballads and songs of violence

D. Songs, Stories and Lore Expressing Attitudes toward Whites

VII. *Prose Material*
(1) Work with two or three famous story tellers
(2) Record emotional speech patterns
1. Anger
2. Boast
3. Pretend anger, etc.
(3) Lying contests

APPENDIX 3

Report on Preliminary Work in Clarksdale, Mississippi by Samuel Adams and Ulysses Young. Oct. 26, 1941.

Coahoma County had undergone a change in the week which elapsed between the scouting trip with Mr. Work, Mr. Lomax, and Mr. Ross. Where everything had been casual and slow paced before, now there was humming activity. The streets in the Negro business district were empty except for the occasional person on some errand. The cafes and barbershops about which people formerly congregated had no patrons. In the interim between my visits cotton had advanced in price and picking was $1.50 a hundred instead of 75 cents. at the end of the week the wages for cotton pickers had advanced to $2.00 a hundred. Not since 1926 had the wages reached that level. Everybody was in the fields. People who had been working for meager wages in the town quit their jobs. All day white women were driving through the Negro residential district seeking someone who would work for them. The usual wages for servants were from three to four dollars a week.

A cook said that she had been working for four dollars a week and in one week of cotton picking she had earned $15.00. A man who worked in a pool room related a conversation between himself and his employer in which he told the employer that his hours of work would have to be reduced and his wages increased from eight to ten dollars a week if he wanted him to come back to work. The employer was reported as saying that, "I'll rack balls myself before I'll pay you $10.00." To which the Negro replied, "Well, it looks like you gonna rack 'em. There's too much cotton in Coahoma County for me to work for eight dollars a week." I inquired if any pressure was put on people to make them work in the fields. Did they practice the arrest for vagrancy which frequently occurs in other parts of the South. My informant said, "No, when prices are good they don't have to do that. They resort to that when prices are bad."

Competition for laborers was great. Street corners were the points at which cotton pickers congregated to be transported to the fields. Trucks were the favorite form of transportation, with some automobiles, and one planter had hired two Greyhound buses. One incident reported was that a truck had been filled with pickers who were to be paid $1.50 a hundred. Another truck drew up behind the first and announced that $1.75 was being paid on the plantation from which it has come. The pickers deserted the first truck and boarded the second. The wage increase seemed to have come about in this way. On Sunday, September 7th two trucks appeared in Clarksdale from Missouri offering pickers $1.50 a hundred and two meals. The wages in Coahoma County had

At the time of the Coahoma County Study, many African Americans in the Delta had already moved off of the plantations and into town. At the harvest, plantations often sent trucks into town to collect day-workers. During his stint in Coahoma County, sociologist Lewis Jones worked in the field to gain a rapport with the pickers and to better understand his subjects' lives. Courtesy of Fisk University, Franklin Library, Special Collections.

been 75 cents at the week end. The next day $1.50 was being paid in Coahoma County. Changes in wages were such that a plantation could not depend on a supply of pickers from one day to the next. Pickers were paid each evening when they stopped work. The next day someone might offer a five or ten cent increase and the pickers may not return to the plantation on which they worked yesterday.

On Sunday, September 14th a truck appeared with Missouri license tags and a Negro was hired by the driver to recruit pickers. In demonstration of disapproval the sheriff and several deputies and the chief of police and a couple of police arrested the Negro at the truck and took him away. The white driver of the truck was not molested but the intimidation had been effective and he had to leave with an empty truck. When he had gone the Negro was released without any charge being preferred against him. One of my informants, the gambler, Kid Simmons, was difficult to find. After seeking him for several days he said, "I just feel funny on the streets. Nobody around but me. They might pick me up as a vag or something." His attitude may be indicated in the following incident. One man was talking about the good jobs and wages being paid in the North.

Kid said, "What you telling me about them for? I don't want these jobs around here. You know I ain't going nowhere looking for one."

Even the children are picking cotton. One man explained, "I'm picking on the _____ place. There's other places where the cotton is better but they got such good 'commodations for children out there. Plenty of sacks and artesian water. You have to give the children a chance; you can't shut them out. My three children made about $5.00 a day all week." He said that the money made by the children from Monday through Friday was taken to buy clothing and handled by the parents but the money they earned on Saturday was theirs to use as they saw fit.

Saturday night is shopping time. Very few people come to town before dark, but about eight o'clock the streets begin to fill with a pushing, surging crowd. Merchants reported that on Saturday the 13th they sold until they were exhausted or supplies depleted and they simply put patrons out and closed the stores. A Jewish woman declared that her stock was depleted and orders for goods were not being filled so her husband had gone away to try to get goods which failed to come on order. Mrs. Sanders, owner of the Negro drug store, said, "These people behave like it is Christmas. They are buying toys for the children and everything. Saturday night a man came in here with a red wagon he had bought."

In regard to our study, Professor Wright suggested that we begin the first of November instead of the first of October because the people were too busy at this time and the plantation owners would be unsympathetic as well as the people themselves disinterested. Mr. P. F. Williams suggested that the study begin the middle of November. He thought the first too early. He said those people haven't had an opportunity to earn money in a long time and they are going to be intent on that. He offered full cooperation that I call on him for any assistance he might be in position to give.

Mr. D. F. Crumpton, superintendent of schools in Coahoma County, pledged the cooperation of the teachers in the county. My request of him was that teachers spot leaders in ring games and the musicians in the community. I said that there would be no request for any of their time from their school duties. He said that he would be glad for them to give time. He offered to have schools arrange game fest days on afternoons just for us.

The new Jeanes supervisor in the county is Mrs. Lillian Rogers who was at Indianola and worked with Powdermaker and Dollard. She offered to be of any assistance we requested of her. Crumpton suggested the former Jeanes supervisor who has been demoted to a classroom teacher, as of possible assistance. She is Miss Ernestine Powell. Mr. Ammons, the county farm agent was enthusiastic about the project. He covers the county with his movie projector and educational films. He also has a record player. He suggested that we give him several of our records and he would play them at his gatherings and tell the people to brush up their repertoires and prepare themselves for our coming. He said he would not begin his community visits until late October because the people worked so late in the cotton picking season that it was hard to have them assemble before 9:30 or 10 o'clock. He suggested that we contact Mr. Vickery who had been the A.A.A. administrator in the county for seven years. Mr. Vickery, he thought, knew the county better than anyone else.

Mr. Vickery is now manager of the S. H. Kyle plantation where an experimental program is planned for the coming year. Mr. Kyle is president of the Coahoma County Farm Bureau. Mr. Vickery suggested these plantations—the King and Anderson plantation which had been in the possession of the Andersons since it was cleared and placed in cultivation. He said that much of the old tradition would be found there. Young Mr. Anderson is willing to allow us access to the plantation.

The Hopson plantation which is highly mechanized. Professor Stone, who has taught the school on the Hopson plantation, was found in the field picking cotton. He was interested in our plans and offered assistance. He accompanied us to see the book-keeper to whom he explained the project. Mr. H. H. Hopson Jr. was ill and couldn't be seen but the bookkeeper is a native of Murfreesboro, Tennessee and knew about Fisk. He and Professor Stone were sure that free access to the plantation would be given. The bookkeeper said that Mr. Hopson wouldn't want us on the plantation during the cotton picking season but when cotton picking was over we would be welcome. I am to write Mr. Hopson when we are ready to begin.

The Sherrod plantation. Mr. Vickery said it would be interesting because there is everything there from oxen to tractors. He said Mr. Sherrod would understand and be sympathetic to the undertaking.

The moderator of the Coahoma County Missionary Baptist Association is willing to give us assistance we need. He said we might be interested in the semi-annual meeting of the association which is held in Clarksdale between the first and second Sundays in November.

Mr. Nelson, one of the undertakers in Clarksdale said that he would post us on interesting funerals. He expressed regret that we were not recording now because a big funeral was to be held on the 17th. A minister died just before the National Baptist Convention and his body was being held twelve days until the ministers returned from Cleveland. There were to be thirty ministers as honorary pall bearers. He said that it would be an all day affair.

The groundwork was pretty carefully laid and will be followed through with letters to the plantation owners, the county superintendent, and Clarksdale newspaper, when the dates of the study are finally decided.

Interviews and notes will be appended to this report later.

APPENDIX 4

Memorandum to Charles S. Johnson
from Lewis W. Jones

MEMORANDUM

To: Dr. Charles S. Johnson
From: Lewis W. Jones
Re: The Folk Culture Study in Coahoma County, Mississippi

August 20, 1942

1. Report on Field Experience

A more adequate acquaintance with Coahoma County was gained in this field period than we had previously. Some contact with all parts of the community was made, if only observation in some areas. A good general impression of the total county organization was secured horizontally in an immediate cross section, and vertically from the oldest to the youngest generation. The historical process in the county was documented through interviews.

Much time was spent in the location of informants who could perform musically and in the recording of the efforts of these performers. From the oldest generation we secured interview material where they were physically unable to play or sing, and in instances where they refused to present secular music because they had become church members and would not violate their reformation. A list of the informants, with brief descriptive notations, was kept, and can be presented later if necessary. A seemingly adequate amount of information was secured on the lives and music of the oldest generation. Children's games were recorded from the youngest generation, and also from the third generation by the performance of children at the Coahoma County Training School, at Friars Point, and at the Moorhead Plantation, and the performance of teachers at the session for teachers at the Coahoma County Training School.

Religious music was recorded at two sessions of the State Baptist Convention and at the Holiness Church. One lack may be the failure to record a service of the A.M.E. Church in Clarksdale, but this performance is so standardized that it might be duplicated in any middle class congregation, white or colored, in almost any part of the county. From special informants records were made of the performance of religious songs which were dated and their current use determined.

Work songs were recorded where possible. A few field ballads were recorded. It seemed impossible to secure an adequate performance of levee camp songs, but from interviews ideas were gained of the character of these songs. The outstanding performance of work songs was that of railroad section songs which came from a most cooperative couple of section hands.

Secular music other than work songs was secured through the performance of the county musician, the roaming professional musician, a blind ballad maker, and an old musician who presented old tunes. Interview material provided a history of the development of music in the area and, as far as possible, a dating of these changes.

The last two days in the field were spent 60 miles from Clarksdale "in the hills" where the people who settled Coahoma County came from. There were found more musicians and a greater variety of music than in the Delta, and which the report on the study will take into account when written. A musical instrument called "quills" was found with which there is little familiarity outside the folk community. In the performance of secular music this side trip was very valuable.

More than 70 records were made during the period in the area and these will contain, at a conservative minimum estimate, four times that many songs.

The general results of the study may be seen in the impressionistic statement which follows as a suggested organization of the report on the study.

2. Impressionistic Suggestions for Organization of the Report on the Study

Introduction. Social Contours

The people of Coahoma County are predominantly rural. There is one town, with a population of 12,000, and four villages, but the familiar names referred to as places by the people of the area are simply plantation headquarters with store, owners, and agents homes, sometimes a gin, sometimes a railroad station, and sometimes a filling station. Such is the character of Hopson, Sherard, Mattson, Cloverhill, etc. The so-called urban population of Clarksdale is close to the plantation. Many of the inhabitants are seasonal laborers who go to the fields in the hoeing and picking seasons. The four generations living may be considered as being the river generation—the oldest people, who are in their seventies and eighties; the railroad generation, from sixty to forty; the highway generation, in their twenties and thirties; and the youth and children.

The economic organization of the area is the familiar one of cotton cultivation, but a dynamic cotton area in which the soil productivity is sufficient to have new machinery and new methods of cultivation reaching a high degree of efficiency for the economy. The economic system with its changes affects the lives of the people in a way which is rendering many of their folk skills useless, uprooting them from the soil, and bringing bewilderment to those who have been subject to the most drastic changes. Some sharecroppers feel insecure in the system which keeps them idle while a tractor breaks their land, plants their crops, plows their crops and turns the crops into their care only for a brief space of "chopping" and for the months of harvest. When these tractor costs appear as charges against their crops at settlement time they cannot understand them. Share tenants are reduced to the cropper status by no wish of their own nor mean spirit of the landlord, but by the system which leaves no uncultivated acreage for pasture and no acreage allotted for feed growing.

Dominant in the culture is the church. There are perhaps more churches than stores and schools combined. The majority of these churches are Baptist, which frowns on the "pleasures" of the people. Those who sin by playing secular music share the beliefs of the church people that they will go to hell if they continue to make music and die unrepentant.

The whole life experience of the people is organized about the means of communication and transportation. The rivers—the Mississippi and the Sunflower—are no longer significant as avenues of trade and travel. They are so controlled as to be considered a menace rather than a value, and have their greatest meaning in the memories of the oldest generation who lived lives organized about them. The railroads are decreasing in importance. The second generation describes the peak of development when many trains ran across the county instead of two daily, on the *Riverside,* and just a few more on the *Mainline.* The highways are new, and with the lack of consideration of the young throw themselves across the community with disregard for towns born and nurtured by the railroad. A new institutional development has begun about the highway.

Part I. The River

The Mississippi overflowed seasonally, depositing an additional layer of fertile top soil over the upper delta. The first white settlers to come to the area in which Coahoma County was marked off found mounds which the Indians had thrown up to provide a refuge about the crest of the waters in flood season. Only sparse settlement had been made in the area before the Civil War. These consisted of small plantation clearings along the Mississippi and its tributary, the Sunflower.

The oldest generation in Coahoma County is composed of people who migrated there in the seventies and eighties. These people came from the "hills" of Mississippi, from Alabama, and a few from Georgia. According to their accounts, they were at first afraid of the delta country because of the reports circulated in the hills concerning the devastating floods which took a heavy toll of life and property. Despite this reputation people migrated there and found that the fertile land produced in a remarkable abundance. The river came to be known, through conflicting reports, in its dual role as a threat and as a promise. Those who first returned from a period of living in the delta, with large sums of money, encouraged others to migrate there. Some of these migrants declare that they actually believed that "greenbacks grew on trees and there were ponds of molasses" in the delta.

This generation who cleared the forests and cultivated the plantations in the seventies and eighties were a hardy pioneering people. They struggled with nature which supplied game and beasts in its stands of forest and cane brakes. Then there were deer and turkeys and wolves and "bear tracks were more common in the fields then than pig tracks are now." Their lives were almost amphibian. They had to know the water as they knew the land, and had to manipulate a boat with skill equal to that used in swinging an axe and guiding a plow.

This was the era of the river culture. The trading settlements and "towns" were steamboat landings. Starting at the northern end of the county, steamboats stopped at Port Royal, Burke's Landing, Sunflower Landing, and Malone's Landing. The most important trade center in the county was Friars Point at Port Royal, which was the county seat. Rena Lara at Sunflower Landing and Hill House at Malone's Landing were centers of the life of the plantation people.

Harnessing the river and the railroad came about the same time. There had been some attempt at levee building before the Civil War but these inadequate earth barriers to the floods had fallen into disrepair during the war. In 1864, the Yazoo-Mississippi Delta Levee district was organized and systematic levee construction began. The story of the levee is that of hard ruthless contractors and rough violent workers who through the stage of the wheelbarrow, the slip and the wheeler to the modern motor driven machinery placed a man-made mountain along the course of the river. Short lines of railroad had been constructed in 1877 from the river to Lula, a distance of 8 miles, and in 1879 a short line was extended from Eagles Nest to Clarksdale. In 1884 a section of railroad was complete through the county as a part of the line connecting Memphis with New Orleans.

The river era was one in which the plantation economy was dominant. The circumstances produced the most benevolent phase of the plantation system. Much of the consumption need of the people was produced on the farms. The swamps and uncleared forests provided game, fish, and wild life. Labor was precious and every inducement was made to hold laborers on the plantations. The tenants made money. They carried their cotton by wagon to the river landings in the dry season and waited through the muddy season for the waters to rise to a point that they could reach the landings by skiff with late produce, and to do their trading in the wet season.

Churches were few and widely separated, and mostly of the Baptist denomination. They sang the "Dr. Watt" songs borrowed from the white churches and translation into the chanting and moaning of the long meter began. The old spirituals or "Hallies" were used as collection and revival songs. The church was an important institution with a very real meaning in the community. Affiliation with the church really meant a difference in the conduct and social attitudes of the people. The church people enjoyed recreation in which the "Rock Daniel" was a peculiar phenomenon. These "Rock Daniels" were not confined to the church meeting but were acceptable to religious people at church entertainments, at quiltings, and at house parties.

The ring game was a form of recreation indulged in by both religious and non-religious people. The dances were for the non-religious and were replete with fiddler and the dance caller who intoned the figures to be executed.

Part II. The Railroad

The first railroad was a narrow gauge line connecting Clarksdale with Helena, through Jonestown. It was the second railroad which stretched across the county in the process of connecting Memphis and New Orleans that took the focus of life from the river. The struggle of the railroad with the river for dominance was to be seen reflected in the contest of Clarksdale and Friars Point for the county seat. Friars Point, at the edge of the county, on the river, was no longer regarded as the most important terminal for trade and travel. Clarksdale on the railroad lay claims to the importance of its central location. The contest was resolved in a compromise to be found in several delta counties—division of the county into two administrative districts—one on the railroad and the other on the river. The railroad later won and Clarksdale became the county seat and the trade center of the county.

The railroad was not subject to natural forces as was the river, which was not man's making and not subject to his control. The increasingly effective levee did not control the river but simply restrained it and ever stronger levees were necessary to maintain this restraint. Levees were built across once fertile fields on the river's edge. Land "behind" the levee, between the levee and the river, was subject to floods and unpredictable seasons, but that outside could be cultivated with some sense of security. Planters with the sense of security the levee gave cleared and drained the swamps and lowlands and put them into cultivation. The produce from the increased productive lands was carted to the stations along the railroad, to begin their journey to market centers at either end of the railroad—Memphis or New Orleans.

Cultivation became more intensive, the plantation system lost some of its self-contained character and became a more commercial enterprise. Fishing spots became fewer with improvements of drainage; old-timers point to fields where once they could "catch a good mess of fish." Game became scarcer as wooded plots disappeared into abundantly producing cotton fields. Tenants became fewer as pasture land became too valuable to be held out of production. The percentage of sharecroppers increased. The farm operator became more dependent on the commissary for food brought by the trains which took his cotton away. The traditional plantation order disappeared into a commercial order.

The height of the railroad's importance marked the passage of the frontier. The "bad men" and bold men became fewer. Law and order and the control of the "system" supplanted the control of the person based on personal strength and personal acumen.

Instead of self-contained small localities organized about the plantation communities, race became important socially. When the A.M.E. Churches had been organized in Reconstruction, the Masonic lodge had been established at the same time. The earliest A.M.E. churches had jointly occupied buildings with the Masonic Lodge. The buildings were two-story, with church on the ground floor and lodge rooms occupying the second story. The two men who organized the A.M.E. Churches in the area were Dr. Stinger and Reverend Dixon. Dr. Stinger also organized the Masonic lodges. Reverend Moses Dixon founded the Order of Tabor, which flourished. Other lodges came—the Pythians, the Odd Fellows, and the Woodmen of Union. "Race" consciousness expressed itself in the development of Negro businesses in the "colored sections" in the towns. World War prices of cotton caused the area to boom.

Class difference among Negroes appeared pronounced in this era. On the river Negro owners were men who had been smart enough to advance from the status of tenant. They were friendly and associated with their friends who remained tenants. In the new railroad town a Negro leadership developed to exploit economically the race consciousness and mutual helpfulness notions of the earlier period. The commercial economy presented a Negro middle class to supplant the earlier "race leadership." The division between the wicked and the respectable became more formal in the towns. The red light district was a formally organized pleasure area in the town.

The railroad era witnessed a more formal and less spontaneous expression of attitudes and feelings. Men were singing their thoughts and fancies on the levee, on the railroad, and in the field, but these expressions were confined to the spot of their making. The social song was no longer the traditional ring play and dance. These songs were divided into the respectable and the wicked. The respectable were the popular written music, while in the brothels in the red light district the blues were taking form and identification. The spirituals were sung less and less, while the "Dr. Watt" song, with its standardized form became increasingly popular. The "gospel" songs were beginning to appear in the churches.

Part III. The Highway

Highway development was slow in Mississippi, being graveled roads which were called "the good road." The main highways followed the railroads closely, usually running parallel. The tributary roads leading into the main thoroughfares were not well developed, and many of them were not all-weather roads, but in the dry season at least they permitted greater freedom of movement than the railroad. The early twenties saw the collapse of the cotton boom, the closing of the red light district, and trouble for the middle class. When the concrete highway came, in the thirties, it went across the country with little regard for the railroad and railroad towns. The movement of people was less restrained than when they were dependent upon the railroad. The filling station followed the railroad station as the railroad station had followed the steamboat landing.

The era of the highway is that of motor driven machinery and the economy rapidly reflected the change. Following the depression, the flat extensive fields lent themselves to tractor cultivation. The introduction of motor driven machinery further changed the plantation system. The folk skills and folk knowledge of soil and plant and animal became unimportant with scientific cultivation. The transition is not complete, and the economy is complicated with the varying degrees of traditional form and practice in cotton production just as a variety of roads lead into the concrete highway—hard surface, gravel, and dirt.

Socially, the organization of the area is also complicated. The complexity is to be seen in the variety of plantation workers and stratification of people in the towns. The churches differ in form of worship from one to the other. The lodges which collapsed in the depression struggle feebly to resurrect themselves. The burial society, which is a form of insurance, offers none of the social values which characterized the lodge. The middle class lost many of its members in the collapse of the cotton boom. Those who remain are simply middle class people stripped of leadership claims or influence. There is greater standardization. The radio and the juke box have made for a standardization of music tastes. There remains a little of the river, much of the railroad, along with the confused beginnings of the highway culture.

3. Outline of Material to Go into the Study Report

I. The River
    A.   Skeletal statistics on population, land in cultivation, occupational classes, from the censuses of 1860, 1870, and 1880.
    B.   General descriptive material on Mississippi river life in the seventies and eighties, from secondary sources.
        1.   Descriptive accounts of plantation life.
        2.   Steamboats and their passengers and trade.
    C.   The river culture as Negroes knew it; using interview material to indicate where the people who settled the delta came from.
        1.   The economy described. Land clearing, agriculture, place of game and fish in the economy. The influence on the economy of the river and the seasons. The steamboat and the skiff.
        2.   Social organization. Plantation life. Life and activities at the steamboat

       landings. The church. Recreation.

3.   Political and other organized social activities of Negroes. Elections. The Fallottatchie (?) riot of 1875.*

4.   Expressions of the culture in song and music.
     i. Land-clearing hollers and chants
     ii. Ring plays
     iii. Dances
     iv. Religious music

D.   The Levees

1.   Story of levee building according to dates.

2.   Meaning of the levee to economic life of the area.

3.   Folk story of levee building. Organization of the levee camp. The contractors and their practices. The levee worker as a social type.

4.   Gambling and violence associated with the levee builders. Gambling in levee camps and on the steamboats. Gambling songs. The "bad man" or "bad nigger" on the levee.

5.   Reaction to life and expression of ideas concerning work and love in the levee camp song and ballad.

E.   The plantation along the Sunflower river. The more fully developed plantations on the eastern bank of the Sunflower.

II. The Railroad

A.   The building of the railroads.

B.   Skeletal statistics on the county from 1890 to 1920. The rise in importance of the towns.

C.   Economic developments. Changing aspects of plantation life. Occupational proliferation, commercial developments.

D.   The World War I boom.

E.   Social organization. Negro class outlines. Negro institutional life in the county. Race contacts.

F.   Farm life—Clarksdale, population in 1890, 781; in 1920, 7,552.

1.   Description of the growth of the town.

2.   The red light district—institutionalized recreation and vice. The brothel, the saloon, the gambling house.

G.   "Advancement of the race" and its implications.

---

*Jones is possibly referring to political riots during Reconstruction. On September 1, 1875, in Yazoo City, white Democrats attacked black Republicans; one white and three blacks were killed. Also, a riot on September 4, 1875, near Clinton in Hinds County resulted in loss of life. This heightened political tension occurred during the lead up to the November 1875 presidential election where the Republican Hayes defeated the Democrat Tildon.

    H.   Economic collapse with falling cotton prices, prohibition, closing of the red light district, the Negro exodus.

    I.   Expression of ideas, attitudes, and culture values by Negroes.

        1.   Religious music. Standardization of the "Dr. Watt" and the increasing importance of "gospel" songs.

        2.   The emergence of "the blues" in the red light district.

        3.   Negro musicians with a well-defined status and significance in the white and in the Negro community.

III. The Highway

    A.   Drawing a new contour of the area with roads suited to motor vehicles.

    B.   Skeletal statistics, 1930 and 1940.

    C.   Motor driven machinery in the economy. The plantation under the impact of the depression. The influence of the New Deal, plus machines, plus efficiency methods.

    D.   Social organization. Disappearance of the political influence of the Negro. Death of the lodges. Emphasis on church and school.

    E.   Wider orientation of the people. The younger generation of ministers and the national church organizations. The radio. The juke box.

    F.   Complexity and standardization of the life of the community. The vestige of a river tradition. The strong but dying railroad pattern. The emerging highway pattern and its significance.

4. Proposed Procedure

1. Examination of secondary materials for descriptive materials.
2. Use of local history materials on which to hang folk accounts.
3. Newspapers examined for account of history making events.
4. Maps of the area for the periods selected.
5. Use of song texts as the ideas and value judgments of the people.

Reading of secondary materials may go on while the record transcriptions are being made.

APPENDIX 5

List of Records on Machines
in Clarksdale Amusement Places

The first coin-operated jukeboxes were invented in 1890, thirteen years after Thomas Edison invented his phonograph. But jukeboxes weren't widespread until the 1930s. In farming areas, mechanization in the bars and restaurants was parallel to mechanization in the fields; the fieldhand and the live musician were both losing work.

As part of the documentation of music in Coahoma County, Lewis Jones went to Clarksdale's five bars on September 9, 1941, and noted the records on each one. We surmise that he was most comfortable at Messenger's Café, where he apparently went often enough to rank several of the songs by the number of times he heard them (note the parenthetical numbers that follow some titles). After Louis Jordan's sophisticated blues sound, the next most popular artists were the somewhat schmaltzy big band sounds of Sammy Kaye and Eddy Duchin. (The note to the song "Daddy" indicates the list was compiled over more than one visit.)

In his article "Clarksdale Piccolo Blues" (*Jazz & Blues,* November 1971, p.30.), Tony Russell has provided further analysis of what Jones found:

> The artists found on every jukebox are [Count] Basie, [Fats] Waller, [Louis] Jordan, Lil Green and Walter Davis. Jordan and Lil Green are spread most widely, each having nine "entries;" Basie has eight, Waller seven, Earl Hines and Artie Shaw six each. Hines's "Jelly Jelly" and Lil Green's "Love Me" turn up four times each; five items appear thrice (by Waller, Basie, Memphis Slim, Sister Rosetta [Tharpe] and Lil Green again). And the one record which sweeps the board, appearing on each of the five boxes, is "Come Back Baby" by Walter Davis. [Davis was a blues pianist from St. Louis often cited by Muddy Waters and others as a major influence.]
>
> So, what of the blues amidst all this? Apart from Lil and Walter and Memphis Slim, pickings are certainly scanty. Lone items by [Blind Boy] Fuller, Sonny Boy [Williamson I], Peetie [Wheatstraw], [Roosevelt] Sykes, Washboard Sam, [Jazz] Gillum and [Tommy] McClennan; a couple of Big Bills [Broonzy] and a two-timer by Ollie Shepard, and that's it. Of the 108 listings on the five boxes, less than thirty are blues within the meaning of Dixon and Godrich [authors of *Blues and Gospel Records*]. And if this was how the Clarksdale jukeboxes looked, back in the summer of '41, it was probably how most other southern black boxes looked, more or less. Even down to Sammy Kaye, Eddy Duchin and all.

Messenger's Café
I Know How to Do It—Sam Price
Going to Chicago— Count Basie (1)
Vine Street Boogie—Jay McShann
That's the Blues Old Man—Johnny Hodges (3)
The Boogie Woogie Piggy—Glenn Miller
Until the Real Thing Comes Along—Ink Spots
When I Been Drinkin—Big Bill
Solitude—Billy Holiday
Daddy—Sammy Kaye (5) Was First, Now Waning Popularity
Julia—Earl Hines
I Like My Sugar Sweet—Fletcher Henderson
I See a Million People—Cab Calloway
Brotherly Love—Louis Jordan (6)
Twenty Four Robbers—Fats Waller
I'll Get Mine Bye and Bye—Louis Armstrong
Love Me—Lil Green
Jelly Jelly Blues—Earl Hines
Come Back Baby—Walter Davis
Yes Indeed—Tommy Dorsey
Maria Elena—Eddy Duchin (4)
Tonight You Belong to Me—Erskine Hawkins
Basie Boogie—Count Basie
Pine Top Boogie Woogie—Louis Jordan (2)
Romance in the Dark—Lil Green

Chicken Shack
There's Something Within Me—Sister Rosetta Tharpe
Beer Drinkin Women—Memphis Slim
Buckin the Dice—Fats Waller
Blue Flame—Woody Herman
Blues—Artie Shaw
Come Back Baby—Walter Davis
Throw This Dog a Bone—Ollie Shepard
Love Me—Lil Green
Going to Chicago—Count Basie
Call Me a Taxi—Bob Crosby
Daddy—Sammy Kaye
Saxa Woogie—Louis Jordan

Pan Pan—Louis Jordan
Down, Down, Down—Count Basie
Jelly Jelly—Earl Hines
My Mellow Man—Lil Green
I'm Falling for You—Earl Hines
Keep Cool Fool—Ella Fitzgerald
Yes Indeed—Bing Crosby
Stand by Me—Sister Rosetta Tharpe

Dipsie Doodle
Romance in the Dark—Lil Green
All That Meat and No Potatoes—Fats Waller
Undecided Blues—Count Basie
Key to the Highway—Jazz Gillum
Beer Drinking Woman—Memphis Minnie
Stand by Me—Sister Rosetta Tharpe
Because of You—Erskine Butterfield
Yes I Got Your Woman—Washboard Sam
Wee Baby Blues—Art Tatum
Whiskey Head Man—Tommy McClennan
Boogie Woogie's Mother-in-Law—Buddy Johnson
Shortenin Bread—Fats Waller
My Mellow Man—Lil Green
Come Back Baby—Walter Davis
Love Me—Lil Green
Pine Top Boogie Woogie—Louis Jordan
My Blue Heaven—Artie Shaw
Rocking Chair Blues—Big Bill
Please Mr. Johnson—Buddy Johnson
Jelly Jelly—Earl Hines

New Africa
Summit Ridge Drive—Artie Shaw
All That Meat and No Potatoes—Fats Waller
Cross Your Heart—Artie Shaw
Undecided Blues—Count Basie
New Please Mr. Johnson—Buddy Johnson
Pan Pan—Louis Jordan
I Been Dealing with the Devil—Sonny Boy
Fine and Mellow—Andy Kirk
Dig the Blues—Four Clefs

Mama Know What Papa Wants When Papa's Feeling Blue—(?)
Knock Me Out—Honey Dripper
Blue Flame—Woody Herman
That's the Blues Old Man—Johnny Hodges
My Mellow Man—Lil Green
Keep Cool Fool—Erskine Hawkins
Blues Part 2—Artie Shaw
Come Back Baby—Walter Davis
Twenty Four Robbers—Jimmie Lunceford
Fan It—Woody Herman
Red Wagon—Count Basie
Do You Call That a Buddy—Larry Clinton
Just Jiving Around—Sam Price
Chocolate—Jimmie Lunceford
T Bone Blues—Louis Jordan

Bucky's
Throw That Dog a Bone—Ollie Shepard
Going to Chicago—Count Basie
Jelly Jelly—Earl Hines
Boogie Woogie's Mother-in-Law—Buddy Johnson
My Blue Heaven—Artie Shaw
Do You Call That a Buddy—Louis Jordan
Good Feeling Blues—Blind Boy
Look Out for Yourself—Peetie Wheatstraw
What You Know Joe—Jimmy Lunceford
Buckin the Dice—Fats Waller
Red Wagon—Louis Holden
Please Mr. Johnson—Buddy Johnson
Love Me—Lil Green
All That Meat and No Potatoes—Fats Waller
219 Blues—Louis Armstrong
Stand by Me—Sister Rosetta Tharpe
Beer Drinkin Woman—Memphis Slim
SaxaWoogie—Louis Jordan
Come Back Baby—Walter Davis
Summit Ridge Drive—Artie Shaw

AFTERWORD

In 1989 I was asked by Paul Wells, Director of the Center for Popular Music at Middle Tennessee State University, if I would undertake a research project. Dr. Charles Wolfe of MTSU's English Department earlier had met John Work's widow. She had told Wolfe that John Work had made instantaneous discs of folk music that had not been donated to the American Folklife Collection at the Library of Congress. The knowledgeable Dr. Wolfe was familiar with the quality and import of Work's Library of Congress recordings and was eager to verify Mrs. Work's information. My background in music and audio engineering (and, most likely, my availability) qualified me to Wolfe and Wells.

In the several months spent going through papers, photographs, and recordings at the Work home on the edge of the Fisk University campus, I came to appreciate Work's deep understanding of and unique approach to the study of Negro vernacular music.

In 1990, I used these materials to produce a radio documentary surveying Work's folkloric activities. With the permission of the Work estate, the recordings and some photos and papers went into the Center for Popular Music's archives. This is the material I shared with Robert when he began work on the Muddy Waters biography. His intelligence and research skills (in addition to his requisite interest in Work's part in the Coahoma project) encouraged me to share my opinion that Work's voice was unique in folklore scholarship—unique, and to that moment, mostly unheard.

I gave him a sample of Work's typescript and asked him to keep an eye open as he researched Muddy. I was looking for some text and musical transcriptions that I knew had existed, but currently weren't at either the house or among the microfilms at Fisk. Gordon went on with the research and writing of the Waters biography, and I heard no more. Meanwhile, the Work residence, uninhabited since illness put Mrs. Work in a nursing home, suffered break-ins, vandalism, and a fire. The remaining papers and personal family possessions were put in storage. Later, by mistake, the storage company discarded them. It seemed to me as if Professor Work was disappearing bit by bit.

But this book is evidence of a providence that cheers the disheartened. Since Robert Gordon located the material you now hold, the Library of Congress has devoted part of its American Memory website to Professor Work's efforts in recording the 1941 Fort Valley College Folk Festival (*http://memory.loc.gov/ammem/ftyhtml/ftyhome.html*); and the Alabama Folklife Association has published Joe Dan Boyd's book *Judge Jackson and The Colored Sacred Harp,* which contains an excellent account of Work's first field trip (available from the Alabama Center for Traditional Culture, 410 North Hull St., Montgomery, AL 36104).

Robert and I were given the good fortune to work together and, with a very sympathetic Vanderbilt University Press team, put this book in your hand. Perhaps history won't be indifferent to Professor Work, after all.

Bruce Nemerov
Murfreesboro, Tennessee
2005

NOTES

Abbreviations

ALA   Alan Lomax Archives, Hunter College, NY.

ALC   Alan Lomax Collection, Library of Congress.

F-LC   Fisk-Library of Congress Coahoma County Study Collection, Library of Congress.

SCFLFU   Special Collections, Franklin Library, Fisk University.

JWW-SCFLFU   John Work III Collection, Special Collections, Franklin Library, Fisk University.

CSJ   Charles S. Johnson Collection, Special Collections, Franklin Library, Fisk University.

TEJ   T. E. Jones Collection, Special Collections, Franklin Library, Fisk University.

Preface

1. Bruce Nemerov, "John Wesley Work III: Field Recordings of Southern Black Folk Music, 1935–1942," *Tennessee Folklore Society Bulletin* LIII, no. 3 (1989): 82–103.

Introduction

1. John Work to Thomas Jones, May 25, 1940, JWW-SCFLFU.
2. 1900 U.S. Census.
3. Personal communication, 2004; unpublished interview with Helen Work by Doug Seroff, March 19, 1984.
4. *Crisis*, 32, no. 1 (May 1926): 32–34.
5. Unpublished interview with Helen Work by Doug Seroff, March 19, 1984.
6. The Julius Rosenwald Fund, based in Chicago, was chartered in 1917 "for the well-being of mankind" with an endowment of $20 million. Rosenwald had been a president of Sears-Roebuck. The fund concentrated on "equalization of opportunities among the various groups in America, contributing substantial sums to Negro education, Negro health, fellowships for Negroes and white Southerners, and general activities with a view to improving democratic human relations" (Rosenwald Fund news release, July 1947, Rosenwald Collection, SCFLFU). Rosenwald stipulated that the fund conclude its work within a generation, spending its entire principal and income by June 30, 1948.
7. JWW-SCFLFU.

8. Personal communication, 2004.

9. JWW-SCFLFU.

10. Work used a Presto model D, which recorded only 12-inch discs; the Library of Congress used a model Y, which could also record 16-inch discs.

11. JWW-SCFLFU, November 1, 1938.

12. Typescript in JWW-SCFLFU.

13. From Work's notebook, some interesting comments on unrecorded subjects:

    Thomas S. King – born Nolensville, Tennessee, in 1885. Lived in Nashville 38 years. 2nd Ave. – 2nd house back of H. G. Hills. Learned banjo from Ida Redd. Self taught on fiddle – 41 years. Saw Eph Grissom lynched in 1898.

    John Carter – born near Murfreesboro [Tennessee] – 1864. Farmer. Learned to play from his brother.

14. Joe M. Richardson, *A History of Fisk University 1865–1946* (University of Alabama Press, 1980).

15. Personal communication to Nemerov from John Work IV, 2004.

16. Edith Work, interviewed by William Garcia, August 11, 1971.

17. JWW-SCFLFU.

18. Ibid. Willis Duke "W. D." Weatherford was a professor of religion and humanities at Fisk in the early 1940s. In 1934, he coauthored a textbook with Charles S. Johnson, *Race Relations: Adjustments of Whites and Negroes in the United States.*

19. Alan Lomax to Library of Congress, September 1941. ALA

20. JWW-SCFLFU.

21. Ibid.

22. Personal communication to Nemerov from John Work IV, 2004. Also see Richard Robbins, *Sidelines Activist: Charles S. Johnson and the Struggle for Civil Rights* (Jackson: University Press of Mississippi, 1996), 138–140. For Lomax's estimation of the project's importance, see Lomax letter to Jerome Wisener, September 5, 1941, ALC: "…we have a study planned, which I believe is going to revolutionize the study of folk songs and folk lore in this country…"

23. Personal communication to Nemerov from John Work IV, 2004; see also William Garcia, "The Life and Choral Music of John Wesley Work (1901–1967)" (Ph.D. dissertation, University of Iowa, 1973).

24. JWW-SCFLFU.

25. Ibid.

26. The drama department curriculum, especially during summer educator's sessions, incorporated Negro folk tales. Since the study would address these, along with games and other folklore, Ross was invited to participate.

27. For the new, smaller research project to which Lomax is relegating Work, he suggests to

President Jones that a university car be made available to Dr. Work for hauling the recording equipment. Jones made no such allocation.

28. Alan Lomax to John Work, July 30, 1941, American Memory, Fort Valley State College Folk Festival Collection:

   http://memory.loc.gov/cgi-bin/query/r?ammem/ftv:@fieldDOCID=mss011

29. Personal communication to Nemerov from John W. Work IV.

30. Alan Lomax, *The Land Where the Blues Began* (New York: Pantheon, 1993), xii.

31. Lomax to Johnson, July 30, 1941, F-LC, Folder 8.

32. Lomax to Charles S. Johnson, August 21, 1941, F-LC, Folder 8.

33. "I believe that this survey and the resultant study will represent the first scientific study in the field of American folk-song. It will be carried out by Doctor Charles S. Johnson and his graduate students in Sociology in collaboration with the Library of Congress." Lomax to Archive of Folksong and Music, Library of Congress, August 21, 1941.

34. The promised duplicates were cut in a cost-saving measure at the Library (Memorandum from Harold Spivacke, August 5, 1942, F-LC Folder 9).

35. Lomax, summary statement to Library of Congress, September 18, 1941, F-LC. Lomax also states: "Dr. Johnson agreed to furnish the field workers to supervise the editing of the material at Fisk. I proposed that the library furnish the recording equipment, the records, and a set of duplicates for the Fisk library, and my own services as a field worker and co-editor of the study." Instead of editing the study, Lomax used it to write his own text, unsuccessfully in 1948, successfully in 1993.

36. Anthropologist Hortense Powdermaker, doing field work for *Growing Up in the Black Belt,* wrote to Charles S. Johnson from Mississippi that once she told her informants she was from Fisk, they became responsive, "taking her for a light-skinned Negro." Recounted in Robbins, (Jackson: University Press of Mississippi, 1996), 91.

37. See also Gordon, *Can't Be Satisfied: The Life and Times of Muddy Waters.*

38. Lomax, *The Land Where the Blues Began,* 41.

39. Ibid. On September 5 Lomax wrote the library's sound engineer Jerome Wisener on the troubles they'd had in the region: "the community situation was so hot, as well as complicated, that I would hesitate to document it, until I knew the place better. Everywhere we went we were asked point blank, were we or were we not union organizers." He also commented on the glass-backed records' fragility, lending credence to the idea that the Library of Congress's cracked Muddy Waters recording has never been played since the day it was recorded: "Three or four have been cracked by being bumped around in the car and one of the best records, I found today, was broken right through the middle." For more information on the broken disc, see Robert Gordon, *Can't Be Satisfied: The Life and Times of Muddy Waters* (Boston: Little, Brown, 2002).

40. Lomax to Library of Congress, September 18, 1941, F-LC; the closing phrase about Fisk's sponsorship was dropped in the final document.

41. Charles S. Johnson to Alan Lomax, September 16, 1941, ALC.

42. Adams, Young, Report on Preliminary Work in Clarksdale, Mississippi, October 6, 1941 (See Appendix 3).

43. Lewis Jones, Report on Preliminary Work in Clarksdale, Mississippi, September 29, 1941. JWW-SCFLFU.

44. Lomax to Library of Congress, September 18, 1941; Dr. Johnson wrote Lomax on September 29: "The seminar yielded, I note, a rich array of materials and a degree of stimulation far exceeding anything expected, although I confess I expected a great deal. You have a genius for hard work as well as for catching, following through and recording a wide range of the most excitingly beautiful as well as culturally significant folk material," ALC.

45. Neither the originals nor the copies of these "field notes and interviews" have been located.

46. Several unsigned, handwritten letters or "reports," written from the Coahoma County Training School, in Clarksdale on December 11, 1941, are included in the Charles S. Johnson Collection (Folder 2, Box 24, SCFLFU). "14 interviews conducted so far, including family schedules and musical questionnaires and supplementary materials. Bad weather. Leads and contacts with many musicians, including Jesse James Jefferson, 'a harmonica and banjo player.' At the time that I met him he was walking down the street on Saturday night singing and playing on his guitar, 'I'm just a poor cold nigger.' He had an interesting story to tell of how he used to make ten and twelve dollars playing for parties, but now the 'seabirds' have taken practically all of his business away and so now he plays at the 'juk' houses in the rurals for $1.75 . . . The people are at home, and for the most part have plenty of time on their hands. The cotton is all picked and the majority of the settlements have been made. This is a good time for interviewing and making contacts. There are two problems in this regard. First, that for the most part only the women are to be found in the homes; the men go hunting or spend the day in town and I have a feeling that it is not the woman in groups like these who possess the knowledge of the story; but the man. The second problem is in this regard—in so many instances in the various homes there are so many visitors that only general questions can be asked during the course of the interview . . . I don't like the mud, nor the inconveniences, nor the rain, nor the cold; but I do have a liking for the people and an interest in the work."

47. Lomax to Lewis Jones, January 21, 1942. ALC.

48. Adams to Johnson, January 8, 1942, CSJ.

49. Report from Adams, CSJ.

50. Lomax to Johnson, March 20, 1942, Folder 9, F-LC Regarding the question of whether "informants" were paid, here is conclusive evidence. Among Work's expenses were anticipated payments to "informants," those whom they would record. In a letter a few days later to President Jones, Work elaborated: "The study of these would involve the occasional payment of small fees to persons in charge to gain permission to record or to stimulate the necessary cooperation . . . Most of these men eke out a living from their music and either demand money for their performances, or, if not demanding money,

perform better when paid" (John Work to Thomas Jones, August 28, 1941, JWW-SC-FLFU). Such practice was not uncommon. In a budget prepared on August 21, 1941 and sent to the Archive of Folksong and Music, Lomax included a line for "Needles, payments to informants" and the amount $150. A similar budget for a two-week trip, prepared August 4, 1942, included "4 sapphire needles" at a cost of twenty dollars. We can infer that Lomax was prepared to pay out over $100 to informants. Furthermore, when Lomax wrote to John Work on February 27, 1942, that he would notify "the authorities at Fort Valley that you are coming down to make records for our use in my place," he discussed the mechanics of being reimbursed by the library: "If you pay the singers, rent a car, or have other expenses out of this item for more than $1.00, you must turn in a receipt for every item."

51. Work to Lomax, March 11, 1942, JWW-SCFLFU.

52. Lomax to Johnson, March 20, 1942, Folder 9, F-LC.

53. Waters to Lomax, June 25, 1942, F-LC.

54. On January 23, 1943, Muddy had someone sign his name to another form sent by Alan Lomax acknowledging receipt of two copies of "Record 18 in Album IV of *Folk Music of the United States from Records in the Archive of American Folk Song* (1942)," F-LC.

55. Lomax field notebooks, July 13, 1942, ALA.

56. Ibid.

57. Ibid, July 15, 1942.

58. Personal communication to the authors from Jeff Todd Titon.

59. The September 22, 1942 letter has not yet been located.

60. One of the counties surveyed for *Growing Up in the Black Belt* was Coahoma. In his introduction, Charles Johnson writes, "Bolivar and Coahoma counties in the Mississippi Delta are active and comparatively flourishing plantation areas not yet seriously affected by the forces which have brought about disorganization in the other areas. Despite falling cotton prices and general unrest, the exceptional adaptation of the Delta to the plantation system has *preserved the traditional order* with only slight modifications" (emphasis added).

61. Folk culture seminar description, JWW-SCFLFU.

62. Work to T. Jones, June 1943, JWW-SCFLFU. Mr. Wheeler was paid the "student work rate" of twenty-five cents per hour, with the work taking 167 hours.

63. JWW-SCFLFU.

64. John W. Work to T.E. Jones, undated, JWW-SCFLFU.

65. John Work to Thomas Jones, July 30, 1943, JWW-SCFLFU.

66. JWW-SCFLFU.

67. Duncan Emrich to Thomas Jones, December 14, 1945, T. E. Jones collection, SCFLFU.

68. JWW-SCFLFU.

69. The original is misdated as 1947, but it's clearly in response to the 12/47 letter; Lomax wrote the old year out of habit.

70.   Other labels involved in releases include Testament, Biograph, Folkways, Verve, Poly-
      gram, and Chess.

John Work's Untitled Manuscript

1.   Nolan Porterfield, *Last Cavalier: The Life and Times of John A. Lomax, 1867-1948*. (Ur-
      bana: University of Illinois Press, 1996), p. 298.
2.   Alice C. Reid, *Gee's Bend: A Rural Negro Community* (Mss). Fisk University, p. 71.
3.   Charles S. Johnson, *Growing up in the Black Belt*. Washington, D. C., p. 140.
4.   The teacher is an important disseminator of Negro folksong. In most Negro colleges
      singing of spirituals is an important activity in the music program. Here new spirituals
      are taught to the choruses. Members of these choruses returning to their home-churches
      and schools teach these there. For this reason, many spirituals reach rural South Caro-
      lina, Mississippi, or Texas by way of Fisk University, Hampton Institute, or Prairie View
      College.
5.   John and Alan Lomax, *Our Singing Country* (New York, 1941); William Arms Fisher,
      Seventy Negro Spirituals (Boston, 1926); John Work, *American Negro Songs* (New York,
      1940); Ballanta-Taylor, *Saint Helena Island Spirituals* (New York, 1925); R. Nathaniel
      Dett, *Religious Folk Songs of the Negro* (Hampton, 1927); Lydia Parrish, *Slave Songs of
      the Georgia Sea Islands* (New York, 1942).
6.   John W. Work, *American Negro Songs*. Page 4 for discussion of this form.
7.   *Gee's Bend*. p. 83.
8.   *Lanterns on the Levee*. New York, p. 253.
9.   W. C. Handy, *Blues*. New York, p. 25.
10.   Alice Morse Earle, *The Sabbath in Puritan New England*.
11.   Alice C. Reid, *Gee's Bend: A Rural Negro Community* (Mss). Fisk University, 1942.
12.   Charles S. Johnson, *Growing Up in the Black Belt*. pp. 148–155.
13.   W. C. Handy, *Blues*. New York, 1927. *The Father of the Blues*. New York, 1941, p. 74–
      121.
14.   W. C. Handy, *Blues*. New York, 1927, introduction.
15.   Thomas W. Talley, *Negro Folk Rhymes*. New York, 1921.
16.   Thomas W. Talley, *Negro Folk Rhymes*. New York, 1922, p. 16.
17.   John McBride, Jr., *The Sewanee Review*, "Br'er Rabbit in the Folk Tales of the Negro."
      1911.
18.   Thomas W. Talley, *Negro Folk Rhymes*, pp. 308–326.
19.   Newman I. White, *American Negro Songs*. Cambridge, 1928, chapter VI.
20.   Ibid.
21.   See biographical sketches in the appendix.
22.   Louise Pound, *American Ballads and Songs*; Campbell and Sharp, *Folk Songs from the
      Southern Appalachians*; John A. and Alan Lomax, *American Ballads and Folk Songs*.
      New York, 1934.

23. Odum and Johnson, *The Negro and His Songs.* Chapel Hill, 1925, pp. 196–98.

24. Lomax, *American Ballads and Songs.* pp. 93–99.

25. See reference to this song in the biographical sketch of Charles Haffer in appendix.

26. Houston Bacon, who began work as a waterboy when nine years old on a Missouri levee has followed construction and railroad work all of his life. Until the last eight years spent in Clarksdale as a section gang laborer, he has constantly "been on the go," and has worked in most of the middle-southern and middle-western states. His songs reflect his travels.

27. J. W. Work, *American Negro Songs.* New York, 1940.

28. Arthur P. Hudson, *Folk Songs of Mississippi.* Chapel Hill, 1936.

29. At one time, about 1910, there were fifteen such bands playing in the vicinity of Clarksdale.

30. W. C. Handy, *Father of the Blues.* Chapter 7.

"Changing Negro Life in the Delta" by Samuel C. Adams

1. C. S. Johnson, E. E. Embree, and W. W. Alexander, *The Collapse of Cotton Tenancy.* (Chapel Hill: The University of North Carolina Press, 1935), p. 35.

2. E. J. Frazier, *The Negro Family in the United States.* (Chicago: The University of Chicago Press, 1939), p. 112.

3. "Cultures change by diffusion of patterns from without, they change by invention from within, they change by the demands and imposition of conquest . . . Social change is habit change." John Dollard, "The Acquisition of New Social Habits," in R. Linton (ed.), *The Science of Man in the World Crisis* (New York: Columbia University Press, 1945), pp. 443 and 446. "The key to change may be sought in invention. The word as here used means any new element in culture . . . a much broader meaning than the term commonly conveys. For a particular culture area social change is due to an invention either made in that area or else imported to it." W. F. Ogburn, "Social Change," *Ency. of Soc. Sciences,* III, 331. W. F. Ogburn, *Social Change* (New York: The Viking Press, 1922); also J. H. S. Bossard, *Social Change and Social Problems* (New York: Harper & Bros., 1938).

4. C. S. Johnson, *The Shadow of the Plantation* (Chicago: The University of Chicago Press, 1934); also A. F. Raper, *Preface to Peasantry* (Chapel Hill: The University of North Carolina Press, 1936).

5. Robert Bedfield in his study of changing folk culture in Yucatan sought to classify four different communities within that territory with respect to the degree in which life in each community was dominated by religious sanctions. In the community most remote from the principal city, all social life seemed to have a religious sanction. In the city of Merida, the dominant mood and temper of the people was secular and individualistic. Between these two extremes were communities exhibiting various degrees of secularization. *Folk Culture In Yucatan* (Chicago: The University of Chicago Press, 1941); James West, *Plainville, U.S.A.* (New York: Columbia University Press, 1945); also Alice

C. Reid, "Gee's Bend: A Rural Negro Community in Transition" (Nashville: M.A. Thesis Fisk University, 1941).

6.   "At first, anthropologists were primarily interested in speculating upon possible stages of cultural evolution. They became engaged in salvaging all possible information about the life that aboriginal peoples had lived prior to the influence of European culture. There was also a tendency to identify nonliterate peoples with the different stages through which it was believed mankind as a whole had passed. The fact that various aboriginal peoples had been undergoing cultural changes and readaptation in mode of life ever since Europeans had come in contact with them aroused scarcely a casual interest." A. I. Hallowell, "Sociopsychological Aspects of Acculturation," in Ralph Linton (ed.), *The Science of Man in the World Crisis* (New York: Columbia University Press, 1945), p. 171. See E. B. Dixon, *The Building of Cultures* (New York: Charles Scribner's Sons, 1928) and B. Malinowski, "Culture," *Ency. of Soc. Sciences,* IV, p. 624.

7.   "Can Progress in Race Relations be Measured?" *Social Forces,* (Forth-coming issue, November, 1946).

8.   A. Hallowell, "Sociopsychological Aspects of Acculturation," in R. Linton (ed.), *The Science of Man in the World Crisis* (New York: Columbia University Press, 1945) p. 183; also B. Malinowski, *The Dynamics of Culture Change* (New Haven: Yale University Press, 1945)

9.   R. E. Park, "Culture and Civilization" in *Race and Culture* (unpublished manuscript), also Louis Wirth, "Urban Society and Civilization," *American Journal of Sociology,* XLV (1940) p. 744. Civilization is cradled in the city, can be bought and sold, constitutes our techniques; things of utility. Civilized life radiates from the city, rationalizes life activities, and tends to displace culture.

10. Another plantation community, New Africa, sixteen miles from Clarksdale was observed to compare findings. This community, being more isolated, provided a kind of controlled situation.

11. See Appendix A for the questionnaire used in this study.

12. See Appendix A for the schedule used in this study.

13.   "The alluvial plain . . . contains some of the richest land in the world. Nearly all of it is bottom land, produced and fed through countless eons by the inundations of the Mississippi River and reclaimed for usage by a system of powerful levees that hold the flood in check. The alluvial deposits have been found to be 35 feet deep in many places." Federal Writers Project, ° (New York: Viking Press, 1938), pp. 31–33.

14. Thirteen Mississippi counties fall within this area. They are Warren, Yazoo, Sharkey, Issaquena, Humphreys, Washington, Sunflower, Boliver, Coahoma, Tunica, Quitman, Tallahatchie, Leflore. See *Sixteenth Census of the United States,* 1940, "Population Characteristics," Vol. II, Part 4; and C. S. Johnson, *Statistical Atlas of Southern Counties* (Chapel Hill: The University of North Carolina Press, 1941).

15. Federal Writers Project, *op. cit.* p. 33

16. *Consumers Market Data Handbook,* 1930; see Clarksdale, Mississippi.

17. Formal songs from published books known as the Dr. Watt Hymnal [Isaac Watts].

18. Form of expressive behavior closely related to the old religious and revival shout.

19. E. B. Reuter, *The American Race Problem.* (New York: Thomas Y. Crowell Company, 1938), p. 329.

20. C. S. Johnson, *op. cit.,* p. 150.

21. E. F. Frazier, *op. cit.,* p. 111; also J. W. Work. *American Negro Songs.* (New York: Howell Soskin and Co., 1940), p. 23.

22. E. B. Reuter, *op. cit.,* p. 330.

23. Personal Document.

24. C. S. Johnson, *Shadow of the Plantation.* (Chicago: The University of Chicago Press, 1934), pp. 150, 151, 178–182.

25. Personal Document.

26. Personal Document.

27. Ibid.

28. Ibid.

29. Personal Document.

30. Personal Document.

31. Ibid.

32. Personal Document

33. Ibid.

34. Personal Document.

35. Robert Redfield, *Topoztlan. (*Chicago: The University of Chicago Press), 1930, pp. 1–2.

36. C. S. Johnson, *Shadow of the Plantation* (Chicago: The University of Chicago Press, 1934); E. F. Frazier, *The Negro Family in the United States* (Chicago: The University of Chicago Press, 1939); J. S. Bassett, *The Southern Plantation Overseer* (Massachusetts: Smith College, 1925).

37. R. E. Park, "Introduction" to C. S. Johnson's *Shadow of The Plantation* (Chicago: The University of Chicago Press, 1934), pp. xii–xiv.

38. Personal Document.

39. Personal Document.

40. Personal Document.

41. In one of his essays, Dr. R. E. Park says:

The Negro folk songs are the Negroes' literature of slavery. They reflect life as he saw it and felt it at that time . . . There are besides rhymes and jingles, sung when the slaves danced at evening around the cabin fire and the songs of longing, sad, dreaming airs, described the more sorrowful pictures of slave life, and sung in the dusk when the slaves were returning home from their day's work.

Whatever may have been the origin of his other songs we know that the spirituals arose spontaneously out of the communal excitements of a religious meeting—a revival or a "shout." The best of these were remembered, repeated and handed down by oral tradition. The songs that were most often repeated were those that most completely and adequately voiced the deep unconscious wishes of those who sang them. Thus by a process of natural selection the songs that circulated the widest and lived longest were those which reflected the profounder and more permanent moods and sentiments of the race. It was through the medium of these religious songs which were sung all over the South, wherever slave plantations existed, that the Negro achieved, in slavery, if not, as one writer has finally put it, race consciousness, at least a consciousness of his race.

"Negro Race Consciousness as Reflected In Race Literature," *American Review,* I (September–October, 1923), pp. 506–507; also see N. N. Puckett, *Folk Beliefs of the Southern Negro* (Chapel Hill: The University of North Carolina Press, 1926); F. L. Olmsted, *A Journey in the Seaboard Slave States* (New York: G. P. Putnam's Sons, 1904); and C. S. Johnson, *The Negro in American Civilization* (New York: Henry Holt & Co., 1930).

42.	"The sinner on the mourner's bench, 'down in the valley,' despairing of this world, with its troubles, its disappointments, and its insecurity, found consolation in the bright vision of another world, almost visible over there beyond Jordan: a world where all troubles vanished, where every day was Sunday, and where the souls redeemed walked in majesty with long white robes and golden slippers, talked familiarly with the angels, with Peter and Paul–and there was no more work." R. E. Park, *op. cit.,* p. 507.

43.	Personal Document.

44.	Federal Writers Project, *Mississippi.* (New York: The Viking Press, 1938), p. 157.

45.	Personal Document.

46.	Personal Document.

47.	Ibid.

48.	Ibid.

49.	Ibid.

50.	Ibid.

51.	Personal Document.

52.	Ibid.

53.	Ibid.

54.	C. S. Johnson, E. F. Embree, W. W. Alexander, *The Collapse of Cotton Tenancy.* (Chapel Hill: The University of North Carolina Press, 1935), p. 35.

55.	"A society is isolated to the extent that contacts among members of the local society (community) are many and intimate and characterized by a high degree of mutual understanding of much of the habitual mental life of one another while contacts between members of the local society and outsiders are few, not intimate, and characterized by a lower degree of mutual understanding." Robert Redfield, *The Folk Culture of Yucatan.* (Chicago: The University of Chicago Press, 1941), p. 16.

56.	R. E. Park, *op. cit.,* p. 508.

57.	J. W. Work, *American Negro Songs.* (New York: Howell, Soskins and Company, 1940), pp. 13 and 44.

58. Changes in folk culture are occuring in other parts of the world, in Mexico, see Robert Redfield, *op. cit.*, p. 3. Also R. E. Park suggests further insights. He says: "It is in art and literature, and particularly the art of the moving picture rather than the newspaper which exercise, I suspect, the most profound and subversive cultural influence in the world today. Anyone who has had an opportunity to observe the influence of the moving picture in any of the outlying regions of the world and upon peoples . . . can have no doubt about the profound and revolutionary changes they have already wrought in the attitudes and cultures of peoples, even in the most remote parts of the world. "Reflections on Communication and Culture", *The American Journal of Sociology*, XLIV (September, 1938), pp. 204–205.

59. Some idea of the extent of literacy can be gained from the following:

TABLE I

Last Grade Completed by Number of Family Heads and Wives of 100 Negro Sharecropper Families on the King and Anderson Plantation; Coahoma County, Mississippi, 1941.

Last Grade Completed:	No. of Family Heads:	No. of Wives:
Total 100	100	100
Not Given	0	14
Less than 2nd Grade	26	8
2–3	20	8
4–5	24	28
6–7	20	24
8–10	10	18
Median	4.4	5.9

60. R. E. Park, *op. cit.*, p. 508.
61. Personal Document.
62. Personal Document.
63. Ibid.
64. Personal Document.
65. Personal Document.
66. Personal Document.
67. Ibid.
68. Personal Document.
69. Ibid.
70. Personal Document.
71. Ibid.

72. Personal Document.
73. Ibid.
74. Personal Document.
75. Ibid.
76. Personal Document.
77. R. E. Park, op. cit., p. 514.
78. Personal Document.
79. Personal Document.
80. Ibid.
81. Ibid.
82. Ibid.
83. Ibid.
84. **TABLE II**

    Songs Known by Negro Sharecroppers on the King and Anderson
    Plantation, Coahoma County, Mississippi, 1941.

Kinds of Songs	No. of Songs	Per cent
Total	260	100.0
Church Songs (Hymns)	78	30.0
Spirituals	48	18.5
Blues	52	20.0
Jazz Songs	42	16.2
Sentimental Songs	26	10.0
Singing Games	8	3.0
Not Given	6	2.3

85. E. F. Frazier, *op. cit.*, p. 274.
86. R. B. Dixon, *The Building of Cultures.* (New York: Charles Scribner's Sons, 1928), p. 116.
87. R. B. Dixon, *op. cit.*, p. 109.

Appendix 1

1. Deputy sheriff William I. Herbert.
2. The structure had been built, according to *The Mississippi Rag*, around 1910 as a lodge hall, then became a Sanctified church, a blacksmith shop, a pop-bottling factory, and a garage. Proprietor Ed Frazier opened the club in 1938.
3. Paige Van Vorst, "Walter Barnes & His Band of Heroes," *The Mississippi Rag*, November 1998, p. 37.
4. United Press wire story, *Nashville Banner*, April 24, 1940, p. 1.

5. United Press wire story, *Nashville Banner,* April 24, 1940, p. 1.

6. Cited in *The Mississippi Rag.* November 1998, p. 37.

7. *The Natchez Democrat,* April 24, 1940.

8. The drummer was Oscar Brown; bassist Arthur Edwards was severely burned.

9. *Natchez Democrat,* April 24, 1940.

10. From *www.lib.usm.edu/~spcol/crda/oh/belltrans.htm:* "It was just screams in the air," said Josephine Clemons Bell, who was thirty-one and lived about five blocks away. She had family at the dance. "I never did find my sister. The next day I found her where they had them all stretched out in the undertaker parlor. That's where I found her and her husband." The deceased couple left a five year old son. Interview conducted October 22, 1996, by Amy McPhail.

INDEX OF TRANSCRIPTIONS

GENERAL INDEX

Page numbers in italics refer to photographs; page numbers in bold refer to transcripts.